ROUTLEDGE LIBRARY EDITIONS:
VICTORIAN POETRY

Volume 3

EMILY DICKINSON

EMILY DICKINSON

A Celebration for Readers

Edited by
SUZANNE JUHASZ AND CRISTANNE MILLER

Routledge
Taylor & Francis Group
LONDON AND NEW YORK

First published in 1989 by Gordon and Breach

This edition first published in 2016
by Routledge
2 Park Square, Milton Park, Abingdon, Oxon OX14 4RN

and by Routledge
711 Third Avenue, New York, NY 10017

Routledge is an imprint of the Taylor & Francis Group, an informa business

British Library Cataloguing in Publication Data
A catalogue record for this book is available from the British Library

ISBN: 978-1-138-67471-4 (Set)
ISBN: 978-1-315-56115-8 (Set) (ebk)
ISBN: 978-1-138-67208-6 (Volume 3) (hbk)
ISBN: 978-1-138-67210-9 (Volume 3) (pbk)
ISBN: 978-1-315-61654-4 (Volume 3) (ebk)

Publisher's Note
The publisher has gone to great lengths to ensure the quality of this reprint but points out that some imperfections in the original copies may be apparent.

Disclaimer
The publisher has made every effort to trace copyright holders and would welcome correspondence from those they have been unable to trace.

EMILY DICKINSON

A Celebration for Readers

Proceedings of the Conference held on
September 19–21, 1986
at the Claremont Colleges
Claremont, California

Edited by

SUZANNE JUHASZ
University of Colorado, Boulder

and

CRISTANNE MILLER
Pomona College, Claremont, California

GORDON AND BREACH
NEW YORK LONDON PARIS MONTREUX TOKYO MELBOURNE

Published simultaneously by Gordon and Breach, Science Publishers, Inc. and Gordon and Breach Science Publishers S.A.

Post Office Box 786
Cooper Station
New York, New York 10276
United States of America

Post Office Box 197
London WC2E 9PX
England

58, rue Lhomond
75005 Paris
France

Post Office Box 161
1820 Montreux 2
Switzerland

3-14-9, Okubo
Shinjuku-ku, Tokyo
Japan

Private Bag 8
Camberwell, Victoria 3124
Australia

This material originally appeared as Volume 16, Issues 1-2 of the journal *Women's Studies.*

Library of Congress Cataloging-in-Publication Data

Emily Dickinson: a celebration for readers: proceedings of the conference held on September 19-21, 1986 at the Claremont College/ edited by Suzanne Juhasz and Cristanne Miller.
p. cm. — (Studies in gender and culture. ISSN 0889-3128; v. 3)
ISBN 0-677-22170-3 : $19.00
1. Dickinson, Emily, 1830-1886 — Criticism and interpretation — — Congresses. I. Juhasz, Suzanne, 1942- . II. Miller, Cristanne. III. Series.
PS1541.Z5539 1989 89-12004
811'.4—dc20 CIP

Contents

Introduction

SUZANNE JUHASZ
University of Colorado, Boulder

and

CRISTANNE MILLER
Pomona College

1986: THE YEAR Emily Dickinson centennial conferences materialized across the continent, each framing the poet differently by the structure of its program, its invited speakers, and its target audience. The Claremont conference began with a clear conception of what its tone and purpose would be. In a flurry of quick meetings, followed up by long two- and then three-way telephone conversations, Suzanne Juhasz, Cristanne Miller, and Ellin Ringler-Henderson decided that "Emily Dickinson: A Celebration for Readers" would focus the attention of its invited and attending participants on Dickinson's poems. This seemed to us an indulgence (when do we get to talk with other Dickinson scholars just about the poems?) but also ideologically important: this conference would structure an occasion for talking with other thinkers instead of talking to them. And we hoped it would be a celebration in fact as well as in title.

In this conference, we wanted to concentrate on Emily Dickinson, to encourage the participants to come closer to her and her art. We wanted depths, not surfaces; complexities, not simplification. Examining in a careful and organized way the poems themselves*, and the ways in which we read them, seemed a good way to accomplish our

*We reproduce here the texts of Dickinson's poems as they were used in the conference workshops. We chose to use Johnson's one-volume edition, because it is more readily available than the three-volume edition to the reading public.

Women's Studies, 1989
Vol. 16, pp. 1-7

goal. At the same time, we wanted to avoid the lecturing and "star turns" that, at so many scholarly conferences, produce glossy summaries of positions, closed circuits which an audience may appreciate but never enter. This system seems to focus more attention on the speaker than on the subject. Instead, we envisioned a "participatory" model, with clusters of short presentations leading to discussions in a workshop setting. Especially, we wanted to focus on individual poems, and on multiple readings of the same poem, to explore the ways in which we come to determine and appreciate the poet's meanings.

We envisioned that each discussion or workshop would be set in motion by three short readings of the same poem. These readings would ideally both complement and provoke one another and, in the process, spark off conversation among all who were present. In such a format, we hoped, there would be no perception of a "correct" or "best" reading and, consequently, the multiple readings would encourage concern about how readers might accommodate more than one reading at the same time.

Behind this format — or rather, embedded into it, was yet another aspiration: to bring together and help to foster a community of Dickinson readers. Although we desired that the subject take precedence over the commentary, the "presenters" or participants would matter crucially. The poetry has meaning only in our reading of it, we all felt; we have to be there, doing it, for the poetry to come alive. As readers of Dickinson, we have a common identity and experience, which can be cultivated and enriched through interaction with one another. Not only do we learn more about Dickinson this way, but about ourselves as readers. The conference structure was developed in order that such interaction might occur.

After building our conference in the air, we began trying to reproduce it on the grounds of the Claremont Colleges. We started with the schedule: the workshops themselves and a frame that would constitute preparation for their discussion of the poems and then response to that discussion. The opening night would introduce Emily Dickinson in the form of a concerted reading of her poems. Five participants would join in giving physical voice to the act of reading Dickinson's work and, indirectly, in revealing how various this one poet's work can sound when read by different voices. The poems, chosen to let us hear Dickinson speak of herself in increasingly wider relationships — to love, to the outside world, to death and eternity — were grouped together to reveal her overlapping attitudes and feelings. There would be no commentary during this reading — only the poems themselves, back to back. The conference would begin with all listening to Dickinson's own words. In a courtyard reception following the reading, the talking *about* the poems and the poet could begin.

The next morning would start with a short introductory talk (followed by discussion) that would place Dickinson in her times and introduce questions of how twentieth-century readers interpret a nineteenth-century woman's poetry. This would provide a common ground or base from which the ensuing discussions would take off and would be the only "lecture" in the entire conference: not meant to honor a particular scholar but to provide a common reference point for the group as a whole. The short talk and long discussion, we hoped, would set the tone for a participatory conference on Dickinson herself and her poems. Next would come the first set of workshops on the poems.

We imagined that we could count on an average participation of around sixty people, and that twenty to twenty-five would be a manageable size for a good discussion. Consequently, we decided to have three workshops run simultaneously on three different poems. To establish the diversity we wanted to encourage in the discussions, we asked three critics to give brief (ten minute) readings of the poem chosen for each group: the first half an hour of the session, then, would consist of three presentations on a poem; the next hour was scheduled for open discussion. The morning session of three workshops would immediately precede lunch, and following lunch would come a second session of three concurrently running workshops.

In choosing the six poems for the workshops, we attempted to balance the participants's personal preferences for a particular poem with our judgement of a poem's complexity or richness; we wanted, furthermore, to give people a chance to talk about a range of the types of poems Dickinson writes. There was also a concern that some of the six poems be well known to a general audience, in order both that the entire audience feel comfortable participating in the discussion and to persuade people to attend the conference who do not work on Dickinson or even in the field of English literature but who may previously have puzzled over one of these poems. The poems chosen were "A solemn thing — it was — I said" (271), "He fumbles at your Soul" (315), "The name — of it — is 'Autumn'"(656), "My Life had stood — a

Loaded Gun" (754), "A Word made Flesh is seldom" (1651), and "The farthest Thunder that I heard" (1581). In choosing the readers for each poem, we also tried to group critics who would approach their poem differently.

After two sessions of workshops on individual poems, we wanted a more analytical plenary panel and discussion on reading Dickinson, or the ways various assumptions about the poet or the poems affect the process of reading. By this time in the conference, we thought, all participants would be eager to talk about their own processes of reading and about what differences they had observed in the two discussion workshops they had attended. Again, we decided on three presentations for this panel in order to continue the commitment to fruitful disagreement rather than either pronouncement or dichotomized views. Similarly, we expected the talks to be brief so that substantial discussion might follow. This discussion would last into the late afternoon; dinner would be followed by a showing of the New York Center for Visual History film on Dickinson.

The conference as planned thus far satisfied us with its focus on the poems, but we wanted to conclude by broadening that focus to include discussion on the poet herself. We envisioned a general session first, jokingly, titled "Who Is Emily Dickinson Anyway?", then more formally titled "Three Views of the Poet." We were aiming for a move from her words to some sense of the person who wrote them: her personality, her presence, her existence in the world. Three of the conference's participants would present brief papers on their view of the poet, to be followed by discussion.

In deciding who to invite to give papers at the conference, we returned first to part of our original decision in planning the conference: as far as we knew, there had been as yet no major celebrations of Dickinson's centennial on the West Coast (and we knew of only one other event planned), in spite of the number of Dickinson scholars and devotees there. We began, then, by inviting scholars from the West who we thought would be comfortable in the kind of participatory, non-hierarchical conference we had planned. We also decided from the beginning to invite a few participants whose primary response to Dickinson was as poets rather than as critics, and hence turned to Marcia Falk and Maurya Simon. As our funds were confirmed and as we ran into the inevitable obstacles of academic and personal commitments that prevented some people from joining us, we shifted more of our invitations to the Midwest and East. We were heartened in this stage of the planning by the enthusiastic reponses we received from people planning to come and from those who regretted that they could not: almost everyone commented on the form of the conference, and one participant wrote, "It sounds so humane!" We felt this was the height of praise.

Of course, no conference ever runs exactly as it was planned; several talks were longer than we had hoped they would be, and there were what is no doubt the normal number of minor glichs in programming. In all, however, we feel that the conference exceeded our expectations. It gave us two days of intense and glorious talking about Emily Dickinson's poetry, a shared sense of community as Dickinson readers and scholars, and a greater understanding and appreciation of the poet herself. Notes we received from participants after the conference indicated that our enthusiasm was shared: "thank you for an *unusually* stimulating and enjoyable conference," "a truly enjoyable conference," "one of the most stimulating, as well as agreeable, conferences of my academic life ... 'The Feast of Reason and the Flow of Soul'."

What we have described so far has to do with the theory and design of the conference. Also needed are a few words about the material of this volume. Along with the papers presented in Claremont, we reproduce here transcripts from the six workshops on the poems — for most participants the highlight of the conference, both because the workshops allowed individuals to receive immediate, multiple response to private questions about a line, a poem, or the poet, and because they provided a format for intense examination of what in Dickinson's poems encouraged such difference in readings and such deep questions about intent, tone, and context.

In the morning session on "A solemn thing — it was — I said —" (speakers: Marcia Falk, Barbara Mossberg, Maurya Simon), discussion ranged from questions of how necessary metaphor is in any theological language and Dickinson's identification of herself with Jesus (as alternate "son") or with God, to questions about the relative physical size of the poet in the Dickinson family. Papers at the simultaneous session on "He fumbles at your Soul" (speakers: Robin Riley Fast, Suzanne Juhasz, Ellen Ringler-Henderson) led to discussion of whether being *receptive* necessarily involves either passivity or activity; again, of Dickinson's identification of herself with Jesus; and of the experience of reading Dickinson's poems. The seldom analyzed "The name — of it — is 'Autumn' —" (speakers: Joanne Feit Diehl, Barbara Packer) generated discussion about the disruption of categories, and more generally of play, in Dickinson's and other women writers' works, and divergent analyses of the language and structure of Dickinson's work as a whole.

In the afternoon, discussions were equally wide-ranging. The session on "My Life had stood — a Loaded Gun —" (speakers: Joanne Dobson, Lillian Faderman, Ellen Ringler-Henderson) focused on the closing conundrum of the poem, partly in the context of conventions in contemporary novels by women; on questions of whether or not Dickinson wanted to publish; on her celebrations of lesbian love; and — as in one morning session — on the extent to which Dickinson demanded that we change both our critical language and critical categories to comprehend her. "A Word made Flesh is seldom" (speakers: Joanne Feit Diehl, Cristanne Miller, Maurya Simon) generated more specific examination of the syntax and structure of the given poem than any other group, but this examination involved broader questions on the extent to which Dickinson was rejecting God's (or the patriarchal) word for her own (erotic and/or poetic) language, or transforming God's word into her own; and, again, questions about the process of reading Dickinson's poems — especially as feminist critics. Speakers Marcia Falk and Barbara Packer, in their session on "The farthest Thunder that I heard", also concentrated on single lines of the poem, their analysis leading to questions about fallacies of form — whether the poem's confusion stems from the poet or from the reader — and the extent to which Dickinson's poems create their reader. This led, in turn, to enthusiastic commentary on the conference itelf:

> "I like your observation that interpreting Emily Dickinson becomes the creation of a reader. And what you're saying is a commentary on what we're doing here: it does create a way of reading that enriches and validates what other people are doing; it's a very collaborative thing, an appreciation of each other."
>
> "... what we're doing today is acknowledging that conversation teases thought out of us."

In another favorite moment, a speaker prefaced her presentation with the comment that she was "revising" an earlier reading she had done of the same poem; and then she, and several other Dickinson scholars on the panel and in the workshop group, proceded to query, critique and expand that revision. "We never get to talk to each other in this way," various people exclaimed; "we always have to get up and expound. What a treat, what a pleasure this has been!"

We are publishing the procedings of the conference, in response to many suggestions to do so, in the hopes of sharing its contents with the wider community of Dickinson readers. We hope that the sense of conversation, and connection, as well as the information it generated, will be communicated in the following pages.

We have done little editing of the transcripts of each workshop beyond the obvious tidying required to present speech in written form. The interruptions, sentence fragments, and occasional lapses into both argument and silliness seemed, to us, worth saving as indicators of a way to pursue ideas passionately in an academic and scholarly setting, and as reminders of the what must be one of the greatest and rarest pleasures of our occupation: reading a great poet's work with a community of readers.†

†This conference would not have been possible without the extremely generous support of the Pomona College Public Events Committee, aided by the Pitzer College Public Events Committee, the Claremont Colleges Women's Studies and American Studies Programs. Thanks to *Women's Studies*, in particular to editor Wendy Martin, and to the Pomona College Research Committee for the opportunity to publish the proceedings here.

Locating a Feminist Critical Practice: Between the Kingdom and the Glory

CHERYL WALKER

Scripps College

IN THREE DIFFERENT letters, numbered by Johnson and Ward 292, 330, and 583, Emily Dickinson uses a passage from the Sermon on the Mount (Matthew 6:13) to privilege power as a category surpassing or incorporating kingdom and glory. One such passage reads: "When I was a little Girl I remember hearing that remarkable passage and preferring the 'Power,' not knowing at the time that 'Kingdom' and 'Glory' were included" (L 330).

As a feminist critic I am concerned with power: both the power language confers and the power relations which affect language use itself. Dickinson was first taken up in a major way by the New Critics who preferred what I would call the glory aspect of power in its synchronic dimensions. This was an era in which the "universality" of Dickinson's poems, particularly those about God, love and death, was applauded along with her linguistic originality. Dickinson herself called glory "that bright tragic thing/ That for an instant/ Means Dominion" in poem # 1660. The "instant" seems to lie outside of time though it might also be said to "remember" time which gives it the aura of tragic limitation.

Kingdom, on the other hand, is a signalling word frequently used to differentiate different forms of time, as in #721 ("Behind me dips Eternity") or forms of power. As a Janus-faced image, the kingdom may look toward heaven or toward earth, but when the word appears, we are usually reminded that on earth the Soul is exposed to time, to

Women's Studies, 1989
Vol. 16, pp. 9-19
Reprints available directly from the publisher

history, and to the power relations which may inhibit her, especially if she is a woman. The poems I am most interested in seem to emerge at the crux, or crossing, of kingdom and glory, in the nexus of power. Holding kingdom and glory in tension, these poems provide a discourse about power which says a great deal about one version of the nineteenth-century female imagination.

Interpreting the poems, however, involves locating one's critical practice itself within the nexus of power. As a feminist critic, I must evaluate a number of critical strategies already in place. If New Criticism tended to prefer the glory of Dickinson's work, feminist criticism inevitably concerns itself with the kingdom, with patriarchy, and with the power relations which affect language use itself.

A recent fashion in feminist criticism is to tell success stories. Having passed beyond telling the stories of women as victims, we now celebrate the way women writers remained undefeated and managed to subvert oppressive male power structures embodied in both social and literary conventions. The virtues of this criticism are often its courage, imagination, and gusto. However, my problem with it is that it seems at times to lack fidelity and sensitivity to the past. Also, by emphasizing transcendence, it minimizes the effects of patriarchy and thus subtly reinforces its hold over our past and our present.

Let me be more specific in respect to the case of Emily Dickinson. It is now fashionable to celebrate Dickinson's withdrawal from the world, to acknowledge her cleverness in avoiding various forms of social oppression many nineteenth-century women who led more normal lives had to contend with. It is also fashionable for feminist critics to feel that they can find ample evidence for Dickinson's essential sympathies with feminism in her poems and letters. Certain facts about Dickinson's life and art provide at least a degree of friction against such theories, however.

Her fearfulness and dependency upon others late into her life, her choice of conservative Judge Lord as a lover, her dismissal of most women and admiration of powerful men, her mental breakdowns: all suggest that Dickinson's life is not quite the model of a successful feminist manipulation of circumstances we sometimes wish it to be.

Furthermore, Dickinson was not unusually concerned about being "a *woman* poet." At least her *conscious* dedication to gender-neutral philosophical issues in a great many poems distinguishes her from most other nineteenth-century American women poets and has led us as feminist critics to return again and again to the same comparatively small number of poems and letters which do address gender in some overt way.

In the space I have left I would like to consider a different way of reading Dickinson historically. The *modus operandi* I wish to adopt, which might loosely be called a form of post-structuralism, is in no sense unique to my reading of Dickinson. In fact, I wish only to confirm a set of strategies used occasionally and with varying degrees of success by many critics.

Though not nearly as often situating herself in a gender-specific context as many of her female contemporary writers, Dickinson is more directly conscious of allying herself with power than they were. Her poems and letters are liberally sprinkled with references to power and certainly her language use exhibits a desire to equate poetry not with release of feeling, as many nineteenth-century poetesses did, but with the assumption of power and the defiance of tradition. One way of reading her historically is to consider the way her representation of power relations might have been affected by her experience of gender. Dickinson clearly admired power but her orientation to it was highly ambivalent and as such it both unites her to other women poets and reflects her position in a power structure which allies power with masculinity.

Susan Gilbert Dickinson was rare among her associates in being a woman who inspired Dickinson with a sense of earthly ascendancy. Even to miss her was power, as she says in letter #364, and from early to late Susan brings the word *power* to Emily Dickinson's mind. As late as 1882 she is writing to Susan: "Thank her dear power for having come, an Avalanche of Sun!" (L755).

It is usually men, however, who represent power in Dickinson's imagination. Higginson is a figure of power who often evokes the poet's most timid self. In the letter with which I began this essay, in addition to reflecting on the relationship between kingdom, power and glory, Dickinson compliments Higginson's letter for a "a spectral power in thought that walks alone," adding: "I would like to thank you for your great kindness but never try to lift the words which I cannot hold" (L 330). (Apparently he has been criticizing her diction.)

She also poses as comparatively insignificant in a letter to Samuel Bowles. After her tribute to his influence in the lives of "so many," she confesses that she has no such range of impact. However, she further muses, "How extraordinary that Life's large Population contain so few of power to us" (L 275). In this reflection, she characteristically turns the tables. Though her power over others is limited, the power of most people to affect her is also limited. These two letters suggest two typical modes Dickinson employed in dealing with male power figures.

Clearly, Dickinson was attracted to masculine forms of power. She writes approvingly of a portrait of Tommaso Salvini in 1884 in terms that bring to mind her feelings about her father: "The brow is that of Deity — the eyes, those of the lost, but the power lies in the *Throat* — pleading, sovereign, savage — the panther and the dove!" (L 948). Her admiration for her father and the Master letters further confirm their attraction to stimulating versions of male force. And we must remember her involvement with the intimidating Judge Lord. She describes his face in these terms in 1885: "Had I not loved it, I had feared it, the Face had such ascension" (L967).

Even Dickinson's definitions of poetry are clothed in the rhetoric of power. "If I read a book [and] it makes my whole body so cold no fire ever can warm me, I know *that* is poetry. If I feel physically as if the top of my head were taken off, I know *that* is poetry. These are the only way I know it" (L342a). *Art* and *power* are sometimes used interchangeably.

But the synthesis power effects in Dickinson is always decaying into antithesis, into powerlessness, and that too is a fundamental property of her imagination and an indication of her shared relation to a gender-differentiated power structure. In order to explore why that might have been characteristic of her, it is helpful to look a little outside the usual critical structure and to bring to bear on Dickinson's work some of the insights of recent French feminist theory.

Helene Cixous begins her strange, provocative essay "Sorties" in *The Newly-Born Woman* with the following set of reflections:

Where is she?
Activity/Passivity
Sun/Moon
Culture/Nature
Day/Night

Father/Mother
Head/Heart
Intelligible/Palpable
Logos/Pathos

Form, convex, step, advance, semen, progress
Matter, concave, ground — where steps are taken, holding-and dumping ground.
Man
―――――――
Woman

Always the same metaphor: we follow it, it carries us, beneath all its figures, wherever discourse is organized. If we read or speak, the same thread or double braid is leading us throughout literature, philosophy, criticism, centuries of representation and reflection.
Thought has always worked through opposition,
Speaking/Writing
Parole/Ecriture
High/Low
Through dual, hierarchical oppositions. Superior/Inferior. Myths, legends, books. Philosophical systems. Everywhere (where) ordering intervenes, where a law organizes what is thinkable by oppositions (dual, irreconcilable; or sublatable, dialectical). All these pairs of oppositions are *couples.* Does that mean something? Is the fact that Logocentrism subjects thought — all concepts, codes and values — to a binary system, related to "the" couple, man/woman? (63-63)

Cixous' provocative suggestion that we read a binary opposition between man and woman as the basis of many other paired oppositions in philosophical discourse is at the heart of my argument for a historical and gendered reading of Dickinson. We can, of course, search the poems for places where Dickinson consciously and directly reflects upon gender. If we are cultural critics, we can look for direct references to historical persons and events. However, we do not need to proceed in this way in order to find the impact of patriarchy on the poet's work. As a poet whose work is necessarily inscribed within the codes of nineteenth-century American bourgeois culture, Emily Dickinson could not fail to reproduce in part the structure of power relations in which she was enmeshed.

No cultural hegemony is absolute, however. Consider, for instance, this pair of statements about women and power made by two men of Dickinson's time and milieu. In his novel *Miss Gilbert's Career,* Josiah Holland, Dickinson's friend, congratulates his heroine for giving up her literary career in exchange for a career of marriage and self-sacrifice. Her need for power is re-routed so that it is no longer her own "imperious will" which she seeks to gratify. Holland writes: "She learned that a woman's truest career is lived in love's serene retirement — lived in feeding the native forces of her other self — lived in the career of her husband" (466). Here we have the common and recognizable version of true womanhood's relation to power: indirect, self-effacing, domestic, and predicated on the virtues of heart and hearth.

Austin Dickinson's description of the impact of women on some aspects of nineteenth-century culture is quite different, however. His opinion is that "the women count in our modern census. They have appeared above the surface in the last generation, and become a power, nowhere more than in parish affairs, where they have found a congenial field for their activities . . . They are hardly longer the power behind the throne; they are a good part of the throne itself" (Sewall, *The Life*, 121-22).

Leaving aside here the complex issues of biographical origins, of sincerity and authenticity raised by these quotations, let us acknowledge that they do point to a situation first experienced by middle-class American women in the nineteenth century: the situation of finding themselves able to operate in a public arena in *relatively* large numbers while they were at the same time deeply afflicted with a sense of guilt for betraying the ethical code of femininity and the domestic sphere. This is the double bind nimbly captured in Mary Kelley's title, *Private Woman, Public Stage.*

It is not enough to say that women were in many ways effectively powerless in nineteenth-century American bourgeois culture. We must also acknowledge that in parish activities, in education, in certain political causes, and *as writers*, middle-class women had more public influence than ever before. Many nineteenth-century women writers supported whole families with the proceeds of their writing. Lydia Sigourney could command $100 for four poems and $500 from *Godey's Lady's Book* for the use of her name on its title page. However, the cost of playing on the public stage, or entering the market, could be great as well. In the nineteenth century we see the first major alliance between creative women and madness.

Catherine Clement in her disquisition on "the hysteric" in *The Newly-Born Woman* gives us a set of highly-charged statements applicable to many guilt-ridden nineteenth-century women writers. Clement, in the essay called "The Guilty One," writes:

> That is the easiest solution: keeping oneself in a state of permanent guilt is to constitute oneself as a subject. Caught up in themes which are not hers, repeating her cues, always somewhere between sleep and wakefulness, between a hypnotic and an excited state, she is not she, but through the play of identifications, she is successively each one of the others. They are going to help her become a subject: they are going to make her guilty. (46)

This is the way Clement describes the simultaneous attraction and threat represented by the powerful male intermediary to the talented but conflicted woman.

These interventions in the on-going discussion about women and power must serve as an introduction to my reading of two poems about power in Emily Dickinson's canon: "My life had stood a loaded gun" and "Behind me dips eternity." Both of these poems have been extensively discussed by others; few critics, however, have attempted to talk about the loaded gun poem as a particularly historical document.

The poem really clicks into place when we consider it as one written by a certain kind of woman in nineteenth-century America.

Let's look at the poem in more detail:

My Life had stood—a Loaded Gun—
In Corners—till a Day
The Owner passed—identified—
And carried Me away—

And now We roam in Sovreign Woods—
And now We hunt the Doe—
And every time I speak for Him—
The Mountains straight reply—

And do I smile, such cordial light
Upon the Valley glow—
It is as a Vesuvian face
Had let it's pleasure through—

And when at Night—Our good Day done—
I guard My Master's Head—
'Tis better than the Eider-Duck's
Deep Pillow—to have shared—

To foe of His—I'm deadly foe—
None stir the second time—
On whom I lay a Yellow Eye—
Or an emphatic Thumb—

Though I than He—may longer live
He longer must—than I—
For I have but the power to kill,
Without—the power to die—

Written about 1863, this poem examines the effects of assuming certain kinds of power. A moral focus is conspicuously absent as a divining rod until the last stanza where the speaker with only "the power to kill" reveals her morally compromised position. The poem does a double take, strangely, in that last stanza. Up until this point, the reader is invited to see the speaker's newly assumed identity as beneficial and even heroic. The Wordsworthian mountains echo her speech, the day done has been a "good day," a strenuous day more satisfying than sleeping on a downy pillow. Only the third stanza with its "Vesuvian face" throws an eerie light over this whole proceeding. It's worth remembering that Mount Vesuvius erupted a number of times during the 1850s climaxing with a particularly fearsome and destructive eruption in 1861. Should we ignore the threat implied in a volcanic eruption? Up until the final stanza the poet seems peculiarly unwilling to judge negatively this assumption of destructive force. A variant for "None stir the second time" is "None *harm* the second time," again suggesting that the gun's destructive force is not morally suspect since it is used defensively.

However, the final stanza clearly introduces a new emotion into the poem. The emotion is guilt. I agree with Barbara Clarke Mossberg that this poem represents "an array of conflicting attitudes toward art and the self, which result in severe identity conflict" (23). The poem is hysterical in certain ways and that hysteria must be understood in the historical context of a continent and a century in which women were invited to assume certain sorts of power while at the same time subtly tortured for their desires to do so.

Let us go back to Catherine Clement's description of the hysterical woman as "the guilty one": she has been possessed by her doctors. They have offered her the chance to become a subject. "Caught up in themes which are not hers, repeating her cues, always somewhere between sleep and wakefulness, between a hypnotic and an excited state, she is not she, but through the play of identifications, she is successively each one of the others. They are going to help her become a subject: they are going to make her guilty." This is the position described by the female gun self.

From my point of view, this poem is not a confession of the poet's personal misery, however. Richard Sewall provides a helpful reminder in his biography that the *Springfield Republican* used the eider-duck image in an 1860 article discouraging women poets from writing "the literature of misery." The speaker here rejects the eider duck's deep pillow. Instead of being a confessional poem, this work is closer to a definitional exploration of a certain kind of power.

My intuition is that Dickinson began this poem with the intention of writing another celebration of her relation to the Master Force. This would connect the first stanza, at least, to other works like "I'm ceded, I've stopped being theirs," "He put the belt around my life," and "A wife at daybreak I shall be." There is a sense of strain in the poem, however, as though as she went along — at first admiring the power conferred upon the speaker by her relation to the Owner — another set of issues presented itself in her mind. What does it mean for a woman to subsume herself so totally in the life of a masculine presence? The metatext begins to unravel the text by suggesting the destructiveness of a pure instrumentality. Negative associations with power lurch through the backcountry of the poetic landscape.

Without the owner, the speaker cannot speak at all. She cannot roam in "Sovreign Woods," that is, in the forest protected for the king's own hunting, the forest of patriarchal power. However, the cost of accepting this empowerment is hunting the doe, killing off her linkage to female life, and surrendering a maternal, nurturing influence like that of the eider duck (known to cushion her babies by feathering her nest with down plucked from her own beast). Though we cannot help feeling the emphatic thumb of the poet's conscious attempt to make us admire this power through most of the poem, we also cannot ignore the accumulation of underground hints of guilt.

At the end, the speaker seems to throw up her hands in horror at the satanic bargain she has made. As a ventriloquist's dummy, as a pure instrument of another's force, she has surrendered her status as a subject. Power can only be understood as part of an oppositional pair in juxtaposition with powerlessness as life can only be lived fully with the knowledge of death as its terminus. Having agreed to speak only for him, the gun seals *his* immortality while at the same time accepting the status of non-being for herself. The power to kill involves the preliminary death of the self recorded in the gun's admission that she no longer has the power to die. She is already dead. The speaker has become not a self, as she had hoped, but a mouthpiece.

As we watch the sovereign female self assume the mantle of power in the poem only to turn that mantle inside out at the end in a confession of guilt and powerlessness, we witness a ritual performed again and again in the nineteenth century by creative women, for whom power, once admired, turns ugly and self-destructive. Toward the end of the century, Ella Wheeler Wilcox summed it up in *Men, Women and Emotions* (1893): "Seen from a distance, fame may seem to a woman like a sea bathed in tropical suns, wherein she longs to sail. Let fame once be hers, she finds it a prairie fire consuming or scorching all that is dearest in life to her. Be careful before you light these fires with your own hands" (291). As in so many statements of its kind, for the more narrow instance of fame, we might very well substitute the broader, more threatening term: power.

Another poem in which fears for a female self emerge is "Behind me dips eternity" (#721).

Behind Me—dips Eternity—
Before Me—Immortality—
Myself—the Term between—
Death but the Drift of Eastern Gray,
Dissolving into Dawn away,
Before the West begin—

'Tis Kingdoms—afterward—they say—
In perfect—pauseless Monarchy—
Whose Prince—is Son of None—
Himself—His Dateless Dynasty—
Himself—Himself diversify—
In Duplicate divine—

'Tis Miracle before Me—then—
'Tis Miracle behind—between—
A Crescent in the Sea—
With Midnight to the North of Her—
and Midnight to the South of Her—
And Maelstrom—in the Sky—

Reading this poem in a gendered historical context, I am particularly struck by the speaker's positioning of herself in terms of these two axes: An east-west metaphysics rendered male and a north-south temporal realm rendered female. In a century which at least paid considerable lip service to the notion of separate spheres of gender, in a country in which those spheres have paradigms in Puritan gender divisions predicated on Adam and Eve, the poet seems both to invoke and to revoke conventional mappings of power. This poem can be read as the poet's self-insertion of the female into history: 'Myself-the Term between." *His* power, from this point of view, looks comparatively lifeless. As under the aegis of the patriarchal god, patriarchal authority clones itself repeatedly in what Cixous might call a "repetition of the same," the speaker understands her position as not merely personal (an *I*'s position) but generic (a *Her*'s position). "With Midnight to the North of Her-/ And Midnight to the South of Her," she has no points of reference to determine her own power, however. Might not this "Maelstrom in the Sky" suggest a whirlpool of male force threatening to derange her "crescent in the sea"? It will take a miracle of a different kind to preserve her from harm.

My intention in this brief textual discussion has been to make an argument not only for the plausibility of historical, gender-sensitive criticism but for its continuing exfoliation. To the extent that we can find new ways of decoding the power relations which operate both behind and within literature we open up new ways of seeing our own linguistic situations in the present. As Toril Moi puts it in *Sexual/Textual Politics*, "It is necessary to deconstruct the opposition between traditionally 'masculine' and traditionally 'feminine' values *and* to confront the full political force and reality of such categories" (160). This means locating a feminist critical practice along two axes, ignoring neither the kingdom which circumscribed an Emily Dickinson nor the glory which she learned to appropriate for her art.

Works Cited

All references to the poems and letters of Emily Dickinson are taken from the following sources and reflect the numbering system used in these sources: *The Letters of Emily Dickinson*, 3 vols. Edited by Thomas H. Johnson and Theodora Ward. Cambridge, Mass: Harvard UP, 1955; *The Poems of Emily Dickinson*. 3 vols. Edited by Thomas H. Johnson. Cambridge, Mass.: 1958.

Cameron, Sharon. *Lyric Time: Dickinson and the Limits of Genre*. Baltimore: Johns Hopkins UP, 1979.

Cixous, Helene and Catherine Clement. *The Newly Born Woman*. Minneapolis: U of Minnesota P, 1986.

Holland, Josiah Gilbert. *Miss Gilbert's Career*. New York: Scribner's, 1860.

Kelley, Mary. *Private Woman, Public Stage*. New York: Oxford UP, 1984.

Moi, Toril. *Sexual/Textual Politics*. New York: Methuen, 1985.

Mossberg, Barbara Antonina Clarke. *Emily Dickinson: When a Writer is a Daughter*. Bloomington: Indiana UP, 1982.

Sewall, Richard B. *The Life of Emily Dickinson*. 2 vols. New York: Farrar, Straus, 1974.

Wilcox, Ella Wheeler. *Men, Women, and Emotions*. Chicago: Mirrill, Higgins, 1893.

Poem 271

A solemn thing — it was — I said —
A woman — white — to be —
And wear — if God should count me fit —
Her blameless mystery —

A hallowed thing — to drop a life
Into the purple well —
Too plummetless — that it return —
Eternity — until —

I pondered how the bliss would look —
And would it feel as big —
When I could take it in my hand —
As hovering — seen — through fog —

And then — the size of this "small" life —
The Sages — call it small —
Swelled — like Horizons — in my vest —
And I sneered — softly — "small"!

c. 1861 *1896*

Women's Studies, 1989
Vol. 16, p. 21
Reprints available directly from the publisher

Poem 271

MARCIA FALK

Stanford University, Palo Alto

IN THE FIRST publication of Emily Dickinson's poem #271 (in 1896, ten years after Dickinson's death), the poem was entitled "Wedded" by the editors. The editorial assumption that this passionate lyric was intended as a paean to marriage is typical of the way Dickinson's work and life have been treated by the critics until recently. It is much to the credit of feminist scholars in the recent past that readers have begun to see the poet and the poetry on their own terms, rather than filtered through the lens of heterosexist assumptions and values. The re-visioning of poem #271 as an expression of the poet's consecration to her art — an interpretation that sees the "woman — white" as Dickinson's private symbol for the role of the poet — falls within this new line of criticism. Insofar as it rejects the idea that the poem is a celebration of traditional marriage, this interpretation offers an important corrective to the earlier view. However, I believe that it does not yet fully take into account the logical development of the poem's argument — its unexpected *turns* of thought — and the literary and social conventions that the poem rests upon and ultimately transforms. I would like, therefore, to propose another alternative, a different dialogue with this poem.

I am going to begin by asserting the view — surprising though it may at first seem in the context of this feminist forum — that the "woman — white" is a double symbol for the traditional female roles of bride and nun, both of which, of course, are marriage roles — that is, roles of dependent relationship to a male other (or Other). Indeed, I think it is impossible to ignore these conventional readings of the "woman — white," no matter what information we have about

Women's Studies, 1989
Vol. 16, pp. 23-27

Dickinson's biography. That Dickinson never married, that she chose to dress in white, that she dedicated herself fiercely to her poetry at about the time this poem was written — these are all facts of interest and importance, but they cannot obliterate, for us as readers any more than for Dickinson as writer, the common symbolic associations of the image of "a woman — white." In our culture, such an image cannot but call to mind the bridal gown and, perhaps secondarily, the novice's habit. Moreover, as we shall see as we read through the poem, Dickinson develops the bridal image thematically as the poem progresses, making it the foundation of a sophisticated poetic structure.

Having said this, however, I want to follow with the claim that the poem is finally *not* about choosing to be a bride or a nun, but about the process by which the speaker comes to reject such a choice. Indeed, the poem is not about the choice of any vocation or the adoption of any role. Rather, it is about the overthrowing of roles and idealizations in favor of embracing an autonomous, self-created life. Such a life is one of real and particular experiences — as contrasted with idealized, gender-determined roles — and no matter how this life is viewed by the world, no matter how "small" and inconsequential it may seem to external authorities and "Sages," it swells proud and large in the speaker's own "vest."

But the poem does not begin with this realization; it ends there. The following is an outline of the sequence of thoughts and events that leads to this defiant conclusion.

The poem recounts a mini-narrative, describing first what the speaker *once thought* ("A solemn thing — it *was* — I *said* —" [emphases mine]), followed by how she came to consider this idea ("I pondered how the bliss would look —"), and finally stating what she now believes and feels ("And then —/. . . I sneered —"). The sequence of actions completed by the first person narrator — I said, I pondered, and then I sneered — summarizes the poem's story, which is, in effect, the tale of a change of heart and mind.

Once, the speaker tells us, she proclaimed it "a solemn thing" to be a "woman — white" (a bride to man or God). She believed this role to be sanctioned by God and cloaked in blamelessness (purity) and mystery (sexuality, passion). While the almost-oxymoronic phrase "blameless mystery" calls to mind the miraculous Virgin Birth (and, hence, associations of the convent), it also suggests the paradoxes of our culture's idealized image of the secular bride, especially the adolescent one: virtuous and virginal, yet seductive and sexual. Consider, for a moment, the classic style of wedding gowns: white, of course, and floor-length, covering the body from top — often beginning at the neck, with lace — to the very bottom, and even trailing beyond; yet form-fitting at the torso and often quite low-cut at the bust beneath the conveniently transparent lace; thus projecting the deliberately confusing message of chastity that seduces, modesty that reveals. To be both virgin and femme fatale was once an ideal shared by many American young women, living as they did in a culture deeply conflicted about sexuality in general and female sexuality in particular. In the first stanza of the poem, the speaker describes the aspirations she once embraced and the convictions she espoused when she declared it "solemn" to be a bride.

In the second stanza, the speaker continues to refer back to this earlier stage of life when she imagined her own future as a woman. "The purple well," another richly associative symbol, seems to emerge out of the symbol of the "woman — white," and to extend its meanings in both secular and religious domains. Thus, as a vaginal image, the well suggests female sexuality, while as a sacred image drawn from the body of nature — an image which is also associated with women, especially in biblical and other religious sources — it can represent a spiritual passageway, a site of revelation, a source of life. Although purple may appear to be the opposite of white — the one the symbolic color of lifeblood and passion, the other of innocence and purity — such a joining of opposites only completes in imagery the paradox implied in the "blameless mystery" of the first stanza. White becomes purple, as bridal innocence yields to marital passion, or religious self-renunciation leads to union with the Divine. To the adolescent imagination, the virgin ideal leads naturally into an idealized life of passion, be that passion sexual or religious. For the youthful persona of the speaker's past, the possibilities of "the purple well" seem infinite, "plummetless"; indeed, this well is a fount of eternal life, promising to "return — Eternity" to her.

The last two lines of the stanza are syntactically difficult, and it is tempting to read "Eternity — until —" as a reversal for the sake of the rhyme. But there seems to be more than rhyme at stake here. Placing "until" after "eternity," Dickinson cuts eternity short, and the word "until" becomes the turning point between the two halves of the poem: I said all of this *until*... I pondered.

In the second half of the poem, the vision changes, as thought supersedes the adolescent imaginings recounted in the first two stanzas. The speaker now *ponders* the "bliss" about which she had earlier only fantasized, wondering whether the life she had envisioned will seem as "big" once she possesses it as it had seemed when she had only imagined it. At a distance, she notes, this bliss was necessarily blurred by "fog," the fog of unreality. The logic of the laws of perspective is reversed here. Normally, things seem larger the closer they are brought into view. But here, the speaker questions whether her fantasies will seem — will "feel," to be precise — as big when they are owned, held in the hand, as they did when they were only glimpsed from far away. The answer, unspoken but already implied in the doubting, implied in the question itself, is a frank and resounding "no."

No, the life of the bride or the nun will not seem so large to her once she owns it. Having seen that her fantasies were misguided, overblown, the speaker now has the insight that her life is *already large.* It is already full and whole as "Horizons" — that is, a world in itself — swelling in her "vest" (a metonymy for her body, hence her Self, to replace the image of the gown or habit implied by the "woman — white"). This is the revelation of the fourth stanza. The so-called "Sages" — male authorities, society's standard-bearers — may have deemed her life "small," incomplete, unworthy. In *their* eyes, she may need to dedicate herself to a groom or to a God in order to be made whole, to be saved. But to this false vision she now replies with defiant and self-confident restraint — "softly," with only a sneer. With a sarcasm strongly implied by the use of quotation marks, Dickinson inverts the meaning of the Sages' word: "small" becomes, by implication, infinitely large. The speaker's choice to be her own Self — not to give her Self over to a male other, or to any other-defined role — seems fully valid now, not needing further argument or explanation. Indeed, her choices do not concern the outside world at all, for they are hers alone to make.

Having achieved this self-sufficiency, the speaker has completed her journey, arriving from adolescence to adulthood. She has gone from would-be bride ("woman — white — to be") to true mother of her Self. Her journey has taken her through an idealized anticipation of sexual, or mystical, union (the life dropped into the bottomless "purple well"), and then through a conceptualizing period (when she ponders). It is in this period of conceptualization/conception that she comes to reject the false "bliss," and in its stead to conceive — virginally, as it were, without union with a male other — a new identity, one which she will eventually hold in her own hands. This embryonic ("'small'") new identity then swells large in the womb of her "vest," until finally she is ready to defy the paternal authorities, become her own parent, and give birth to a new Self.

In poem #508, Dickinson will subsequently write:

I'm ceded — I've stopped being Theirs —
. . . .
A half unconscious Queen —
But this time — Adequate — Erect,
With Will to choose, or to reject,
And I choose, just a Crown —

The speaker of #508 makes clear just how crucial was the choice of her own identity, an identity contrasted with the one imposed on her by others. The speaker of poem #271 describes a similar choice and provides a similar contrast; however, she reveals not just the end of the process but also the internal stages along the way — and this revelation is what makes the poem so poignant. Thus poem #271 depicts the temptations that are at first succumbed to, the robes that are eventually cast off, and the idols that must finally be overthrown before the Crown of the Self can be donned.

The genius of poem #271 lies in the subtle interrelationship between its imagery and its structure, and in its bold appropriation and transformation of elemental cultural conventions. By an exquisitely crafted use of her art, Dickinson has taken the theme of bride-become-wife-and-mother (or, virgin-become-nun-or-Madonna) and converted it into the story of a woman's creation of her Self. She has done far more than reject tradition here; she has passed through it, transcended it, and made from it something wholly new.

Poem 271

Dressing for Success: Emily Dickinson's Accomplished "A solemn thing — it was — I said"

BARBARA MOSSBERG

U.S. Scholar in Residence, United States Information Agency
University of Oregon

EARLY IN HER poetic career, Emily Dickinson celebrated her decision to live a life as a poet. In p. 271, "A solemn thing — it was — I said", one of her first fully developed treatments of interwoven issues — her self-image as a poet, her confidence in her renunciation of a conventional woman's life, her rejection of majority opinion in her pitting herself against the "Sages", and her size — we see themes which will emerge as pivotal: self-reliance, creation and control, the giving of the self over to art, the concept of stature (the Economy size is the largest), and finally, the focus on the process of writing itself,

P. 271 introduces the connection Dickinson makes between a poet's life and a renounced woman's life, a connection she develops throughout her poetry. Dickinson describes taking responsibility for her own life, and whatever action is necessary to achieve success. Dickinson is famous for her whites — the dresses she wore, the way she describes her soul at the "white heat." In this poem she makes explicit her use of white to describe a life of renunciation as a woman, associating white with purity, cleanliness, holiness; white is "blameless," "mystery" — unknown, virgin.

How does she propose, then, to live a "white life"? By dropping "life" itself into the "purple well" — a witty image, playing on ink well, perhaps

Women's Studies, 1989
Vol. 16, pp. 29-34

in the sense of Sylvia Plath's "bloodjet is poetry" as well. Purple is Dickinson's word for royalty, eternity, splendor, and art. She gives up life as a traditional woman (a bride in white) for art.

To **drop** something, as into a well, to let it fall, in this case is not an accident, but a deliberate act; it is controlled; one drops something one has in one's hand. To drop something sounds like a casual act. Yet Dickinson contrasts "hallowed" with the specific act of **dropping** a life, letting it go, of her own volition. She drops her life for her writing, plunges herself into the purple well. As she immerses herself in the purple ink, which while deep will return to her an immortal life, we see her control her life, the shape it will have, the ultimate weight and stature, through her writing, **her hand** — holding the pen, controlling the ink, making life. Thus when Dickinson says in the last stanza, "when I could take it in my hand" — we can understand that "it" is her life as an artist; her blissful life is controlled, created, **hand-made**. We see a focus on the process of writing again and again in Dickinson's poetry, the appearance of her **hand** at work.

The sense of her being in control is developed from the first stanza, in which she is "to be" a woman "white." To **wear** mystery, to put it on: this is a **decision**. Dickinson's use of "the bliss' as a synonym for her achievement as an artist — a function of her renunciation of traditional fulfillment as a woman — reinforces our sense of the deliberate nature of her decision to re-create her own life, take her life literally into her own hands. Bliss is a state of feeling, what Dickinson would experience if she were to drop her life into the purple well, yet we note that Dickinson gives "bliss" dimensions — it has a size, a life, a heft, a look, a feel; it is the life she creates when she "drops a life" into the well — by way of her art.

If the world sees her dropped, virgin, life as "**small**," as if she had not really lived, as if she had not lived significantly, it is wrong. Her attitude towards the "Sages" then is defiant, scornful. Their values are undermined by their blindness to her worth. Dickinson writes in this same time period "I'm Nobody" (p. 228), which expresses this attitude towards "them" and what they presume about her life. From the outside, she looks like a "nobody," and given those values and perspectives, she prefers to be unknown. It is better than being compromised by "their" limited viewpoint of who matters, someone who is "somebody." She even is willing to risk being considered a man by us, have us see her with a beard, with no breasts, in her renunciation of a woman's life, as her late companion piece to this poem makes clear, p. 1737, "Rearrange a "Wife's" affection!" In this poem, Dickinson makes clear her sense that one cannot be both woman and poet. She has had to choose, and she chose art. She renounced love, trust, emotional and physical bonds which could fulfill her; she endured anguish, and loneliness; she was a martyr to her art, living a life unknown, unrecognized. Yet she had no doubt that we would be reading this poem, that she would have made herself immortal by her decision to write, to forfeit a woman's traditional successes.

Dickinson deals with this self-conscious decision throughout her poetic career. P. 343, for example, says

My reward for Being, was This.
My premium — My Bliss —
. . .
When Thrones accost my Hands —
With "Me, Miss, Me" —
I'll unroll Thee —
Dominions dowerless — beside this Grace —
Election — Vote —
The Ballots of Eternity, will show just that.

The "This" in the first line is the poem before us, as "Thee" refers to the poem, and "this grace" as well. We see again the notion of "bliss," the presence of the hands, the issue of eternity, the idea of a reward for renunciation.

P. 349 also deals with this theme;

I had the Glory — that will do —
. . . with one long "Nay" —
Bliss' early shape
Deforming — Dwindling — Gulfing up —
Time's possibility.

Bliss is a function of renunciation (see also P. 356, P. 359):

I gained it so —
By Climbing slow
By Catching at the Twigs that grow
Between — the Bliss — and me —

This focus on her strategy to create poems is made explicit and is present throughout Dickinson's work. In P. 528, we see the renunciation, symbolized by "white"; P. 657 shows Dickinson gathering

Paradise with her hands; P. 801 shows her hands, writing the poem; P. 486 shows us her strategy of gaining poems by leading a "small" life. But in every case her strategy with her hands leads to a success as a poet, to immortality. In Dickinson's opinion, her life, she has us know, is only small in quotation marks: it really is huge, and it grows and "swells."

The poem is technically crafty; thematically about development, size, growth, about the ways both daunted and undaunted she creates her art and life out of her self-image as an artist, the poem structurally develops an illustration of growth. In terms of the poem's imagery, we see a progression in the four stanzas from a "woman white" — an esteemed life — to a life as a woman dropped into a purple well. This dropped white/purple life becomes "the bliss" in the third stanza. Finally, this white dropped life, this bliss, is revealed as not a "small" life. The conditional state of the speaker ("a woman — white — to be") in the opening stanza is equated in the last stanza with the fact of being such a woman. The humility of the first lines becomes arrogance at the end, as the speaker revels in her abilities to become such an esteemed person agains all odds, tradition, advice — moving from a solemn mood of modesty, hoping that God would approve of her, to sneering at the notion that anyone, even "sages," can judge her. In an intimate aside to the reader, she describes herself talking back — softly, true — but *sneering* — an attitude Dickinson emphasizes by the alliteration of **sneered, softly, small**. She moves from sobriety to bliss, dependence to self-reliance.

What fuels this progression is her imagination. Dickinson's narrator grows by use of her own words and her self-conscious reasoning process ("I said,") as she imagines her life. She goes on to tell us that she "ponders," and the question she asks herself leads to an answer, so that she predicts, writes a self-fulfilling prophecy ("and then"), demonstrating the power she draws from herself, the poet: writing, thinking, imagining, dipping her life, forever, into the purple well. The contrast between the holy reverence of the first stanza and the attitude towards the sages who don't know anything in the last is extreme: what Dickinson shows is that the process of thinking and speaking about her life decision, about her art, leads her to the confidence of saying that the sages are not right about her; they are not "sage," in fact. Finally "small is not small."

As P. 454 and others make clear, Dickinson feels poetic power in a conventionally defined "small" life. Thus the boldness we see emerge here comes out of her confidence in her decision to live precisely this life she lives by writing: "the difference made me bold." What we will continue to see again and again is the narrator overturning public opinion about her life. She is really not poor:

"Rich! 'Twas Myself — was rich —
To take the name of Gold —
And Gold to own in solid Bars —
The Difference made me bold —"

She is not small but she celebrates a "small" life:

I was the slightest in the House —
I took the smallest Room —
. . .
So stationed I could catch the Mint
That never ceased to fall — (P. 486)

In the same language as "I pondered how the bliss would look —" she considers her wealth:

I wonder how the Rich — may feel —
An Indiaman — An Earl
I deem that I — with but a Crumb
Am Sovereign of them all — (from P. 791)

Therefore we can understand a context for the resolution of P. 271, "And I sneered — softly — 'small!'" and that of other poems: P. 612, for example, or P. 248, show Dickinson living "small" as a gnat, having a "timid" and little hand. But P. 613, "They shut me up in Prose," P. 791, "God gave a loaf to every Bird —," P. 1282, "Art thou the thing I wanted?" P. 288, "I'm Nobody," each end with a tossed head, a triumphant defiance. The spirit of "small!" which ends P. 271 is repeated in "Still!" in P. 613, when Dickinson is "shut up in Prose" and told to be "still" as she was as a little girl. She feels "sovereign of them all," she "dines without — like God", and she dismisses with scorn a publically affirmed life.

We see the technology of success — what it requires for Dickinson. This is not a poem about aspiration, but of achievement, achieved. It is all the more significant, then, that it is an early poem — evidence that at the outset, Dickinson established her sense of purpose, her way of seeing herself and her work, as successful. This is not to say that

Dickinson did not ever suffer anxiety about her art or life, or did not grow as a poet, or develop her ideas about poetry further, but simply to emphasize her own understanding and sense of accomplishment: she dressed for success, but to be judged only on her own terms; her designer's label would read: "Original. Made by Hand. Size Small." The price? "All — is the price of All."

Poem 271

MAURYA SIMON

University of California at Riverside

PERHAPS I MIGHT, in opening, make a stark confession, and thus qualify and disqualify my critical responses to Emily Dickinson's poems. I am a poet and not an academic; thus, I have perhaps a vested interest in these volatile, impassioned, disturbing, tormented, ecstatic, dazzling, cladestine, and fierce poems. Dickinson's poems matter to me, because they seem to achieve the impossible. Her obscure and complex life matters to me, because it is the model of a poet's life lived in extremity: lived, as she would have it, between the limits of an "Awful Vacuum" and "A Geometric Joy." Dickinson's language both seduces and repels me; for it manages both to diagram a visionary consciousness and, ultimately, to plumb the depths of despair, desperation, and terror.

When I read Emily Dickinson, I find myself confronted with some of the questions and conflicts she faced as a writer: for instance, what is the relationship between my identity as a woman and my identity as a poet? Is it necessary for me as an artist to create for myself a life in language that is to some degree independent of family alliances? How do I balance a need for Experience with the need for its suspension in order to contemplate its significance? Must the Soul select her own Society?

Most likely the answers to these and other questions will continue to elude me. But what is clear is that Dickinson embarked upon what Richard Howard has called "the most relentless epic of identity in our literature." With unsurpassed courage this poet who feared much, but who did not fear her own mind, explored the farthest reaches, the margins, of the universe. Thus, she empowers all her readers and

Women's Studies, 1989
Vol. 16, pp. 35-37

urges us to inhabit "A fairer House than prose —," that is, to "dwell in Possibility —."

In poem 271 we have, I believe, a poet's poem; that is, one that focuses upon the poet's relationship to her own power and that ultimately exposes her willingness to submit to that power. For Dickinson, it is, indeed, a "solemn thing," to don the "white" vestment, the poet's mantle. For, like a novice nun, an initiate, a bride to Christ, the poet must consider the finality of her vows, the deliberateness of her sacrifices, and the immense demands such a vocation — that of being a poet — impose upon her. A "solemn thing" this chosen path, and yet how considerable are its intellectual, emotional, and spiritual rewards.

As Robert Hass writes in *Twentieth Century Pleasures*, "Art is foremost an activity of the spirit, and when we lose track of what makes an art an art, we lose track of the spirit." The art of poetry, in particular, is an art of transformation. To be worthy of its mystical possibilities, of poetry's "blameless mystery," Dickinson must be willing to sacrifice living a conventional life. She must be prepared "to drop [her] life/ Into the purple well," to forego living in the world at large, to excuse herself from the passing amusements and passions of sex, the calls of matrimony and motherhood. Dickinson drops the garments of her past identity down the well of time: only on Judgement Day, in the blaze of Eternity's light, will she again confront her cast-off secular life, the life that might have been, and her life as it is.

The poem is held delicately together by the use of this extended metaphor of the poet's donning a white vestment or dress. This white garment represents the uniform appropriate to Dickinson's literary/ religious vocation: the garment is virginial, pure, blank as a page of paper, the color of light, of holiness, of God, of transformation and bliss. In the third stanza, the poet "ponder[s] how the bliss would look" — and the entire poem suddenly takes a turn, as if to approach the incomprehensible, that "Thunderbolt —/ That scalps your naked Soul," the very nature of Being, which is both macrocosm and microcosm, clay and Atom, small enough to fit (like a pen) in Dickinson's hand, yet so immense it hovers as though seen "through fog."

Dickinson associates the bliss of being a poet with the awed pleasures of engaging in a sacred act and pact with divinity. She feels that to be inspired, to breathe life into art, into language, is to be empowered by, and with the Spirit. Such bliss, like the best poetry, is mysterious by nature; it is elusive, baffling: it defies analysis. But even barely glimpsed, the bliss of being a poet affords Dickinson such a sense of intense and enormous power that she is moved to exclaim triumphantly, at the poem's end, that the Sages — whoever they may be — are wrong to condemn her for living a so-called "small" life. Indeed, so convinced is Dickinson of the importance of her calling, the necessity of being a "woman in white" — a poet — that her heart, her very life, swells "like Horizons in [her] vest" to think of the bliss it brings her. Her pride in her genius (for I do believe that genius recognizes itself), and in her literary talents, allows her to sneer at those Sages. Thus the tone of this last stanza is quite defiant and boastful, and in a vague way echoes the claim made in the poem's opening lines: "A solemn thing — it was — I said —/ A woman — white — to be —." I think these lines ask us to acknowledge Dickinson's conviction that womanhood and poetry may coexist: that one needn't disassociate oneself from either identity. Indeed, Dickinson asserts that there's a duplicity involved: a poet is both flesh and mind, woman and Soul. The one fact of being necessarily coexists with the other. She suggests that language mediates between the self and the world, the conscious and the unconscious, and thus strives to achieve what Coleridge considered the basis of art: "the harmonizing of opposites." Such "harmonizing" pervades Dickinson's life and work.

Poem 271
Workshop Discussion

Speakers: MARCIA FALK, BARBARA MOSSBERG, MAURYA SIMON

I think this is anger in the last stanza. Did she ever express this anger directly to the people in her life?

Yes — in many of her letters, especially as a teenager and as an adolescent. Her persona in her letters was of a self-indulgent, witty brat — angry, fed-up, cynical and sarcastic. At one point she's in the kitchen talking about her mother who is ill and she's having to do some of the chores, and she says she's: "looking around my kitchen . . . *My* kitchen I think I called it — God forbid that it was, or ever shall by my own — God keep me from what they call *households.*" In another letter she says that nobody ever gives her any time to write in her family; "they run me all day like a summer dog in a [pant]." She says "What need have I of affection?" and "*mind* the house and the food, *sweep* if the spirits were low, and for what neighborhood, what so full as my own — the infirm, the blind, the halt, the utterly hateful to me and ugly, and these to see and be seen by? An opportunity for cultivating meekness. I prefer angels who sing bad songs." Whether or not this is hyperbole, there really is an angry, sarcastic and sharp-edged tone to these letters, and she had the reputation in her family for having a sharp tongue. Not quite so sharp as Lavinia, whom you didn't want to cross; she really did have a sharp tongue.

But, I still need to know if she, for example, turned to one of the sages

Women's Studies, 1989
Vol. 16, pp. 39-52
Reprints available directly from the publisher
Photocopying permitted by license only

in her life and said, "Listen, back off. I've become this person and I'm pissed at you. Don't bug me." Was there anything that direct?

There was one interchange between Austin, her brother, and herself where she exalted the power of metaphors. She would write him very literary letters trying to impress him with what she could do with metaphors — he was at Harvard studying law. Apparently he wrote her back and said, "Calm yourself." So she wrote him back and, in a way, said "I will never again try to express myself to you. Here I try to be so exalted and you come out in your slippers and say as calmly as you please" — and so that's why we have the lines: "I'll be a little ninny, a little pussycatty, a little robin red breast." There was a real bitterness in that exchange that I found haunting in later letters.

It feels in a lot of poems she's getting [that] out. It's true she tells it slant, but she tells it all.

It seems like the wise people didn't care whether anybody thought they were wise or not. And to me it seems a very masculine question — excuse my bias — because through history women have just done things whether they got credit or whether they spit back and said, "you said I couldn't do it." Critically, we haven't been overly praised, but I don't think we women really give a hang — in a lot of instances.

Well, I remember a story that when ED was at Mount Holyoke she was often running against the mainstream (although I think some people or person noted her real talent, her genius); she refused to go to chapel because intellectually it seemed nonsense to her. So she did assert herself before she decided to retreat — well, retreat's the wrong word — closet herself with what she had to do. She was outspoken; she did use her tongue and wasn't afraid to say "No." Whatever this poem means, it marks some turnabout; she stayed in that house, and the garden.

I really am curious to know how other people read the poem itself.

I read exactly what you did; in fact, I wrote a paper on it (and the professor agreed with what the other two speakers said) but [now] I totally disagree with you. In the second stanza I chose not to reverse

"Eternity — until" and I read "Too plummetless — that it return — Eternity" to mean that it warrants eternity. This dropping of my life, this retreat is too deep, it's too much apart from real life that I will get anything out of it, that eternity will be mine.

The "too" is really difficult, isn't it? One almost wants to read "so" for it . . .

But the plummet can't ever find the bottom. There is no way that it can.

But couldn't it be more accurately read plummet-full; it was too much plummet, because the plummet is going down, and if you're plummetless . . .

But you cannot *plummeted*; you cannot really dive into it because it's an endless abyss.

It's endless because a plummet is a metal weight you drop overboard to see how deep things are.

But why can't something be "too plummetless" at this point? In other words, it can't return. It's too plummetless to return until . . .

Irretrievable.

But it's not true. You can retrieve . . . it would be death, but you can do it.

But for her the decision was absolute.

She must have seen it that way because that seems to be what she's saying; and she lived her life in a certain way.

What is her connection between God and poetry?

We probably have very differing points of view on her relationship to God and the connection with poetry. For a long time, I have seen Emily Dickinson's God as basically an enlarged father figure, having much of the characteristics and personality of her own father and of fathers in her community and culture. She would address this father in her poems with sarcasm and wit. In a way she was like a lawyer bringing briefs to the judge/lawyer/father, trying to reason with him: "Let Us play Yesterday — / I — the Girl at school — / You — and Eternity — the / Untold Tale —." She's always bringing this case up: "Papa above! Regard a Mouse," and so on. In one of my favorite poems of hers, she equates father, burglar and banker, and talks about God as this crafty business person who has a grand scheme where he can't fail. First, he comes and takes somebody away and so we have loss. How are we going to console ourselves? Well, we have to go to God. So it's like a burglar/banker combination coming and robbing you and then saying "I'll give you a loan." He's moonlighting, he's the fence. So now she says, I've lost, and here you've done this to me again, burglar/banker/father; I am poor once more.

Her linking-up the trinity as the secular combination burglar/banker/father indicates a kind of disrespect and a teasing of his authority. The rest of the world acknowledges his great power and authority and sagacity. They pray to him, taking him as godly, not just the father; and yet look what God has done to her. God has made her powerless. God chose a son; when God needed help with the world, he doesn't choose a daughter or a wife or an aunt. It's a father-son team. In my reading of the letters, she has a lot of trouble with that. Many times she talks about the son in quotes — Who was the "Son"? — trying to make it ambiguous (the son's sex and personality). In some of the poems, she is even trying to say, "It really was me, I'm the son."

I think that the way religion was institutionally presented to her in church was unacceptable and an affront, but that she had a sense of a larger God who approved of what she wrote, who knew that she was a spiritual person who loved creation and gloried in it, and did not think she was heretical or a naughty child. So many of her poems where she talks about going to heaven and being kicked out — she's too loud, she's cross, she's like a schoolgirl waiting for recess and God never takes a nap, she considers running away — I think those play on the God and the heaven that was passed down to her, not the one she really knows. She says, "I know that He exists. / Somewhere — [and makes no demands on her]". He's basically supportive — she counts on Him.

Do you think that in her earlier poems she perceives a God that's more like an Old Testament God, remote and mysterious and punitive, but in her later poems she expands or maybe even dispenses with those notions, and that the god she perceives is more abstract and less punitive, less remote — still as mysterious! Perhaps it goes along with her maturity. There is certainly a change in terms of her leaving behind the personal and talking more about philosophical and universal things in her later poems. Maybe this is a parallel development, with a change in her perception of God.

I would be very interested in seeing that established. When I was doing work on chronology of the poems, one of the things that I saw that I would have to go back and work on was how ambivalent she was early on, and how her ambivalence was maintained, so that even in the late poems she could say, "Of Course — I prayed — / And did God Care? / He cared as much as on the Air / A Bird — had stamped her foot — / And cried, 'Give Me.'" At the same time, she could write the poem "I know that He exists. / Somewhere in silence" and that "no God ignited this abode to put it out." She was capable, in my reading of her at this point, of entertaining both Gods throughout; it would be so interesting to see in fact a development of her maturity.

I intuit a bit of what Maurya intuits here, and I think it's true of the way she uses "he" in general. She plays with patriarchal language, but one senses that she has another vision of it; "reader, if you would only see my meaning, you would understand that I am using these metaphors to say what I have to say — although I understand that they're only metaphors. I will speak in them because that is the language which I have inherited and the only way that I can communicate, and [because] we can't ever totally transcend that language." But [there is] much less of a sense of literalness than with other poets in the Christian tradition. The "He" of both the Son and the Father, I think, becomes something else for her. This is the kind of reading that is very hard to prove, because I think she would have us take God much as she would have us take many of her other symbols — thunder, lightning, white woman; she never defines the equation, but we bring to it so much cultural definition that it's easy to plug right into the Christian meaning. I wonder if she always had that in mind or if she had a vision of transcendance.

Even though she didn't go to church, even though she said, "Some keep the Sabbath going to Church — / I keep it, staying at Home —," I don't think she ever really saw herself as a heretic.

You don't need to see yourself as a heretic, if you can use the metaphor — if you penetrate the metaphor and know that it is a metaphor. All God-language is a metaphor.

You mean the metaphor, God as father ...

Yes. God's not a father. If God were really a father, God wouldn't be ineffable. If God were really a "he," God wouldn't be ineffable. Anything infinite cannot be expressed in finite terms, so theological language is necessarily the language of metaphor. If as a poet she understands the stretchability, the flexibility of metaphor, she needn't see herself as heretic. She can face herself right in the tradition, recognizing that she's using a language that other people may have seen more narrowly.

And her criticism is really not with God but with the interpretation, with the people who wrote the metaphors — the metaphors of the "hallelujah ..." And she felt they didn't work, that those metaphors kept her from an ability to console herself with her religion that she really did need.

One imagines that had she lived a hundred years later, she might be doing feminist theology and coming up with new metaphors. But that in her own time, it was in more private interpretations.

Barbara, when you were talking about the burglar/banker/father God that she conceived, you mentioned something about her reaching a point where she was able to see herself as the "Son," in quotation marks. Would you elaborate a little on that, because that, too, certainly, is metaphorical. But she must have been as angry and as arrogant and assertive as she is in the last stanza [here].

In the poem I'm thinking of right now — where she says, "Jesus ... Don't you know — me?" or "It was love, oh, punish, pray" — in a way she was saying, "Don't you recognize me, I'm not the

Son"; she almost develops this idea that God mistakes her for the son, because of her devotion, and she's having to clarify to God that she isn't Jesus. Her use of the "Son" is very complex; it isn't always angry. In her letters the play with "father and son" is more sarcastic, but in some way she's showing off for an audience in her letters. A lot of her letters are her kind of saying, "Look, I'm not daunted," showing off, but being a little bit racy for her readers — these are her early letters, not her late letters. In the poems, Dickinson's "Son" is much more complicated.

Perhaps I've misunderstood what you said, but I thought at one point she did equate herself with Christ.

Yes — well, she thinks that God has mistaken her for Christ.

But in a negative way, like something she's trying to get out from under.

I think that in a way she's building her confidence, that she's saying how holy and special she really is: she is so devout, she is so beloved, that even God can't tell the difference between his son and her, the rightful heir to the throne. There are many poems where she approaches Jesus as a colleague, in a way, and really does see it as a brother-sister relationship.

So the two of them can stare together at the smallness of "the sages."

But the sages who don't do justice to who God is.

But even though God is mentioned, is this poem really about doing justice to who God is?

I didn't see God in this poem. I loved their reading, that "if *God* should count me fit." It was just if God was going to let her live this life. But I was very intrigued by this notion of putting away adolescent vision and accepting reality. That makes a lot of sense to me, although I don't know where "he," whether it's the secular or divine "he," comes through.

Well, I deduced that just from the interpretation of "woman white" as either bridal or nun-like image of the marriage itself to other ... a purifying of self, and a giving over of self. I think that in the third stanza she is not mocking, but — how should I put it — she's cutting down the list in favor of what she's then going to bring up in the last stanza, which is her own life. In other words, what you read as identical I read as a contrast. Of course, I don't think there is any way of knowing — it's a question of what dialogue you want to have with the poem. But I say, when she asks the question, "Would it feel as big — / When I could take it in my hand — / as hovering, — seen — through fog," I just hear the answer, "No, it would not feel as big, unequivocably as big," as though she's planting the seed of doubt as quickly as she's overthrowing it. And that's the point at which we see that the others were also idealizations, stereotypes.

Or maybe I identify too strongly, maybe I just wanted that perfect life — and here I don't mean necessarily the bridal image, or the nun image, neither of which attracted me as an adolescent, but that life of perfection somehow in a way that others saw it, as opposed to an acceptance of a life of process that would always somehow be considered "small." You know, the meandering life that the woman leads that never quite fits into the role or the track and never achieves the kind of greatness that others stamp with credentials, with titles.

Hmm, would you equate this poem, then, with a reading of a poem that was explicated by John Cody in *After Great Pain* — where he says: except for the smaller size, apples aren't round; lives are only perfectly round if they're small, but if you want a larger life you're going to have to settle for no circular perfection, more irregularity. Could you make that a companion to this reading of "smaller"?

That's very interesting. That's wonderful! — because we *do* think of Dickinson as small in many ways — for one thing she crafts and carves these small, little dear poems — but my God, she crafted 1775 of them, you know. And they don't all line up; she contradicts herself. Isn't that terrific? Whitman wasn't the only one who contradicted himself. There's a sense of messiness, a perfection that can't be had.

She was not regular. What did Higginson want to do, as soon as he got Dickinson's poems? He says, well, maybe we can market these if we "regularize" them, if we change this word to make it rhyme, and if we could just work that meter out and put a title on it. In fact, when he gave her that kind of advice, that's where she said, "Never mind, I'll just keep my poems to myself. Readers will know better in 1986." She counted on it; I believe that she lived her life with absolute faith that we existed, and that we'd know.

Was there much talk about small breasts in that age? Did people make a big deal about it? It does seem like a "breast image" in the stanza.

Oh, "like Horizons" swelling in her "vest"?

What was the style of dress?

A bodice — the hourglass, during the Civil War . . .

As for physical size — my grandmother, my great-grandmother, and my great-great-grandmother were very tiny people, and my sense of those people is that they were very small. How tall was she?

Well, she was 5′6″ . . . they measured her dress.

5′6″! How could she have fitted — her room was so small!

Well, we always thought that she was 5′2″, but then I read an account that she was really larger. They measured her dress and they said that she had a 35 inch waist.

Still, my grandmother was 4′10″ and my great-grandmother was smaller than she was . . .

You know, she was obsessed in her letters with what she called her "small size," and when she wrote to her sister-in-law and her brother and when they had liked the poem that she had written, she said, "If someday I could make you proud, 'twould give me taller feet." She thought that poetry would make her larger; she wanted "taller feet." On one hand, she keeps saying, "OK, smaller things are better," because I was small, "I could catch the mint that never ceased to fall."

On the other hand, she isn't small at all — "I am large, I contain multitudes."

She loved paradox; she loved oxymorons and playing mysteries.

If she's 5′6″ and weighs, say, 97 pounds, and has no breasts to speak of, then talking about smallness makes sense.

She was not small in her family or context, she was large in her context — which makes it ironic that she described herself to Higginson as she did. She took advantage of the fact that he didn't see her. What if we all could describe ourselves to a correspondent? I would say, "I'm this gorgeous creature, 5′10″, I weigh 100 pounds." She says, "I'm small like the wren." She could say anything about herself, but she was not known in her family as "tiny, petite Emily." That was part of the persona that she cultivated, perhaps to win over his paternal sensibilities, that he would take her in hand; it was part of her submissive guise. "I'm a little baby. Would you take care of me?"

Do you know how large the men in her family were?

The physical size of the Dickinson family!

People were generally smaller, but from the images in the poem, I think of her father as a huge man. Did she see herself as small in relationship to her father?

That's an interesting question.

Well, it seems to me that — I don't want to get psychological about it, but if you are a person, large or small — a woman — who is full of force and anger and funny, you are going to be ever so careful about how you approach men in the 1800's. You're not going to rush in there like "Annie, Get Your Gun." You're going to come in saying, ever so small, like a mouse, "Nothing will happen if you let me in the room." Giving that little voice. You really hear that in her voice: "I'm just so small . . ."

Because she had an awareness of her power, right?

You know it's interesting that her letters to men are so much more humble than her letters to women. When she introduced herself to Higginson: "Oh, I'm small, like the wren, and my father, too busy to notice what I do, I'm this little neglected child." But she describes herself to Kate Anton, "Do you know the sun? Do you dwell where Eden dwells?" She set herself up as the intimate acquaintance of immortality and God and . . .

Do you agree with what Cheryl said this morning — about her relationship to women?

That it was not a very successful feminist paradigm?

Yes. Do you agree with the observation that she disdained women and admired men more?

No, I don't. I think that her attitude towards men in her letters was self-consciously manipulative; she was giving them what she felt they wanted to hear. It's very hard to read her Master letters straight sometimes: "Oh, I'm a little daisy" — that kind of thing, when you see that right next to it she is presenting herself as a dignified, wise, eloquent and deeply compassionate woman to her female correspondents.

And that implies a lot of respect there, doesn't it.

It does. And when she is writing to them, whether it's consoling them about the death of a child or something [else], she writes as if she has something to offer them — not really arrogantly but like, "I have thought and felt a lot, and I share this with you; here's something that I have to give you through my words." She's not playing the same kind of games with women in that way, she doesn't have to put up a front — either as clever little child or beautiful daughter or a woman who's going to interest them. She can be mature Emily Dickinson. I think she had great respect and love for the women in her life. And I think she also despaired at how women were known. The sneering remarks that she has made about women were made when she was trying to cultivate the favor of male correspondents. That's my reading of Dickinson. I don't see her as anti-feminist or that she rejected women, although I think that she had great problems with her own identity.

How could she not?

How can *we* not?

We know this though: her civil war was in herself when she says "me from myself," you know, "to banish" — "had I art." Who of us has not felt this. If I could only get rid of myself. And she realizes it is futile to try. This sense of division within herself was profound, but I don't think that she projected rejection of her own sexuality on women.

Barbara, I'm intrigued by both of your statements about religion and how she viewed Jesus. In the new Testament, Jesus viewed himself such as she — she viewed him the way he wanted us to view him, and yet churches have set it up to think you're blaspheming if you say "I can do what Jesus did, and I can even do greater things than Jesus did." Jesus said, "These things you're astonished at, that I do? Well, you can do these and greater things than I do, you will do." But tell that to ministers of today and they'll hang you. He never wanted to be set up on a pedestal, you know; he was always saying "Look to a higher being than I. I'm the son, we can all be the son." I'm intrigued by your statement, though it seemed sarcastic, that, yes, we would all identify with that sonship, rather than making it male or female. I'm pleased that she saw herself as Jesus would have wanted her to in that station.

Nonetheless, it does remain a bit of a problem for us, that the embodiment of it is male.

But it had to be one or the other!

I don't know, there are traditions in which it's both.

But look what they did to Mary.

Wait — they made it a virgin birth so that a man could not be ... male-female again, but the woman didn't do it with the male, she did it with God direct.

That only makes her an instrument, though. I don't want to get too deeply into theology here, but —

but it takes you away from personhood.

I just wonder if she didn't speculate even beyond that, really pierce that imagery and see it for what it was — which is a male creation, in the sense that the birth is an implantation of the male.

But Jesus did, too.

Well, be that as it may ...

I was struck by the words you recited from a letter she wrote to a woman, "Have you seen Eden?" Instantly I thought of God speaking to Job — she's stepped even one further step and equated herself almost with God, it seems to me, if I heard you right on that. I've been struck today, and I really appreciate the insight that all of you have given me, of the self-confidence of the woman. There are so many arrogant images; this sneering business in the poem at hand, is marvelous. It's something I never knew about her before. Thank you for having shared it.

You know, in a way I think that — this may sound wrong, I don't want it to sound wrong — in a profound way, she identified with God, not as male or female, but as Creator. And creation, for her, was the greatest thing in the world, to be able to create was the greatest power and the glory. That was language she could really understand and use and did use, to talk about herself. I don't even think she felt she was being heretical to say "the power and the glory." As the creator, she identified with the creative act. In a poem, "Art thou the thing I wanted?" when she's finally going to get something, she says "never mind": "I tell thee while I waited / The mystery of Food / Increased till I abdjured it / [And dine without] Like God —." Creation still means, for her, renouncing a kind of fleshly life, and creation was purely spiritual. To the extent to which she could deny herself, she could be like God. In another poem she talks about "This abstinence of mind / Produce a purer food." She felt that she could really serve God, and have God's role to console people, through what she denied herself to make "the word." But the pivot for me is the issue of creation itself.

And that's the terrible choice that this dualistic, patriarchal civilization has given us. We have to deny the flesh to choose the spirit. It's something that we're obviously questioning and challenging today. I'm not sure whether that was in her power to challenge but I do — at the risk of sounding ... I don't ever want to become pitying or condescending toward Emily Dickinson! — I do want to understand through her that terrible choice, that patriarchal choice. Because after all, bodily creation, where it all began ...

What if William Luce was right in "The Belle of Amherst," where he took great liberties with her life and text. Dickinson's father had come up to her and said, "Emily Dickinson, it's great that you're writing poems! This is a great poem! Now you write more of these poems and I'm going to take these with me to Washington. I know a publisher and we're going to publish you, my dear! You're going to be great, you just keep this up." Not only would she not have written the poems she wrote, but poetry and writing would not have had the same meaning to her. Would she have used language in the same way if it had been all right to be a woman poet, and not to feel that she has to renounce her flesh to write poetry? I'm not excusing it, I'm just saying that as a recipient of what she wrote, we benefit from her sense of that dualism.

Well, I like to think that she was such a genius that had she lived in that better, more whole world, that what she would have produced would have been at least equal or greater. But who knows? I'm grateful for what we've got!

Poem 315

He fumbles at your Soul
As Players at the Keys
Before they drop full Music on —
He stuns you by degrees —
Prepares your brittle Nature
For the Ethereal Blow
By fainter Hammers — further heard —
Then nearer — Then so slow
Your Breath has time to straighten —
Your Brain — to bubble Cool —
Deals — One — imperial — Thunderbolt —
That scalps your naked Soul —

When Winds take Forests in their Paws —
The Universe — is still —

c. 1862 *1896*

Women's Studies, 1989
Vol. 16, p. 53
Reprints available directly from the publisher

Poem 315

ROBIN RILEY FAST

University of Akron

This poem is typical of many of Dickinson's poems: we're thrown straight into the action, with no background or explanations, and the result is that as we read the poem, we're both absorbed by the experience it describes, and uncertain of its meaning. All that is clear is the quality of the experience — not its precise significance. ("Your thoughts don't have words every day", [# 1452] — and when they do, they don't necessarily take the form of fully articulated explanations to yourself or to others.)

The first thing I did when I sat down to this assignment was to go through the poem, line by line, noting my responses to the things that caught my attention. When I looked over my list I found I had recorded basically three kinds of things:

1) suggestive or perplexing words and phrases
2) connections to other poems (via imagery, analogies, or "plot" elements)
3) structural devices — parallelism, balance, dashes; paradoxes; and the break before the last two lines.

I'd like to go through the poem, line by line, and comment on them.

Line one makes us ask "who's He?" Dickinson's critical history may make this seem to be the central question (so many critics have spent so much time wondering about the "He's" in the poems), but I'm going to assume that a definite answer is *not* essential. The poem, I think, is quite effective as "just" the description of an experience defined not by being named but by being evoked. Still in line 1,

Women's Studies, 1989
Vol. 16, pp. 55-59
Reprints available directly from the publisher

besides wondering about "him," I thought about "your" — the speaker is either talking to herself, or talking to another person, or to us, in an inclusive manner: "it happened to me, it can happen to you," so to speak. And then "Soul" — despite the physicality of "fumbles," this is not an exclusively physical experience. Lines 2 and 3 introduce the poem's dominant analogy: "he" is like "players," and the soul is like the "keys" of a musical instrument. Dickinson, we might recall, played the piano wierdly and wonderfully, according to her friends.

This analogy to music could recall many of Dickinson's other poems. The ones that came to my mind were poems 503 and 321. In "Better — than Music! For I — who heard it —" (503), she recalls a transcendent music which is both evanescent and *hers* ("Let *me* not spill — its smallest cadence"), which both connects her to Eve (and the tempting music *she* might have heard) and assures her own access to heaven. "Of all the Sounds dispatched abroad" (321) seems even more relevant here: it describes the ethereal music produced by the wind in the trees, and asserts that the "gain" of this music is "inner than the bone." The emphasis on the wind's *hands* and the "*Charge*" of the "old measure in the Boughs" in 321 also recalls "He fumbles at Your Soul." And like lines 6 and 7 of "He fumbles," both "Better than music" and "Of all the Sounds" characterize music in terms of paradoxes that could suggest that music is an emblem, or a proof, or a source, of what I call heaven-at-home, the evanescent nature of the palpable.

Still in line 3, I note that "drop full Music on" seems to imply that the music is not in the keys or Soul, but that they and it depend on the players or "Him." (This might recall "To hear an Oriole sing," poem 526, where the tune is asserted to be not in the tree or the bird, but in the hearer.)

Lines 1-3 together anticipate the next eight lines, which elaborate, variously, on the movement described in the beginning of the poem. Lines 4-6 recall poem 1129:

Tell all the Truth but *tell it slant* —
Success *in Circuit* lies

The unknown "He" seems to be operating according to a similar understanding as he "*prepares*" you "*by degrees*" for a "blow" which your "*brittle Nature*" may otherwise not withstand (recall "our *infirm*

Delight" in 1129). The comparison of truth to lightening in 1129 seems to echo the "imperial Thunderbolt" that comes later in 315, and this connection reinforces the sense of the elemental, irreducible power of the experience described in our poem (315).

Lines 6 and 7 present some paradoxes — the "Ethereal Blow," "Fainter Hammers," and "fainter . . . further heard" — to what effect? They reinforce, I think, the uniqueness of the experience, the fact that it seems to take "you" out of the realm of normal existence, and suggest a quality of unearthly earthliness.

Lines 7-10 made me notice Dickinson's structure. The parallelism ("Your Breath has time to straighten — / Your Brain — to bubble Cool"), alliteration (the preceding lines, and "By fainter Hammers — further heard"), dashes, and rhythmic balance combine to create a kind of back-and-forth, see-saw effect that could be either tantalizing or teasing (as in a cat-and-mouse game, perhaps), which makes me wonder whether this experience is desired or dreaded or both.

Lines 9 and 10 tell of the breath "straightening," the brain "bubbing cool," and thus imply that the subject, "you," has been extremely agitated, perhaps panting, then gasping for breath, as "He" has "stunned" and "prepared" her. Students sometimes ask whether these images signify death. I think, rather, that they represent a momentary respite before the blow that occurs in the next two lines:

Deals — One — imperial — Thunderbolt —
That scalps your naked Soul —

I notice the different pacing of these two lines. In the first, the dashes slow us down and reinforce the power of the "imperial Thunderbolt" which is, remember, analogous to the "full Music" of line 3. (I note, too, that this line is one of the few in the poem with more than four stressed syllables.) The second line, simply by lacking dashes (as well as having a regular iambic beat) seems and becomes faster — the "scalping" is sudden and swift. Of course, and this seems crucial, the line reminds me of Dickinson's famous response to a question from Higginson: "If I feel physically as if the top of my head were taken off, I know *that* is poetry" (*Letters* II:474). (This is the most explicit invitation to interpret the poem as being somehow about poetry, and it reinforces the possibilities of taking "music" and, as we'll see, "winds" that way.)

But the "scalping" is *not* the end of the experience. Dickinson's dashes often suggest, as here, a kind of non-conclusion. Besides, more questions arise — like "then what?" — and there is that provoking blank space before the poem ends.

The blank space might signify a number of things: the shift to an apparently new subject, the silence after the thunderbolt, "your" "stunned" condition, ... an opportunity for us readers to catch our breath before confronting those last two lines.

I have wondered about Dickinson's tone in these lines; after a sometimes tense, step-by-step narration, leading to a resounding crash and silence, we seem to be hearing a different voice making a matter-of-fact statement. Is she explaining it all to us (perhaps condescendingly — "in case you didn't get it")? or teasing us? what might these last two lines mean to the "you" who has gone through the experience of lines 1-12 (as the speaker presumably has)?

The lines at first seem to present a new topic, perhaps a contrast to the previous one. If they did, the tone might be teasing. But I don't think so — there are several connections between these lines and the rest. To start at the end this time, "still —" describes that white space that sets these two lines apart. It is "the Universe" that is still, which is appropriate to the power of the "imperial Thunderbolt" (especially when we recall how often Dickinson uses the language of royalty to describe heaven). "Paws" suggests the initial clumsiness of "fumbles," and the fact that they are the "Winds'" paws suggests a paradox similar to that of "Ethereal blows." "Winds" also, like "Ethereal," and even (in Dickinson's poetry) "imperial," evokes the spiritual, and thus metaphorically as well as literally recalls again poem 321 and "That phraseless Melody — / The Wind does."

But what about "Forests"? "Forests" calls to mind poem 1634, which now seems to me almost a gloss on 315:

Talk not to me of Summer Trees
The foliage of the mind
A Tabernacle is for Birds
Of no corporeal kind
And winds do go that way at noon
To their Ethereal Homes
Whose Bugles call the least of us
To undepicted Realms

This poem makes the earlier metaphor explicit: the "Forests" taken in the winds' "Paws" (315) can now be identified as "The foliage of the mind." And "Talk not to me of Summer Trees" repeats the ethereal quality of 315, but without any of the frenzy, agitation, breathlessness and pain of the earlier poem. Here, the voice is calm, assured, and the focus is interior. Yet the speaker seems to be hearkening back to an earlier experience. As in 315, she starts in the middle: "Talk *not* . . ." Someone, maybe she herself, *has* been talking of summer trees.

So I think the last two lines of 315 might name the experience (hearing the wind in the trees) that *literally* inspired the poem, which may be "simply" a description of hearing the wind (in which case "He" might be the wind, or nature personified — though this seems unlikely to me — or divinity manifesting "him"/itself by acting through nature). *Or* (or *also*) the poem may describe an experience somehow analogous to hearing the wind as "you" do — an experience of "His" power and "your" powerlessness, of pain and awe. But this is also an experience that, as poems like 321 and 1634 show with their similar imagery and figurative language, can be exhilarating and *can* imply "your" power, too. (Going to these other poems at this point may seem suspicious, but I think with Dickinson's poetry we often have to. She uses and reuses the same images, as she explores the same experiences or moments — loss, marriage, sunsets, death — from endlessly varied points of view, and these different poems and perspectives don't replace, but do illuminate, each other.)

I think, then, that this experience, analogous to hearing the wind, is related to poetry — poetic vision or inspiration, perhaps, or the moment (or more) of powerlessness *before* you can write. A case could be made for the experience's being religious — maybe a conversion — or (to me it seems less likely) sexual — a chase, an assault? Poetry, or some experience related to its creation, seems to me this poem's *most* likely subject because of the involvement of body, brain and soul; because of the analogy to music; because of the "imperial" quality and the "winds," as well as because of the similarity of the naked, scalped soul to the poet with the top of her head taken off. (And if it's about poetry, or being a poet, various related identities for "he" can be imagined.)

Of course questions still remain. Are we ever finished with a Dickinson poem?

Poem 315

SUZANNE JUHASZ

University of Colorado, Boulder

I WANT TO begin at the beginning: with the first line, "He fumbles at your soul." Dickinson's first lines are as problematic as they are explanatory. For every piece of information, there is usually a question. Which is why we need the rest of the poem. Here a "he" is acting upon a "you": but who are these actors? We can't say, having only a sense of subject and object, and yet, the customary correlation of these roles with active (subject) and passive (object) is curiously reversed. Because the "you" is the consciousness experiencing the event, "object" becomes "subject" here. And, since the active agent is identified by gender only, "He," we might assume, especially since we do know the gender of the poem's author, that the "you" is female. Consequently, we may go on to surmise that in this poem the traditional object, the woman, speaks, thereby expressing her suppressed subjecthood in a poem that takes gender relationship as its concern.

'He" is encountered acting upon your soul: something at the very heart of the person, its defining essence. What is he doing to this particular soul? Fumbling at it, as if it were a lock he is having trouble opening. To what end, we do not know. Here we are struck primarily by the sense of agency, of power being exercised upon a resistent entity.

To understand this situation more clearly, we eagerly read on — to encounter an analogy: "As Players at the Keys / Before they drop full Music on —." Such a comparison gives tangible form to the situation, not in terms of interpersonal relationship, but of artistic creativity. The "you" becomes "keys," or a piano, while "He" is the "Players": the fingers, I think, of the pianist. Here metonymy provides a closeup; we

---

Women's Studies, 1989
Vol. 16, pp. 61-66
Reprints available directly from the publisher
Photocopying permitted by license only

see fingers at the keys; we understand music-making. Now we begin to understand the "fumbling" better. Either this is a poor pianist, or the fumbling is meant as preparatory activity, awkward but transitional. It is a warming up for the real thing: the full music.

This analogy helps us as well to understand better the active/passive elements of the situation. For whereas the piano needs to be played to make music, the pianist can make no music without it. A double meaning therefore emerges from "Keys": the "ivories," surely; but also, the means of gaining entrance; and even, that which provides an explanation or solution.

Therefore, although it is too early in the poem to resolve the matter, we are faced with our first intimation of contradiction, or multiplicity of meaning. Ought we to take this experience of being acted upon as invasion, implied by that fumbling at the soul, or as potential, implied by the piano analogy? Again, is the fumbling offensive or enticing in its awkward physicality? Statement plus analogy provides, not a simple conjunction, but a complementarity that complicates.

The following line, "He stuns you by degrees," is prefaced and concluded by dashes. Consequently, although in itself it is an independent clause, restating the first line, it can be seen to refer both backwards, summing up the first three lines, and forwards, introducing the more complete description of the same event that follows. The dashes, in other words, can function as colons as well as periods. From one perspective, this hardly matters, since the poem keeps repeating itself; from another, since that repetition complicates, and what is complicated is the "you's" experience of the event, the syntactic overlapping here underscores the way meaning in the poem is created. "He stuns you by degrees —" introduces the long verse sentence that comprises most of the poem, detailing the sequence of the central event. The elements of this longer version are, however, the same as we find in the opening summary: the aggressive albeit objectified outside agent, characterized through verbs alone (stuns, prepares, deals, scalps), the consciousness of a receptive subject; an invasion of momentous proportions. Yet the event, now broken down into its components, has to be read sequentially, as a process whose significance has everything to do with its "degrees." First preparation, then the blow. He has no existence other than his outward manifestations; she displays a complex subjectivity.

Now analogy is replaced by metaphor: outer is inner, for this experience is at once physical and spiritual. It is clearly a "Blow"; nevertheless, an "Ethereal" one. Its effect upon the recipient is to "stun" her: to deprive her consciousness as a result of such violence; but also, perhaps, to astonish, amaze.

The preparation is experienced as sound and pressure: "fainter Hammers" "further heard — / Then nearer — Then so slow." We comprehend a growing volume, and intensity, "Hammers" connoting violent blows, as well as the striking of those musical keys referred to earlier, now as ominous as it was artistic. Yet as we read, the steadily growing noise and pressure forms a background for the soul's response, as the "brittle nature" (or "Substance," in another version) is seen to "straighten," then "bubble Cool." These are comparative terms: straighten implies a previous crookedness; cool implies an earlier heat. Inside the woman's outward passivity there is much activity, for, as in the relationship between piano and pianist, this preparation is as much the soul's work as his. The straightness and coolness implies a readiness: a calmness and a cognizance of what is to come.

The fainter blows have prepared for a climactic assault; it comes, finally, as "One — imperial — Thunderbolt — / That scalps your naked Soul —." The final line of the stanza parallels the first line of the poem, at the same time exaggerating it. He is now entirely god-like and powerful; she is, conversely, vulnerable, available. And if "fumbles" had seemed an act redeemed by its clumsy tentativeness, "scalps" leaves no doubt about its murderous brutality. At the same time, there is something as ecstatic as masochistic in the image of a blinding light, an electricity that, in striking, somehow purifies further a soul prepared, receptive, naked. A variant for "scalps" is "peels," reinforcing our sense of something stripped, reduced to essence, and possibly, transformed. This is, we remember, an "Ethereal" blow, a stunning one at that.

This culminating moment occurs elsewhere in Dickinson's poetry. In poem 1581, for example, "The farthest Thunder that I heard," the same image of a thunderbolt leads to a similar denouement. The speaker is struck by lightning, and she observes, "But I would not exchange the Bolt / For all the rest of Life —." She goes on to compare her specialness to the condition of ordinary mortals, their "Indebtedness to Oxygen" to her "obligation / To Electricity —." And again, in poem 974, the lightning image is used to explain the opening assertion that danger or calamity "disclose" "The Soul's distinct connection / With immortality." "Lightning on a Landscape," we are told, "Exhibits Sheets of Place — / Not yet suspected — but for Flash — / And Click — and Suddenness." Danger, in other words, as poem 1678 explains, "disintegrates Satiety," for it "Begets an awe / That searches Human Nature's creases / As clean as Fire." All of these poems use the thunderbolt to represent the concurrence of danger and revelation, and they help us to see how, as in #315, the soul seeks out and benefits from this calamitous collision as well as is violated by it.

This is the crucial doubling at the heart of the poem. There is no way, at this point, to eliminate or choose between either of these attitudes. Neither can we come to a simple conclusion about who the participants in the drama are, nor the exact nature of their relationship to one another. Helpfully, there remains another stanza: a couplet about winds and forests. What is its relationship to the rest of the poem? The couplet takes the form of aphorism: "When Winds take Forests in their Paws — / The Universe is still —," a truism that, because of its position at the conclusion of the poem, seems placed there to comment on and sum up the preceding events. But, both because it is introduced by the ambiguous dash and because the figurative vocabulary has altered — from thunderbolt to winds and forests — the connection is not readily clear. Still, Dickinson has made this same kind of switch before in the poem, first from the opening "fumbling at your Soul" to players and keys, then from the piano imagery to the thunderbolt sequence. In each case, however, the relationship between participants in the drama has stayed the same, and this is equally true in the final couplet. "Winds" are aggressive, "Forests" are receptive; the winds take (or "hold," in a variant) the forests in their *paws*, this further anthropomorphising (winds like brutes — brutal) reinforcing our sense of violence. If this is the same situation once again, then the key line, because it describes result, becomes the final one. When this kind of event takes place, the universe (or "Firmaments," in a variant) is still. Is this death? Revelation? Transcendence? An end, or a beginning? Not specifying becomes another kind of specification, because once again we are forced to entertain all of the possible meanings here. The stillness which is the result of winds taking forests in their paws seems comparable to the scalped or peeled condition of the naked soul, which in turn is comparable to experiencing full music. Something utter, something ultimate. I am reminded of the concluding lines of poem 1247, "To pile like Thunder to its close," which again uses thunder imagery to show how ultimate experience — here identified as poetry and love — results in what Dickinson calls consummation — and likens to the vision of God: "For None see God and live —." Even as the poem implies that this not-living need not mean sheer death but rather a revelation that leads to transformation, so in #315 we get similar intimations, similar ambiguity.

Reading the poem this slowly forces us to encounter it on an experiential level. Consequently, we have a rather clear idea about what is in the poem and what is not, so that any interpretation we subsequently make can be firmly based in this information.

Let me begin with the not's. We do not find out who the actors are; we do not find out when this action is taking place; we do not find out the literal reference for the metaphors. But, instead of trying to fill in by ourselves these so-called gaps (he's a lover; he's God; he's her father; this is sexual intercourse; this is religious conversion; and so on), we might better use these "omissions" as important information.

That is, if the "He" and the "you" are never specified, this may well be because they are not specific but general, or archetypal, as Dickinson projects her personal experience into more general or universal categories. The persistent present tense is informative in this regard, suggesting that the event is recurrent and typical, rather than one of a kind or once in a while. If the literal equivalent for this internal, psychological, and therefore metaphoric experience is not provided, we might understand that the event itself is conceived of as generic, indicative of the soul's encounter with an aggressive force that attacks, invades, transforms it. Sexual intercourse or religious conversion are, then, as much metaphors for what is happening as are piano playing and storms. Because gender *is* explicitly associated with this occurrence, I would feel justified in reading it as a quintessential pattern in a culture that is structured along gender divisions. The encounter of inner with outer, negative with aggressive, reflective with projective, may be more generally signified in terms of gender difference: female behavior/male behavior. If this is the case, Dickinson's poem both describes that kind of experience and evaluates it, in terms that are of a both/and, or double, nature. At once critiquing and participating in traditional gender arrangements, Dickinson as well reinterprets the meaning of these arrangements. She demonstrates how the female, even when she is behaving according to traditional norms, is nevertheless not object but subject: possessing, in fact, a subjectivity so complicated because it is usually not externalized. At the same time, Dickinson shows both how the kind of violence described here is oppressive and destructive and how there exists a need for endangering the self in just this way: putting oneself at the mercy of some force beyond one so that revelation and transformation might occur. Others of her poems less specifically gender-identified point to this same cultivation of a vulnerability that seeks out danger and benefits from it. This poem shows how gender difference is linked to such critical situations.

Thus, poem 315 is a multi-faceted analysis of the nature and uses of power itself. Even as it reveals the abuses of aggression, so it also shows why and under what circumstances it might be attractive. Demanding only one interpretation of this situation — for example, that Dickinson is attacking typical male-female interaction, or, conversely, that she is submitting herself to it — denies the complex double reality to which this poem attests.

Note

1. This paper, along with my other talk in this volume, "Reading Dickinson Doubly," are earlier versions of my essay, "Reading Doubly: Dickinson, Gender and Multiple Meaning," scheduled to appear in Robin Riley Fast and Christine Mack Gordon, Eds. *Approaches to Teaching the Poetry of Emily Dickinson*, New York: MLA.

Poem 315

ELLIN RINGLER-HENDERSON

Pitzer College

COMING TO Poem 315, "He Fumbles at your Soul," — and to all of her poetry — not as an Emily Dickinson specialist but as a generalist of American and women's literature, I found myself nervously scanning the critics. I experienced all the anxiety engendered those many years ago by my (mostly male) scholarly preceptors when they assigned me a graduate seminar paper on a poem, let us say, to be read aloud in class. The other students had similar assignments; and we were, of course, in direct competition for the best grades. The formula for success was very clear: we were to read all the criticism relevant to our poem, then try to come up with a theory or stance that was different — a new angle. Finally, perhaps, we might read the poem itself, with the main aim of making it fit our theory. The approach was obviously pretty backward and, with its mechanistic and competitive elements, distinctly unfeminist. So, in honor of Emily Dickinson's centenary, let's revise the formula somewhat, looking first at "He fumbles at your Soul" in its own right and then, perhaps, with a bow in my former mentors' direction, at a critic or two.

Poem 315 fits centrally, it seems to me, into the large group of Emily Dickinson's poems about grief, many of which were written in the great year, 1862. It records the process by which the painful experience of loss encroaches slowly upon mind, soul and body, rendering you vaguely — even fearfully — uneasy, until, with a sudden blow — a related experience, another loss perhaps? — you are made to confront the pain directly. Anguish at loss lies like a dull ache fumbling at the center of your being and creating a sense of dread whose "faint hammerblows" — your throbbing pulse? — become progress-
"faint" hammerblows — your throbbing pulse? — become progress-

Women's Studies, 1989
Vol. 16, pp. 67-71

ively stronger. You have only time to pull in your breath and brace yourself before the lightning strikes, and you are hit physically and emotionally with the full force of your grief. It is a process, Dickinson tells us, that occurs "by degrees" and that leaves you finally numb, paralyzed, "stunned" and "still." Reading the poem, one is struck yet again by the poet's familiarity with despair, her deep insight into all of its psychic sensations.

For, the fact is that quite a number of Dickinson's other poems share 315's imagery and echo its drama. For the sake of brevity, let me refer you to a few by title only: "Nature — sometime sears a Sapling — / Sometimes — scalps a Tree —" (314), "There is a languor of the Life/ More imminent than Pain—" (396), '"Twas like a Maelstrom" (41), "We grow accustomed to the Dark —" (419), "The Soul had Bandaged moments —" (512), "There is a pain — so utter —" (599), and "The Whole of it came not at once — / 'Twas Murder by degrees —" (762). One of the works which seems most to mirror 315 is 410:

The first Day's Night had come —
And grateful that a thing
So terrible — had been endured —
I told my Soul to sing —

She said her Strings were snapt —
Her Bow — to Atoms blown —
And so to mend her — gave me work
Until another Morn —

And then — a Day as huge
As Yesterdays in pairs,
Unrolled its horror in my face —
Until it blocked my eyes —

My Brain — begun to laugh —
I mumbled — like a fool —
And tho' 'tis Years ago — that Day —
My Brain keeps giggling — still.

And Something's odd — within —
That person that I was —
And this One — do not feel the same —
Could it be Madness — this?

Also probably written in 1862, "The First Day's Night" is another of Dickinson's accounts of the process in which grief "stuns by degrees."

Here, the poet records a two-fold experience. There is the first Night which prepares her for the greater pain by snapping her strings and blowing her song to atoms; the anguish attacks her here by implication every bit as aggressively as it does in "He fumbles." And, as in 315, there is a brief reprieve, a pause, for the poet to try to mend her strings and bow, before the real horror twice as huge as the first (the "imperial thunderbolt") blinds her and reduces her to a mumbling fool. While 315 remains in the present tense throughout and ends at the moment of the blow, poem 410 is cast almost entirely in the past tense, which allows Dickinson to carry the drama farther, to look back at the later consequences of her grief and wonder whether it has led to madness. What the poems have in common, though, is a pervasive sense of fear, a relentless inescapable pain which when it finally arrives in all its power blocks the consciousness and 'stills' the brain.

There are some interesting ways in which "He fumbles" resembles a Shakespearean sonnet, however much it obviously deviates from that form in meter and rhyme. Like her contemporary, in many ways her artistic brother, Gerard Manley Hopkins, Dickinson was quite capable of adapting (fumbling with?) the sonnet form, though of course *he* was attracted to the Petrarchan variety. As in the English sonnet, the ideas of "He fumbles" are organized into three quatrains and a couplet. Each quatrain develops a separate image or set of images, and each builds to the climax at the end of the third quatrain; while the last two lines serve as an intensifying summary of the preceding twelve.

The first quatrain poses the conundrum in a typical Dickinsonian mode (who is "He"?), offers some clues ("He" "fumbles" and "stuns") and presents a simile which suggests the prelude-like quality of the experience of grief. The fumbling of the players at the keys arouses a sense of uneasy expectancy, even foreboding: (what "full music" lies ahead? when will we have to "face the music"?) The fourth line, "He stuns you by degrees," summarizes the gradual process being described in the first three and continues the motif of being struck (stunned), as players strike the keys before "dropping" music upon you, or hammers strike blows, or thunderbolts or paws stun their victims.

In the second quatrain, the hammers recall the piano keys of the first stanza and complete the sense of brittle and blow in lines 5 and 6. The hammers are also beaten out with the alliterative brittle/blow and the repetitions of fainter/further/nearer/then/then in lines 7 and 8. The pattern begun earlier with the words "stun" and "blow" in the first and second quatrains is developed in the third by the "thunderbolt," which, described as "imperial," fittingly takes a scalp as its trophy of victory over the soul.

The concluding couplet suggests at least two possible readings: one — that the clutch of grief (of the "wind's paws") is so brutal that it obliterates consciousness ("stills the universe"), the final "still" returning us to the word "stun" in line 4. Another implication of the couplet is that the universe is indifferent — "still" meaning both silent and unmoving — to the plight of the individual caught in the grip of pain.

Finally, it seems to me that the poem as a whole suggests the rising of a devastating psychic and emotional storm, from the earliest rumblings (fumblings?) and faint hammers of thunder to the crash of lightning and rush of wind gathering the trees in the later lines.

Many of the critics who deal with this poem focus on the gender of its subject — the "He" — and concentrate on the implications of seduction and sexual violation that they detect in the work. At one extreme, Clark Griffith tells us with wonderful straightforwardness that the subject of 315 is masculine lechery and that the poem simply records the fear of impending rape. More subtly and persuasively, Joanne Dobson assigns 315 to the category she calls "poems of the indeterminate He," reflecting the "pure energy of the masculine," the threatening animus, which Emily Dickinson must finally learn to master and internalize in order to become a whole poet. I find these suggestions provocative, as I do Adrienne Rich's association of the erotic and religious motifs in 315 with what she reads as a description of Dickinson's "relationship to her own creative power," her awareness of daemonic possession.

My own reading of "He fumbles" as a description of the way in which grief plays itself out in the human psyche does not contradict the views of Dobson and Rich, though I'd like to suggest that Dickinson's linking of pain and fear with creativity — her conviction that poetry is the "gift of screws" — depends not only on her awareness of the risks involved in assimilating the powerful "He" of her being. What the writing of poetry also does (as Sylvia Plath's example reminds us) is to call up past experiences of pain, uncovering the poet's earliest fears and grief, and forcing her to relive them even as she describes them. When, in a conversation with Thomas Higginson,

Dickinson defined poetry as that which made her body cold and took the top of her head off, in images startlingly reminiscent of poem 315's third quatrain (in which the "brain bubbles cool" and the "soul is scalped"), she expressed her sensations of great vulnerability in the face of art. Her exploration of terror and grief in "He fumbles" touches so centrally at these feelings that they must inevitably have been rekindled in herself as she wrote. She rendered up the price of her art here — as in dozens of her other poems — in full coinage. Dickinson's talent was indeed an awful privilege, her "bolts of melody" paid for by an immeasurable psychic and emotional dowry.

Poem 315
Workshop Discussion

Speakers: ROBIN RILEY FAST, SUZANNE JUHASZ, ELLEN RINGLER-HENDERSON

Why don't we begin by you making suggestions about the stuff we didn't talk about, the things you thought about that we overlooked. I'm sure there's more. And then we can throw all that together into the pot and see what happens.

You all included this in a way, but the metaphors of going back to part of the 17th century and religious revelation are so tremendous to me in this, thrown of course into an almost naturalistic interpretation. For example, the winds which are the angels and the sentinel of God, and which in the 19th century the novelists — for instance Melville, Hawthorne — pick up as the symbol of divinity, if you think about Hawthorne's winds and trees. And Hawthorne too, of course, would see this ambivalence of God as "the paws" in the poem. But "fumbled" ... I can't explain ... but the last two lines suddenly throw this whole thing into the realm of a kind of "nature-brittle, God-imperious" — which is again sexual imagery, for the 17th century, particularly.

I think we've followed up on that, Gretchen. A number of students in my senior seminar — I asked them to write about these poems, to compare them, and several of them pictured the "key" as a Zeus figure from that imperial image.

Women's Studies, 1989
Vol. 16, pp. 73-84
Reprints available directly from the publisher
Photocopying permitted by license only

But the 19th century, of course, included both the Greek and the Christian interpretation of that.

Dickinson wasn't a very good Christian.

No! So it's an animal force.

She may not have been a good one, but she certainly was conscious of it. She struggled with Christianity, I think.

No, that's what I mean. If she wasn't a good one, she knew what she was supposed to be doing, and as you all know she fought it tooth and nail. And at the same time, turned it around and took the same image ... I think what we have here is very interesting, is that she always used the available coin ... she used the imagery that people understood, and then sort of ironically twisted it. When she does it here, the interesting thing is, is she just saying "for once, I'm just going to do it straight, or am I not?"

I think she did it straight, and then she backed away and did it crooked.

When you say she wasn't a good Christian, it depends on what you mean. She was not a conventional Christian in any way, but I think she was sincere.

She believed in a power ...

Oh, and in Jesus ...

I think she thought she was Jesus.

But to go back to what you say about the word "fumbles" — because if this is God, then indeed he fumbles ...

He's a fumbling God with paws.

Yeah, it's a little problematic. I think it's Thomas Johnson who reads this poem as almost the evangelical preacher. And the shouting, so that she's sitting in the congregation and feeling her soul being played upon by that creature. And if so, if he is a fumbler, then that goes back to the image in the poem that was read last night about "much gesture from the pulpit / strong halleluiahs roll . . ."

But what I always thought very interesting about this poem, is that one of the reasons I got to the place that I did is that a lot of us who have done this reading have picked up on "fumbling" and then say . . .

Sex for sure!

But the fumbling may be fumbling in the beginning, but it sure isn't by the time you get to "scalped." You can't just dismiss it. And that's why I was trying to move it along to . . . because the power is really there; you've got to deal with the power in that poem.

It seems to me there's an awful deception here. It seems that things have gone on quite well, your tongue's straightened out and your brain's bubbled cool and everything like that, and then it all comes back again and my heavens, this is a mean, nasty force, no matter what, whether it's God throwing Paul off his horse on the road to Tarsus or something . . . nothing nice about it at all. And is it her being dragged screaming and kicking into Christian revelation, or the life of the poet, or what? I don't know, but certainly she doesn't embrace this experience one little bit, does she? I think getting at "fumbles" right there in the first line sets it up. She doesn't take away any of the nastiness of "fumbles" anywhere in that poem.

I don't see the fumbling as wicked; it's interesting, I don't see it as wierd.

When Robin talked about teasing, I thought that was very important. Because what we didn't talk about was seduction, you know . . . There is this kind of playing with her as well as upon her that the fumbling doesn't necessarily include.

Do you think that the fumbling is a kind of ineptitude and indifference?

When you actually play the piano, and you fumble on the keys, it's like a warming up process, it's like a testing in a way. And then your power begins to come to your fingers and then you're able to play.

So fumbling in that sense and not ineptitude.

The third line doesn't seem to say that. The power is dropped right on you, when he wants to.

And he's preparing you by degrees already, pretty early on.

I'm not even so sure that the fumbling is entirely nasty. Even though it's painful and horrifying in a sense . . . it is an ethereal blow that she's being prepared for. I have a sense, maybe I'm backing away too much from the elements of violence here, but this is necessary to be cognizant of what's happening. The important thing is how you read the "breath has time to straighten — / Your brain — to bubble Cool," because the way I was reading was that's her preparation; it's not her relaxing because she thinks it's not going to happen.

You mean she's getting ready to get scalped?

Yes! Yes!

And no complaints?

Well, she's working on herself so that she can meet this . . .

Girding the loins . . .

What I think, maybe we want to talk about this . . . there's a way in which, when we talk about gender now as feminists, we simply want to throw out anything left over from sex role structures that has to do with passivity or being taken over by anybody else, with receptivity: that baby has gone out with the bathwater. And yet, for me, what's sort of exciting about the poem is that she is suggesting that that also is a human experience, and it's an experience that women have participated in a lot. So should we just automatically say (I'm bringing up pornography here, I'm bringing up a lot of stuff) we will no more ever be in a situation where something else has power over us; power *over* us, you know. Mutual shared power is lovely, but do you know what I mean? The poem raises those questions for me, and that's what I wanted to get at by talking about it.

Well, in a sense it's not totally passive, really, but it's helpless. The blow is coming from a superior force. But she is in a sense reacting.

But if she worked that hard to get herself into a position of taking it, she's doing as much work as he is, which is what the player of the piano thing is about. She is getting herself to the place to receive the blow.

The one problem with that is that there is something very automatic and instinctive about breath having time to straighten and brain to bubble cool. I don't get the sense of a conscious bringing of anything to bear here. I have a sense of a gasp before it hits. Almost an instinctive kind of thing rather than something which is consciously being able to control itself. It's almost a reflexive thing.

The scary sense of it is that this thing takes a long time. It doesn't just go "wap!".

Maybe another way of thinking about this is Dickinson's insistence on — in lots of poems — the totality of an experience, of enduring every experience: how much can I take, can I then rebound from it? There may be an element of something akin to Emersonian compensation, in the sense that this incredible force, fumbling, stunning, whatever (if I can sustain it, if I can survive it) may, at least if you take the forest and the winds and so on the way I'm inclined to — may give me something. I may be able to turn them into something, I may be able to make them into a sonnet.

But in the last two lines, she's stilled; the subject is "stilled." You don't have that hope, necessarily, but … the universe and, don't you think she's part of it?

I think that's what is interesting, though, about the poem, as we move away from the very specific questions, who is he? what is this? what's the narrative? what's going on here? It's a remarkable evocation of the experience of art. When you think of all the great peak experiences where there's revelation, conversion, the perfect experience of art, the experience she would have in making a perfect poem, all of these I think relate here or are created in this poem.

I want to come back to the fact that I also feel pain here, I really do.

You know, I didn't pay much attention to that word "still" until you brought it up. It is so ambiguous. "Is still"? It still can do something? I consciously put a beat on it, I said "still." It isn't that, probably, but it could be.

I don't know if it's a good thing that the universe is still or not.

You don't know, but you never will know.

When winds take the Forests in their paws, the winds are not still, the forest is not still, but the universe ...

I mean why is it still, is it listening to the wind?

Does it not care?

What do you think about the fact that you'll never know?

But may I throw a reaction into the reading? I think this poem's about sex.

Since I wrote that article, I've moved to the study of popular culture and popular literature, and I see in this poem, I haven't begun with this thought at all because it just occurred to me, that she is experiencing very much what a female character in popular romance experiences.

Being swept away?

For the large body of the text she's between two men, and both are sinister; and she's not sure which one is going to be the savior. And she's experiencing all this confusion and all this pain and being bashed around. Then you have this space, this hiatus here, and then you have something which is very much like an active blow, of the text, when she finally finds out who is the right man. Who will mother her, who will take her?

That's back to what's the matter with sometimes giving yourself up to someone who will, to something that will embrace you, enfold you, whatever that is.

Where do you get embraces, enfoldings?

I don't mean embrace and enfold in a tender way; I mean take you over. Which is not to say that one thing excludes the other. The urge to get to that place, which is the "swept away" urge of the Harlequin . . .

It contains a lot of pain along the way, but perhaps . . .

We are naked here, we are being scalped!

What does it get you? It gets you to the result, the result is the universe is still. What is the route to that place? And everyone who talked has suggested that you're getting both pain and some kind of pleasure. But the interesting thing is, what does it mean when you get there? You know there's seduction, there's teasing, there's her own coming to it . . . you know, it's not either one way or the other. You really can't . . . if you decide for the one, you're throwing out information that's there that you don't want to use. That's really true.

I don't know if there's pleasure in the first part . . .

But there's fascination.

There's enormous attraction . . . I love that, I think that really adds a layer to all the different layers that have been described.

One of the other things we've touched on a lot, and I wondered whether it helps to explain "the universe is still," is the sense almost of a symphony that's being started here and comes to a tremendous kind of crescendo, "that scalps your naked soul," and then there's the coda. It's so nice with that space and then "the Universe is still."

I really want to push a little, because really almost all of the discussion has been about who is going to do the best reading, and that we're going to decide which is the right one.

Are we going to vote?

No, but you know what I mean. Someone says something, then someone else says "no, because it's not that, it's this because of that." Then you say, well, no, it's "y" because I see the 'y" there. And it seems to me what we're all behaving like is, when you're talking about your graduate education, and you mention some unpleasant parts of it, but I think the worst one is the sense that if we have this puzzle, it's going to be just decoded; we will come out with the right answer. The answer.

Surely that's not what we're suggesting.

There are layers of answers — for the same experience, though. Don't you think there's a universal core of experience, the subject, the reaction we ought to be able to arrive at? It may be a sexual one, it may be a religious one, it may be a musical one, it may be grief. But don't you think we ought to be able to feel the emotional reaction in a sense, and grant that this can be the same in all different areas, in sex, in religion, in grief, in music? But I think we should be able to decide whether there's a pleasure or pain here, somehow. You don't think so?

No.

Can they be separated?

I think we can, I hope at least that we can arrive at a sense that this is about an experience which we can characterize as going through these stages or involving these perhaps contradictory, perhaps not, feelings. And in that sense, yes, I think I agree entirely with you. Where we diverge is perhaps in regards to which possible interpretation we give some kind of primacy, while acknowledging other ones as also contributing, being analogous, being appropriate, at this moment or that moment or whatever. Because I don't think I've heard any suggested interpretation here that sounds to me impossible, and what I come up against in myself is, I suppose, the remains of that, well, but there must be one right answer," and my constant response to my students, "well, no there isn't a right answer and she's built perplexity in here," because that's also one of the things that's painful to her, and also productive. I'm going to say this afternoon that the unknown is the greatest meat of the intellect, for no one thinks to thank God. And that's going on here too, I think.

And who needs the right answer. I mean, why do we need a right answer?

Once we're not competing for A's, perhaps we don't.

I thought, listening to the discussion, that a lot of times in the religious literature and religious practice in Western Civilization the goal was to concentrate on the wounds of Christ and all this pain, and then to experience that pain as a prelude to ecstasy. And I think probably it applies to the creation of poetry. And to religious experiences. So maybe, she's not coming at this from a conventional way, but there seems to be some connection between pain and ecstasy.

I'm convinced, certainly, that's true of her. I mean, in her poetry there really is the notion that poetry is the gift of screws, very extraordinary ... suffering is quite analogous to creating something.

I think one thing that would be important in trying to decide whether the emphasis is on the pain or on some sort of pleasure is to decide whether the closing couplet is an analogy for the experience that goes before, or an aftermath, a result of the experience?

That word "still" is the word that suddenly reverberates. And Ellen's analogy to the symphony, because it begins in music in a sense. The wind is music in the trees in a lot of 19th-century literature. It is basically a musical analogy, in the beginning and the end.

What's interesting about the couplet, that makes it very different from the rest of the poem, is the "when — then" structure, because the rest of the poem is all ongoing present tense. So she doesn't give us any sense of what happens after; is there any after? All we have is "the universe is still" — that's what we get. And we have the word "still."

That's a wonderful word, really.

That's the word. And the image just resonates with possibilities of stillness. The poem leaves you with that question of ... it's not so much a question, I think it's a sense of ... since she doesn't tell you which meaning of still, you have to entertain a lot ... and that's where you stop, with the dash.

This inexpectation.

I thought another thing that was very interesting, just in the sense of the reading that went on, was the way everybody had recourse to the other poetry. Again, I was brought up as a good new critic, and we were told that there was this poem and it was unto itself and we never went beyond it. I see all these little nods in the room ... and so that the way we read I thought was very provocative: that everybody did that, everybody said "this poem is not a discrete object, it's not a well-wrought urn." Part of the reading experience that we all seem to have is that it echoes, it opens up, to the other poems. We all started hearing, and we use them kind of analytically; but to me it suggested something more profound or central to what it's like to read Emily Dickinson, which may or may not be the same way you read any other poetry. You know, Dickinson did not publish her poems into these volumes where she edited them and decided, "these will go and these will stay." All we have is this book, where the dashes point us on to the next poem. And it always struck me that the structure of a given poem rests upon the parallelism that we talked about, such that it keeps repeating itself, it keeps on illuminating itself. And that the poems do that as a group to one another. That as a whole, her ouevre works the way an individual poem does, because if you want to know what Dickinson thinks about death, one poem won't do it. You've got to go on with all of them. It struck me that the way in which she composes is always this — what we were just talking about earlier — this sense of not solving a problem, ever.

Well I think Dickinson maybe calls attention more to the need to read her poetry in the context of all of it, just because of the constant, intense ambiguities, deletions, telegraphing that she's doing. Sure, you need to read everybody's works in order to have a full sense of what a given poem is saying, I think you could safely say that. But you're more desperate, at least I am more desperate for the context, the variations, for having the blanks partially filled in by the other poems that give you the next link.

But there are many, many poems that within the space of the individual poem work to solve the problem that the poem raises. Think of the traditional sonnet structure.

Shakespeare's sonnets, though, raise the problem.

No, I think most of the time when they get to the end they've solved what they've set up for that individual day. You might say, "OK, for a full understanding of the relations between death and art and love, read them all." But you take the given structure, it's very logical that way, don't you think? It comes to a conclusion.

No, no, I think many of them have built in ambiguity of the sort that Robin was talking about in Dickinson.

Maybe, of course again with Shakespeare, we have the best of the lot. But . . .

I think perhaps simply to repeat what I suggested in the paper, I think there are some wonderful ways in which this poem has got its back on Shakespeare's sonnet. I think it's fun to see it almost as a parody in the sense that the last little couplet doesn't do what the Shakespearean couplet frequently does.

But there are some Shakespearean sonnets which function in exactly this way. The concluding couplet is analogous, but the link is not there in the way you would expect it, so there is a disruption of expectation just as we have here.

Whether that's true or not, the point that I'm after is that Dickinson builds into her discourse the gap or whatever; it is a part of the actual sentence. Not that she didn't get there, it's not that she tried but she couldn't quite pull it all together — it's that she didn't want to — it's part of what's there. I don't want to talk about her intent, but it's part of what is there constantly, the irresolvable, what Cris calls the "unrecoverable deletions." And that's a fact, that's not a problem, that's not an "oh, too bad." It's there, it's information; what do we do with it? And that's what I'm pushing today. Because it really changes how you read poetry, it seems to me. It really changes where you think you're going and what you think you're doing.

This 19th century skepticism is in Melville, Hawthorne, in the prose, in Emerson — not so much in Emerson but in Melville and Hawthorne. The irony, the indeterminacy, of how you judge a thing runs through the 19th century.

One of the things that struck me was the description you were making of Emily Dickinson's poems needing to be seen as a whole. Perhaps that is the case, that kind of organic connection that one wants to make among her poems ... maybe that's one of the things the dashes mean: "don't stop here!"

Well, that's a good line to end the discussion on, "don't stop here!" Don't stop, come back for more!

Poem 656

The name — of it — is "Autumn" —
The hue — of it — is Blood —
An Artery — upon the Hill —
A Vein — along the Road —

Great Globules — in the Alleys —
And Oh, the Shower of Stain —
When Winds — upset the Basin —
And spill the Scarlet Rain —

It sprinkles Bonnets — far below —
It gathers ruddy Pools —
Then — eddies like a Rose — away —
Upon Vermilion Wheels —

c. 1862 *1892*

Women's Studies, 1989
Vol. 16, p. 85
Reprints available directly from the publisher

Poem 656

Terrains of Difference: Reading Shelley and Dickinson on Autumn

JOANNE FEIT DIEHL

Bowdoin College

WITH FIGURAL and philosophic audacity, poem 656 disrupts conventional literary distinctions between the internal and the external, between nature and culture, between the body and all that lies beyond it. In addition to its brilliantly descriptive view of autumn, Dickinson's text constitutes a re-examination of the relationship between nature and the human, presenting a vision of the world as body and of seasonal (therefore cyclical) occurrence as a willed or volitional event. Dickinson's poem thus re-evaluates the relationship between natural events and the boundaries created by the human imagination to control and so render less threatening those natural forces.

From its opening, "The name — of it — is 'Autumn'" creates a sense of estrangement, for, by drawing attention to the act of naming, the poem implies that autumn itself is a verbal construct defined by perception and mediated through subjectivity. Thus, the poem appropriates the natural to its own definitional objectives. Through the syntactic parallel between the first and second lines: "The name — of it — is 'Autumn' — / The hue — of it — is Blood," Dickinson asserts a correspondence that is not supported by a real epistemological equivalency. By presenting "name" and "hue" as syntactic equals, by choosing "blood" rather than the anticipated "red," Dickinson refuses the difference between describing an aspect of a phenomenon and the activity of naming; thus the premises of definitional logic are, from the poem's inception, violated. The opening lines' anomolous

Women's Studies, 1989
Vol. 16, pp. 87-90

syntax and diction gesture, moreover, toward the text's and Dickinson's larger revisionary conceptual project, the disruption of the very foundations of rhetorical figuration itself.

In the poem's self-described landscape, one discovers traces of a dismembered body: "An Artery — upon the Hill — / A Vein — along the Road." One views parts of a corpse already dissected, turned inside out upon the place that becomes a possible scene of victimization, of accident or of violence. If we are not apprised of the event that has caused such dismemberment, we are, more disturbingly, also not informed whose artery and vein these are. By refusing to distinguish between inner and outer, between agent and object, Dickinson dismembers tropological discourse, based as it must be upon the preservation of such distinctions. Because the reader cannot distinguish between what lies within or beyond the self, the poem erodes both rhetorical and physical boundaries.

Before pursuing the implications of this rhetorical disfigurement, I turn to another poem about autumn, Shelley's "Ode to the West Wind" with its equally de-idealizing and grim vision. I undertake this brief comparative reading to assess the linguistic radicalism of Dickinson's text (and of her poetics more generally). Shelley's Ode envisions the "hectic red" of autumn, its "pestilence-stricken multitudes" and its "winged seeds," "each like a corpse within its grave." Yet, in the face of such desolation, the Ode strives to recover the possibility of a viable, uncompromised, even mutually advantageous relationship between human subjectivity and the natural world. Through this desire, Shelley reinforces his presence as "other" in the natural scene by questing for a relationship with the devastating natural processes over which he actually exercises no control. Through recollection and simile, "If I were a dead leaf ... / If I were a swift cloud, ...", Shelley explores the recuperative possibilities of relationship. The poem, moreover, affirms Shelley's need to discover in himself a reason for being that will lift him beyond his own victimization: "Oh, lift me as a wave, a leaf, a cloud! / I fall upon the thorns of life! I bleed." Shelley's final plea is that he become the west wind's lyre, that his capacity to serve the wind, to speak for it, rescue him. Yet the similitude envisioned between the autumn and the self, "What if my leaves are falling like its own," while painful, preserves the difference between inner and outer through the presence of trope. Shelley moves beyond simile to admonishment: "Be thou me," imploring of the wind an identity that effaces all distinctions. By yearning to incorporate the wind's power through speech and by preserving the difference between speech and wind that permits that yearning, Shelley would discover a reason for being, for being as voice that promises triumph over the inevitability of death.

Dickinson's poem, despite certain overt similarities to Shelley's autumnal vision, nevertheless redefines the relationship between the self and the external, re-mapping the terrain of difference as it dissolves the Shelleyan distinction between the imagination and nature. Through its purposive, deliberate figural exploitation — the great globules in the alleys, the "Shower of Stain" — this poem continues to anatomize landscape. Winds, in Dickinson's autumn, do not "blow," they "upset," an arbitrary accident rather than a natural, hence predictable occurrence. That autumn leaves should be figured as "scarlet rain" is not only to emphasize their color and the fact of their fall but ineradicably to convert them into something other — into a blood-rain (cf. Shelley's "black rain," II, 28). The extremity of such metaphoricity pushes the poem over the edge of the surreal.

Dickinson, moreover, implicates a distinctly feminine culture into her anatomized natural description as bonnets are sprinkled with this unearthly blood, as the decorous rhetoric of costume luridly merges with the grotesque. The bespattered bonnets themselves, it could be argued, represent a crossing over of natural and cultural descriptive categories, creating a conceptual chiasmus that informs the poem's closing lines as the "ruddiness" of health turns into the softer tones of rose and "vermilion," of the season's or the day's close. In this final, apparently decorative description of autumn's departure, ("it eddies like a Rose — away — / Upon Vermilion Wheels —"), one notes the utterly conventional sentimentality of "like a rose" and the decorative quality of "vermilion." These descriptive images further distance us from the just-stated origins of all that lovely, ruddy glow — the carnage of the wreck; for the wheels, as the poem has taught us, are "stained" not by any store-bought paint (or, literally, the leaves) but dyed in blood. Whether deploying the violently aggressive figuration of the poem's first eight lines or the conventional, indeed sentimental, tropes of its final quatrain, Dickinson writes off any representation of authentic feeling. Thus, "Vermilion Wheels" may also synechdochically represent the corpse of an affective self silenced in spite of the poem's overtly dazzling verbal display.

That this poem is frequently read as merely vivid or playful, that it invites such a reading, only reinscribes the power of Dickinson's rhetoric. What permits these naive mis-readings, however, is somewhat more complicated. By deleting any overt expression of feeling from her poem, by excluding an emotionally inflected narrative voice, Dickinson presents her intensely subjectivizing vision as definition. By denying the poem its frame of authorial reference, Dickinson asserts figural audacity as if it were fact. The subjectivity that enacts the very fusion betwen the imagination and the external world itself abjures any overt signs of presence. Thus Dickinson pursues her dismantling of figural discourse by rejecting an affective discourse that would draw attention to a consciousness distinct from that of autumn's. Through such rhetorical evasions, Dickinson creates a hidden space wherein she may dis-able the Shelleyan hope for salvaging a motive for being from the ravages of time. By violating rhetorical boundaries and re-positioning the self *vis-à-vis* the natural world, Dickinson interrogates that world and the rhetorical distinctions that living in such a world conventionally demands. Over against the Romantic imagination's quest for a compensatory consolation, "The name — of it — is 'Autumn'" reveals a terrain of blurred boundaries, of overturned and spilled interiority that can be neither protected nor contained, but itself stains or taints all decorative costumes, whether they be the bonnets of convention or the tropes employed by art.

Poem 656

Dickinson and the Contract of Taste

BARBARA PACKER

University of California, Los Angeles

LAST SPRING I taught a seminar in Dickinson that bore a strong resemblance, in format, to this conference. Students were required to write brief papers on a series of poems chosen in advance, and then to read their "readings" in class. Three or four weeks into this strenuous discipline a student read a paper whose opening sentence mingled resentment with relief: "In this poem," she wrote, "Dickinson mercifully tells us what the subject is in the first line."

Anyone who has ever tried to solve one of Dickinson's riddles, unscramble her elliptical syntax, locate any stable referent for one of her anti-allegories, lay out in temporal sequence the involuted equations that profess to measure time and eternity, or map the spatial convolutions of "circumference," can sympathize with the student's confusion. The contract Dickinson establishes with her readers can frequently dissolve into a relationship of malice, in which the poet toys with our efforts to comprehend her as a cat toys with a mouse.

But our comprehension is not the only thing Dickinson can toy with. Poem 656, at first glance, appears to be a merciful one, since it names its subject in the first line. But by the third line the poem has created a different kind of problem. Not a logical one: the poem is nothing if not logical. "It" is *named* Autumn; it is colored red, like blood; blood is found in veins and arteries; it coagulates in globules, which are collected in surgical basins — it is all perfectly logical. The

Women's Studies, 1989
Vol. 16, pp. 91-94

poem toys not with our comprehension, but with our powers of literary discrimination. It teasingly invites us to consider it in execrable taste.

For the recipe by which Dickinson constructs her lyric seems to have been confected by Martinus Scriblerus in *Peri Bathous.* It has the single-minded devotion to deductive logic, and the heedlessness of tone, that mark the adept at the Art of Sinking. "We cannot too earnestly recommend to our Authors the Study of the *Abuse of Speech.* They ought to lay it down as a Principle, to say nothing in the usual way, but (if possible) in the direct contrary," Scriblerus advises, and then goes on to recommend specific figures. Under "Metaphor" he advises: "The first Rule is to draw it from the lowest things, which is a certain way to sink the highest." And the next rule comes shortly after: "whenever you start a Metaphor, you must be sure to *Run it down,* and pursue it as far as you can go." Later on he extols the virtues of anticlimax, "where the second Line drops quite short of the first, than which nothing creates greater surprise," and especially recommends the use of technical terms "which estrange your Stile from the great and general Ideas of Nature: And the higher your subject is, the lower should you search into Mechanicks for your Expression. If you describe the Garment of an Angel, say that his *Linnen* was *finely spun,* and bleach'd on the happy Plains." Most of all, the bathetic poet should consider himself as a "*Grotesque* Painter, whose Works would be spoiled by an imitation of Nature, or Uniformity of Design. He is to mingle Bits of the most various, or discordant kinds, Landscape, History, Portraits, Animals, and connect them with a great deal of Flourishing, by Heads or Tails, as it shall please his Imagination, and contribute to his principal end, which is to glare by strong Oppositions of Colours, and surprize by Contrariety of Images."

The first stanza of Dickinson's poem is relentless, anticlimactic, and indecorous all at once. The red of autumn is the red of blood — a metaphor so hackneyed that it can only be galvanized into life by the surgical grotesquerie of "An Artery — upon the Hill" and — in case you didn't get it the first time — "A Vein — along the Road —." Martinus Scriblerus holds Blackmore's *Job* up to ridicule for the ludicrous series of images in which God is represented by turns as a Recruiting Officer, an attorney, a fuller, a mercer, and finally a butler:

He measures all the Drops with wondrous Skill,
Which the black clouds, his floating bottles, fill.

If Blackmore's God is a skillful butler, Dickinson's Autumn is a clumsy surgical assistant:

Great Globules — in the Alleys —
And Oh, the Shower of Stain —
When Winds — upset the Basin —
And spill the Scarlet Rain —

In the final line of the second stanza the comparison of leaves to blood, having been run down about as far as it can go, suddenly slides into that catachresis Scriblerus sees as the essence of bathos. The globules of blood spilling out of the upset basin suggest raindrops, and this metaphor in turn causes a dizzying shift in perspective. We have been looking at Autumn as if it were a patient etherized upon a table, but in the final stanza it suddenly "sprinkles Bonnets — far below," and (what is harder to visualize) at the same time "gathers ruddy pools." The last phrase manages to sound odd, though there is nothing really ungrammatical about it. Since Dickinson has been referring to the "Globules" of bright leaves that incarnate autumn, it would be logical to expect the second line of the final stanza to read, "It gathers *in* ruddy Pools —"; instead, the poem suddenly returns us to the mode of the opening stanza, where Autumn is not aggregate but agent.

But how does anyone "gather" a pool? The luckless figure seems to have been introduced only to provide a transition to the final set of figures. Pools eddy, if they are tidal pools, and roses may be said to "eddy," metaphorically, when they lose their petals as they blow. But whatever dim sense of poetic appropriateness that connected pair of metaphors might have conferred upon the final stanza of the poem is exploded by the glaring contrariety that follows, in which Autumn departs on a gaudy Circus wagon with 'Vermilion Wheels." It is as if Dickinson had been set a kind of school exercise: *What is the chief attribute of Autumn?* it is Red. *Name three red things.* Blood. Roses. Circus wagon wheels. *Put them in one poem.*

The ineptitude and crudity with which this exercise is carried out — the grotesque and lovingly detailed exposition of the blood/leaf comparison, the confusion and weakness of the "eddying rose" lines, and the final surprise of those vermilion wheels — ought to lead us to judge the poem hilariously bad, one of those naive productions that are the delight of the Alexander Popes and Mark Twains of the world. I have in fact met readers who see Dickinson this way; but most of us here would defend Dickinson's violations of decorum in this poem and in hundreds like it as intentional.

But what kind of intention does it embody? In a famous book Hugh Kenner pointed out that the techniques of Dryden's, or Pope's, heroic poetry are indistinguishable from the techniques of their mock-heroic poetry. We would have no way of knowing, from internal evidence alone, whether *To Augustus* was sincerely blundering panegyric or deadly satire; to know how the poem should be read we must know something about Pope's intentions.

With Dickinson the case is more complicated. No one who reads the *Collected Poems* with care can fail to become sensible of a frightening power of mind, so that the question of intentionality is in one sense easy to answer. The simple blunder, the sort of thing for which Wordsworth is famous, seems hardly to occur in Dickinson. There are bad lines and bad poems, but they seem more like experiments carelessly discarded than embarrassments offered up in all innocence.

But the deliberate violation of every principle of lyric decorum evident in 656 does not look to me like a failed experiment. Instead it seems a new kind of poem altogether, which attempts to see how far the language of comically bad verse can be made to serve the ends of lyric pleasure. Dickinson is acutely aware of the intimate relation that subsists between imagination and catechresis: all tropes are abuses of language, and the vivid or successful metaphor inhabits a narrow strip of land between the "howler" and the cliche. We are familiar with this shift in the images of the famous poems, as when the "certain slant of light" suddenly becomes oppressive with the "heft" of cathedral tunes; but the same deliberate yoking of contrarieties, of sudden shifts between different universes of discourse, is repeated time and time again in the "lesser" poems as well. For this reason the experience of reading the *Collected Poems* is radically different from reading even the most generous anthology selection, as watching a gymnast's complete tumbling run is from seeing a single cartwheel. The inspired tastelessness of "The name of it is 'Autumn'" is Dickinson's own brand of deadpan humor, which, like the comic routines of a lead character on a situation comedy, tends to become more endearing over time. And the discomfort it creates in us as it jolts us from one crude trope to another is only a wilder variant of the shock all fresh metaphor must necessarily give.

Poem 656
Workshop Discussion

Speakers: JOANNE FEIT DIEHL, BARBARA PACKER.

BOTH BARBARA and Joanne discussed what I'll call the comic element, Barbara calling it more deliberately comic and grotesque, Joanne veering off into the grotesque. I wondered if you think that Dickinson strove for the comic effect as a response to Shelley in — not parody of him exactly, but in a response similar to her treatment of "I rose because he fell," which is a direct paraphrasing of *Jane Eyre.* If you look at the passage where Jane comes back to Rochester after he's been blinded, you actually find phrases that are echoed in that poem. I wonder if there's something similar going on. In another words, how conscious do you think that response to Shelley is?

That she knew Shelley's work I think can be proved if you look at it, and it's impossible to say what she was thinking when she wrote it.

I wonder, it very well might be a direct response. Dickinson, more than I think most of us realize, did respond in very literal ways to the romantics, both the poets and the novelists. It seems to me that that approach really gives both of your readings a kind of focus; it seems to me that they both take on another dimension in that context.

The other question I have is, to relate this to Cheryl's paper earlier, [about] the issue of differentiation vs. ranking. I thought that a very exciting area of discourse came out of that discussion. Joanne suggests that there is a kind of testing of the boundaries and a breaking apart of the conventional relationship of nature and culture, creating an addi-

Women's Studies, 1989
Vol. 16, pp. 95-113

tional space for Dickinson's vision. The whole notion of dismembering tropological discourse and eroding the rhetorical and physical boundaries is a very interesting one.

In the fascicle copy of the poem, the last lines are "That eddies like a rose away / Upon Vermillion wheels," and there's an "x" beside it and the additional variant "makes Vermillion / And leaves me with the hills." The "leaves me with the hills" was a wonderful discovery for me. I did my homework after I wrote my paper, which in some sense is fairly typical, but I felt vindicated since I was so interested in presence and absence, where she is in the poem. By rejecting "And leaves me with the hills," I think she much more subtly removes herself from the poem and so presences herself through her abandonment, by not mentioning herself, by not being there.

That makes it a more conventional kind of romantic pathos. Like "it passes and we stay."

And it makes it possible that she's the one spread out on the landscape...

I think she's been, sort of. The veins and arteries have been rolled up and she's been put on the cart. She has been carted off in some sense. But what remains is the consciousness of watching herself being carted away.

I think the difference in Barbara's tone and mine is important to note —

I thought that in fact you had touched on a point of similarity between what we are doing when you talked about the displacement of affect or the derangement of the expected affect, which seems to be characteristic of all of Dickinson's poems. I can't think of the term for what I want. It's not humor, it's not parody. What it comes closest to reminding me of is something that Max Brod said of Kafka; he talked about Kafka reading "The Metamorphosis" aloud to him and just roaring with laughter as he read it. There was obviously something about it that Kafka himself found profoundly funny. And I find — not reading Dickinson's poems in isolation but reading, say, practically the whole collected poems — that that quality of macabre black humor comes out again and again, and is the hardest thing to introduce to people who don't know Dickinson.

It really is an unholy glee. It's seeing what she's done, it's not so much laughing because anything is funny.

It reminds me of — what is the word Elizabeth Bishop uses, in "The Sea and its Shore" — she talks about the "joke effect." Mr. Boomer discovers a fake nose — his job is to clean the beach every night, and to pick up litter; and the litter is texts, of course — and he discovers this false nose and puts it on. She said that's an example of the joke effect. Part of [this poem's] humor — I would gloomily insist — is a joke effect; it distances the subject so that humor then protects ... Obviously, in a Freudian way, humor is a defense, a way of distancing and displacing oneself from affect, so that one doesn't fall into what for Dickinson may have become a romantic bathos rather than a romantic pathos. It becomes a kind of redeeming irony, perhaps, that enables distance and disguises feeling.

And maybe also, to bring up the question of how it connected to Cheryl's talk, it seems to me that the kinds of hierarchies of tastes that I was discussing are based upon a very hierarchical notion of what kinds of emotion are appropriate to what sorts of poetic subjects. It's a very masculine tradition as well. What is a low word, what are the words you have in a nursery ... I've always felt that Dickinson's subversion of the normal categories of taste was sort of subversive in a feminist way and is akin to, say, writers like Christina Stead. In *The Man Who Loved Children*, Stead does the same kind of writing — which is macabre and comic and profoundly metaphorically imaginative at the same time. The only place that I can think of it in a masculine way is in odd places in Lewis Carroll ...

I sometimes wonder if the notion of high seriousness isn't something ... Women writers like to be comic.

I have begun to delineate a tradition based upon that kind of rhetorical dismantling and disruption. We certainly see it in Marianne Moore and her use of business manual diction and very privatized kind of language, the higher grand style, and I think [here] one definitely sees the ambitious use of nursery rhymes. It's wonderful that you mention Lewis Carroll, because at the end of "Efforts of Affection," Bishop's memoir on Moore, she stares at the name of Marianne Moore and gets stuck on the "M"; she says, "Like Alice, I find myself bemused." That sense of disruptive playfulness and a willingness to disregard and mix categories certainly is present in Bishop's "One Art."

I was trying to think last night of what seems different. Dickinson often seems to me extremely modern in the way that she does this kind of rhetorical subversion — but usually when I think of it in a twentieth-century writer like Eliot, the disruption of categories becomes a symbol of the pathos of the breakdown of western culture, whereas it doesn't seem to me that that's what Dickinson was doing at all. She was doing something much more radical.

Yes, but it's also more playful in its formula. You would never find a sentimental phrase in Eliot used the way Dickinson does.

Not unless it were in quotation marks.

Right, but Dickinson throws it in so lightly that it's hard to know the tone as clearly as you can in Eliot — although Bishop and Moore are playful in that same way.

I think it's a playfulness, [but] I don't think it's a playfulness that attempts to trivialize — rather instead to reappropriate and to question and to make more radical a whole way of speaking.

Do either of you have a sense that the whole tone and mood of the poem changes in the second stanza? It seems to me that the first is very sedate, and then the second one is ebullient: "And Oh, the Shower of Stain" and "spill the Scarlet." It seems as though she shifts gears, she starts one way and then does something else.

Well, the capacity to get intoxicated by language itself — you introduce it in all seriousness and then suddenly [see] the comic possibilities, and then you go with that for a stanza or two. It seems to me that conventional notions of poetry, particularly lyric poetry, would lead you to exclude anything that effected a radical shift, unless it was part of an ode or something like that. Dickinson does it all the time.

Even though we all love her and want to treasure her, I just don't think "eddies like a rose away" is a very good line. It leaves me cold.

I think in its very lack of success it is making a jest ...

But it sounded like you were saying it's presented here in order to make the point about conventionality.

But this is the whole question of intentionality. Does an intention have to be absolutely successful all the way through? What seems to me to make Dickinson's poems so difficult to come to final judgments about is that you can't settle the question of intentionality once and for all. At certain moods you read it and say, "this is a lousy line she left in because she wanted a cliche," but other times you think maybe she left it in because she didn't have time to go back and fix it up. You have the feeling when you're reading Wordsworth that he wanted every line to be absolutely good and perfect, so when he blows it, you know he didn't mean to. But with Dickinson you never — it's like being toyed with by a cat, if you're the mouse. You don't know whether you're criticizing her or whether she's making a fool of you.

I think she's toying with the form of conventional lyric poetry, too, by coming in with the pastoral first stanza, and then you have a shift in geography to the alleys as though you have globules in the alleys. The whole tone, as Cheryl says, changes, so that instead of having the pans of blood out there, these same zephyrs out of the hills come in and slop everything around.

And in turn this ruins the landscape of the first stanza. The bonnet's out wandering around, and the pastoral hills are besmearched with sort of acid rain. And then you have a kind of conventional Blakeian sick rose that whirls away in a metaphorical circus, but it speaks to the first stanza and it's a subversion of that pastoral Shelleyan lament for the pastoral world.

I think she uses synesthesia here, too; the submerging of texture and sound and color scrambles our perceptual categories in ways that create a new space. And I read her as being linguistically radical. I tend to see her irony and humor as always controlled and usually directed toward a deliberate writer — and that's why I think Joanne's reference to Shelley is fascinating. I think [the poem] may in fact be a conscious upsetting of his pastoral conventions.

She never talked about Shelley in a letter.

[But] he was a big deal and was included in the anthology of British Romantic poetry that she owned. And her copy of "Episychidion" has lines that are underlined.

We've been told that Dickinson never underlined in her books and that the underlining belonged to somebody else.

I think one can distinguish, I have distinguished, between heavy pencil marks and light pencil marks — light pencil marks, of course, being Dickinson's and the heavy ones being Sue's. Having gone through page by page, I know there are marks.

I had assumed they were Dickinson's, then I came across a passage by somebody from the immediate family that said, "Emily never made a single mark in her books. She felt very strongly about this." And I said, "Oops, I guess all those things that I made so much of were . . ."

She did it on the sly. She couldn't help herself.

Just like she never wrote poems, you know.

I wanted to ask those of you who teach Dickinson if your experience is at all similar to mine. In a survey course, I find it possible to teach anthology pieces as little iconic neocritical poems and they work very well and people admire them, but I always feel that there's something false to the experience of reading Dickinson in doing that. The only way I really enjoy teaching her is in seminars where we spend at least half a quarter reading hundreds and hundreds of Dickinson poems a week. Because I find that the answer to the riddle of the interpretation of one Dickinson poem is usually another Dickinson poem. And it becomes kind of intoxicating in the way that the poems process you and bounce you around between sort of inspired goofiness and sudden deadly seriousness and fear and silliness. And everybody says, "Oh let's do . . ."; the students take over and they say "can we do 256" or can we do some other one. Which isn't something that usually happens to me teaching any other lyric poet that I can think of. Again, Dickinson seems to have qualities for which I don't have any critical vocabulary.

I think "inspired goofiness" is great.

But that sounds trivializing, and it doesn't seem to me her kind of macabre humor is at all antithetical to seriousness.

Well, it reflects a conflict that women have now and I think must have had then about seriousness, and how seriously to take anything. Women often, I think, see what men do and realize that it's very important, it's war or it's starvation and things that matter. But, on the other hand, we see it as kind of silly, the way they're being and the way things have turned out. And there's a real conflict there — that things that are important are also silly. You can see that her words are the most important things in the world to her, but I think she also sees that people are going to call them silly, and that maybe she should think that way too.

That's certainly borne out if you look at the history of Dickinson criticism. I like the point you made that everybody used to apologize for her . . .

I had a wonderful quote from Ivor Winters — I have to read this to you. "Her meter at its worst, that is, most of the time, kind of stoops along. Her diction, at its worst, is a kind of poetic nursery jargon, and there is a remarkable continuity of manner of a kind nearly indescribable between her best and her worst poems."

I think one of the things that you're saying, Barbara, indirectly, and that I run into when deciding which poems to teach, is that I don't find it so easy to distinguish between her best and her worst poems. There are poems that I love and then there are poems that I passed over when I read them for the first time ten years ago, and somebody reintroduces one to me and I say "this is a great poem!"

Everytime I read through the selected poems, selecting maybe one third of them for an undergraduate seminar, I make a different selection. I go through and as I'm reading through I say "how could I have left out that one, that's a perfect illustration of x-y-z." She doesn't fall into the neat division of canonical and non-canonical that most poets seem to.

We seem to agree that she's scrambling conventional categories of excellence or of literary style. What is she putting in their place — or is it just the sheer diversity that her improvisational and playful genius creates? I wonder if there's a deeper political or epistemological implication or not.

I would guess that perhaps she is covering her tracks, questioning the relationship between poem and another consciousness, or an imaginary reader — and that the figural play and the difficulty describing tone are in some sense at the service of rhetorical masking, defending against what she's actually about. I would suggest that it functions as a defense that enables her to say things that are threatening both to the culture and perhaps to a constructive sense of self.

OK, but is it that she's relieved to step out of a constructive sense of self and finds it an extraordinary freedom but is at the same time frightened by the multiplicity of possibility and the sheer overwhelming confusion, the lack of epistemological hierarchy? Or is there another agenda? Joanne said that there was a space that she created. What is in that space? By deconstructing, say, the Shelleyian approach, what is she, if anything, constructing?

It's a perpetual motion machine.

I was thinking of this because when I was working on Emerson — he hated the notion of a poem that became a fixed set of tropes; it seemed to him deadly. The only time the mind was alive was in "shooting the gap" between one trope and another. His ideal, which he never found realized in any poet that he knew of, was to have a poem that would keep processing you from one trope to another and then start you back over again, like a kind of washing machine. It's frustrating to read him because you think, "the poet you were looking for was in existence and you didn't know it"; in fact, he was staying overnight in the house across the street [from her]!

I think there's a psychological corollary to that continual sense of process, that washing machine. It is a way of allowing one to keep doing what it is necessary to do. To stop is to fix, indeed to establish a hierarchy of trope, and tropological discourse, and she will not do that, or she does it and then inverts it or then laughs, or she moves from one extreme to another. It's in the poise between these leaps that she is able to sustain that sense of language experiment which is at the heart of Emerson's desire.

At the same time you're asking about the sense of space that is established between the elements here; if you go with Emerson's thought, that the poet can only write what he sees, you turn that around: the access to the poet herself is through what she sees and what she writes. If what she sees and what she writes is cartwheeling, experimenting, a sense of crux between different forms, then you never can access the poet. She can stand apart within her own space and maintain her own mystic kinds of boundaries.

That's what Emerson said of Shakespeare, that the greatest poets have no biography. He picked Shakespeare as the person who comes the closest in his mind to offering perpetual-playing tropes.

I think it's important to remind ourselves, too, though, that there may be a lot of poems that are not entirely successful. She wrote an enormous amount; she had a lot to do in her daily life that didn't include five or six hours of writing poetry; she wrote on the back of paper bags, very quickly. It just may be that some of these effects that we're constructing grand theories about — how they deconstruct everything and shake up language and all of that — maybe the poem we're looking at was one she didn't play with a whole lot, and so we're "shooting the gaps" in ways she may not have intended.

But what's wonderful is that she offers us the possibility to shoot the gaps. I may never in my life shoot a real gap; I need my texts to be able to do that. I think, not to be funny about it, that that is part of the process; the reader then is invited to discuss it, to judge, to be the poet. She gives us a chance to be the poet.

I too think that not all the poems are successful, but I think I gain a great insight into her good poems by reading her bad poems. Someone tells a wonderful anecdote about when an art dealer was trying to bring in paintings that were allegedly Picasso's to Picasso, and Picasso kept saying "Fake, fake, fake, fake . . ." And the art dealer was getting furious, to the point where he didn't believe Picasso, so he secretly bought one he knew Picasso had painted and showed it to Picasso, and he said 'Fake." He said, "But you painted that!" and Picasso said "I always paint fakes!" That seems to be the spirit in which Dickinson's failed creations are right among . . .

I'd like to push the discussion in a slightly different way. We seem to be valorizing slipperiness of one kind or another, rich possibilities of all kinds. But what if, as many critics — Toril Moi and other post-structuralists would say — what if slipperiness is a kind of decoy? Slipperiness is what you make of it; it may or may not be radical, it may or may not be conservative. If we always think of dominant ideology as fixed hierarchies, oppositions, all the things that we know and have been very good at isolating — if we think of it only as that, we don't know really what's going on, we don't know how to live in a world in which things are a lot more complicated than that. What if in fact the most effective kind of dominant ideology is precisely a kind of slipperiness that gives us the feeling that we are creating meaning, we are the writer as well as the reader of the poem. Should we push ourselves a little further and question our own assumptions about what we want to value?

What do you see as the consequences of adopting an ideology that values slipperiness? You seem to feel that it's dangerous . . .

Well, it's the kind of self-satisfaction that I myself feel when I write. I take the line, "Oh, good, slipperage in direction, deconstruction of this and that . . ." My nineteenth-century male authors — "bad, bad";

look at these great females — "good, good ..." But I'm quite aware that I'm creating a fiction of a certain kind.

Maybe it's capitalism ... I was thinking of a paper on the relationship between trusts and nineteenth-century culture, especially this notion of Christ implicit in Emerson. The notion that you always want to keep your assets liquid so you can keep reinvesting. Fixity is bad for your portfolio.

Everyone's laughing, because there's something to that ... I guess what's troubling too is that really, we're not valorizing slipperiness in a way; we really want to say that Dickinson is our poet because she says things that we want her to say, right? It isn't because she says in a slippery, incredible way that men are terrific and women are ridiculous, right? We're already within a field in which certain kinds of readings are possible and certain other kinds are not possible. Right? Our basis for discussion is not that Emily Dickinson is conservative and ridiculous for creating a world, poetic or otherwise, in which there are hierarchies ... do you see, we want to valorize a certain kind of discourse.

What I was going to argue in my paper this morning is that there are a lot of things we know about Dickinson that create a certain kind of friction against appropriating her entirely for our own time and place. I think you can say that she was attracted to certain kinds of power, certain kinds of people, and that there are other sides of her that represented a conflicting point of view. Her poetry often comes out of struggles to deal with these things, and she's not always speaking for us. I think most of us are willing to agree that there are things that Dickinson says or does which don't entirely agree with our politics. And I don't think that we have to accept the idea that we're trying to appropriate her utterly for our purposes.

I would also wonder about slipperiness as quite the right word. I prefer the figure of shooting the gap.

What do you mean "shooting the gap"?

If you think of one trope and another as two fixed pieces of language that the mind leaps across, like a canonball going across Niagara. Two tropes or pieces of a trope ...

But with Dickinson you've got all kinds of leaps that you're making — within the metaphor, between metaphors. A lot of her metaphors put three things together, so it's like you're leaping two directions at once.

I would suggest that there is a deeply hierarchical structure in Dickinson, in her view of the world. One again and again sees this enacted in her sense of betrayal of and by that structure that inherently incorporates the puritanic as well as the Emersonian. One can see conflicts in self and in other. It's in the play between those that the excitement can occur. So it is not as if she is somebody who sneaks around or slips or slides, but rather it is in the very sense of struggle and the emotions that are involved in the struggles.

If you're talking about slipperiness of language in terms of indeterminacy, indeterminacy that has a positive value and aesthetic all of its own . . .

I think it's very easy to invoke deconstructive vocabulary in Dickinson's situation, but it doesn't feel right.

All I was asking us to do, in fact, was not to say we don't valorize, we won't have values, but rather to say we are aware that we are having certain kinds of values — and possibly to examine the assumptions that underlie our values, to know what exactly we are standing for — whether we're on steady ground or not.

Joanne, I had a question about your answer to Peggy, and I think it's partly because I didn't understand it. At the risk of sounding like I'm jumpy at the very use of the word "hierarchical," I don't know what you mean when you say you think that there is a deeply hierarchical structure in Dickinson's poems.

"Art Thou the thing I wanted / Begone — my Tooth has grown." I would suggest that there's a hierarchy of desire, that she questions, against which she expresses resentment, resentment at her own desire.

Are you talking about when she wants some things more than others? That she's clear that some things are more important to her than others?

I think the passion for certain others is clear, and I think those others are often identified, as I think you have suggested, with the male, male power and male authority, and love, and something that she cannot do for herself —" I thought that nature was enough / 'Till human nature came" — that sense of the importance of the other, of the person. I think she interrogates that desire, and we can create a story out of the interrogation of that desire and her rising above that desire. That for her is one story of victory. It's not always victorious, but I think there is for her a hierarchy . . .

She desperately wants to say, you know, this is better than this; others have thought this was better but I say this is better.

She's choosing constantly, yes.

That sense of choice, and the necessity that she feels to make a choice, would suggest a world in which there are opposing hierarchies that she cannot accept. So then she asserts her independence by presenting those hierarchies and saying, "Here is how I align myself, given those possibilities." Often that alignment will be a victimization or a defeat, and at other times, when perhaps she's feeling more hopeful, there will be triumph.

Maybe also hierarchies in the sense of a series of progressive annunciations which move from one level of value to another, where — say, in a medieval poem, love within the poem will be seen as much better than anything in the world outside of love, and at the end of the poem erotic love will be renounced in favor of Christian love, which makes it look ridiculous. Troilus goes zooming up to the eighth sphere and turns and laughs at the scene which it was tragedy to be in the middle of. I often get that kind of feeling from Dickinson, where you're suddenly uplifted from one point of view of the universe to another.

What you also might be seeing is a kind of competition. I think the poems are in places highly competitive. They are poems of struggling: there are competing values hierarchically established, in which Dickinson positions and continually repositions herself.

I guess I have a problem with the word hierarchies in the context partly for that reason, because it seems to me that her hierarchies aren't set. She's always choosing — something better or not as good. It seems to me that part of your argument about this poem, Joanne, is that she takes something, the romantic vision of nature, and she does this with it and then she does something else, and then she does a third thing ... so she doesn't leave a hierarchy in place.

It seems to me that she has some real absolute values.

I would stick to hierarchies.

It's like in Emerson's essay "Experience," where, after giving all the arguments for relativity, he says there is something else in our consciousness which is not a sliding scale and which ranks all our exhilaration; he rejects all the female names for it — like Fortune, Minerva, and Muse — and finally settles on "vast, flowing vigor," which seems to me a wonderful expression for the kind of power that Dickinson has.

How are we reading "it" in the first line and in the second line and then in the third stanza —" It sprinkles Bonnets," "the name of it"?

She's pointing to a larger experience that resists naming, and begins, as she often does, with the most limited kind of approach. We can name this experience "autumn," but then she does other things with it.

She seems to me also profoundly interested in categories of grammar. I'm fascinated by the way she uses, for instance, a pronoun to represent a phenomenon, as she does here, as if it were a thing — "spread out like an artery." "It" is used to give a subject to a verb, so that you can say "it sprinkles." You're not actually thinking of a thing up there sprinkling.

It's a grammatical subject.

Yes, which of course can be turned into an allegory if you're writing a poem, but exists all the time in language as a kind of quasi-personification.

She plays with that all the time. Remember when Joanne talked about the two words when she changes from "it" as a thing to "it" as an agent to "it" as a grammatical subject — and they all seem to be the same, because "it" is what she begins with, but "it" has varying syntactical references. But somehow, it's all the same: it's a season, it's some completely unfocused thing — it's what makes the season happen, it's what happens.

I think the poem substantiates Barbara's point, that the extent to which the "it" changes in the poem itself from the verbal use, to "it" leaping up high and then sprinkling down —. "It" becomes an agent, "it" becomes a subject, so that what is a definitional term, "Autumn," then becomes what is responsible for the agency of the sprinkling. There is a sense of perspectival shift.

I always do a week on syntax alone for Dickinson, which is a real revelation to the students. Just as we perceive and do not see what we're looking at, we use language all the time without thinking about it. What Dickinson is forcing us to do in all those poems where she makes you supply the syntax is to become aware of how much activity has to go on in the mind to come up with any sentence at all. I guess that's one of the things I'm most interested in, in her. The metaphors are beautiful and obvious, but what she does with syntax seems to me the most innovative and creative game of any major poet.

I agree. And also I think that to draw attention to the game is to raise the question of hierarchy. To privilege the occupation of making choices is to render problematic the choices that one makes.

I think one of the most interesting things she does with syntax is to create sentences or poems in which there are multiple ways of recreating the sentence and what you do in reading the poem is recreate the sentence in multiple ways — some you can cast out as being totally meaningless in the context of the poem, but usually, or in what I think are the great poems, you've got a couple of ways that will have to stand. Although as a reader, to trace through the poem, you'll pick one, then you have to go back and take another one and go through it again and then go through it again; and the poem itself is all those balls in the air at one time. So the act of reading at any one moment is hierarchical in the sense that you're making the choice and you're pulling this one forward, but ultimately you've got to keep them all there.

"Renunciation — is a piercing virtue" is a great example of that. Where she says "Renunciation — is the Choosing / Against itself — / Itself to justify / Unto itself." It sounds like some mad piece of the Summa Theologica, where grammatical categories also take on theological significance — where the relation of the Father, the Son, and the Holy Ghost is explained in terms of the syntax. The whole language of grammar, the whole terminology of grammar, is not just hierarchical but sado-masochistic! This thing governs that, this is the ablative supine. It's all based on the language of conquest or manipulation.

Is there any way you can say that Dickinson is characteristically American? I'm thinking back to the reference to her as a capitalist poet, which goes along with process and that Emersonian phrase, "vast, flowing vigor." Is her character in some sense a manifestation of our economic system and our valuing of mobility and change and experimentation and improvisation and motion and process?

Joanne's book addresses that issue directly, from seeing her as both similar to and different from the British romantic. But I don't know if it does it quite in the terms that Wendy was introducing. I always think of her in terms of landscape, and the nineteenth-century distinction between European landscape and American landscape, like in that William Bryant poem to Cole the painter, where wildness represents America. I see her as a wild poet, in a way that I really can't imagine a British poet occupying ...

That is the comparison to make, but I would suggest — this comes in part from Sandra Gilbert's response when somebody in a recent conversation asked, "What about Hopkins?" Dickinson feels the freedom to move into non-poetry, whereas if one reads, let's say, Hopkins' letters to Bridges, he is concerned with concentrating and focusing and distilling the metrical stress to refine and to intensify ...

... and to control, to dominate language really. That sense of difference between the American and European relationship to speech comes up in the difference between de Toqueville and Whitman. In *Democracy in America* de Toqueville makes some interesting comments about American use of language and their fondness for abstract terms — like a box with a false bottom, you can keep putting any thing in it you want. He talks about the way democracy encourages the constant change of language, where a person picks up a word and does something to it and passes it on; so it keeps altering. De Toqueville's usually sympathetic to things American, but at that point he's absolutely French. He draws back and says, "I hate this idea of the change of meaning of words." Whitman, in his essay on slang, sees it as the essence of American speech. He says it's the Protestant element in speech, the constant bubbling up from below of creativity — the rankness and wildness of linguistic virileness that upset de Toqueville so.

Even when somebody was being wild, like Blake, he's tearing down one order to replace it with another. Somebody like Whitman is sort of tearing down one to set up his own shop. It's entrepreneurism.

Though I might make this more vexed by then asking a question of gender: is that valorization of an American self different for Whitman and for Dickinson, or are they both up to this same kind of writing of non-poetry, in the service of the self? And I might place the distinction that Dickinson does that at the risk of the self rather than at its valorization, or exclusively its valorization.

Yes, and Whitman seems to me a more conventional poet than Dickinson in that he likes to draw from traditions ...

— and he sanctifies his tone so that he and Eliot sound strangely akin, in a way that makes a demotic kind of diction, mixture of diction sanctified through the Whitmanian voice — whereas Dickinson in her disfigurations doesn't quest after that kind of sanctification of diction.

I was thinking that if you don't want Whitman, how about Williams?

I don't think that Williams proclaims for himself or asserts for himself that kind of authoritative appropriation of landscape that Whitman does. But I think that Williams is inheriting a tradition.

A weird experience that I've had teaching Dickinson is using the Oscar Williams anthology, *Great American Poets*, which has lots and lots of poems from several poets that I do in the survey, and I've often in the past said, "In conjunction with reading Dickinson's poems, read Henry Wadsworth Longfellow. You'll be able to see right away how different she is." And they all come in and look at me very seriously and say they couldn't tell the difference. So I started going back and looking at the poems that he had chosen for her, and I realized that he had chosen a lot of poems that had no syntactical problems, very moderate kinds of poems, and that he could actually find forty or so to put in that didn't seem that bizarre next to Longfellow.

But it's not the dominant strain — it seems to me that simplicity is more of a dominant strain in Williams than in Dickinson.

He chooses a rhetorical mode and follows it through, whereas she consistently juxtaposes ...

And he chooses a mode that's conversationally acceptable.

I think Stevens does a lot of the same sort of things.

So my question would be if there is a gender difference?

When I teach Dickinson in the context of other American writers, I find that the way I describe American writers in contrast to British writers or European writers is very, very close to the way I describe women writers in contrast to male writers. What I take as at the heart of American literature I also take, in many ways, as being at the heart of women's writing. And so I see it partly as a difference in degree and as a difference in emphasis at different points. American literature is doing a lot of those same kinds of breaking away, experimenting with new things, trying to create some sort of new ground, even though it obviously takes a lot of the old along with it.

I think psychologically the sources are related in the sense of being displaced, of not being in the privileged position, of not being associated with the aristocracy, having to prove oneself. The psychological paradigms are not so different. The anxieties of gender are related to those anxieties of patriotism.

I wonder if we could go back to something that you mentioned before when you were talking about Yvor Williams. I was wondering how radically the canon of Dickinson poems that we read to validate our sense of what Dickinson is has changed over a period of time. Because Winters seems to be particularly upset with poems that, to my way of reading Dickinson, are the ones that fall more easily into the category of fixed allegories. They're the poems that I'm just not teaching. These days I find myself, for instance, teaching 721, poems like that, that are disjunctive, synesthetic in a lot of ways. That is not the Dickinson that they anthologized previously, at least looking at anthologies before the 1950's.

The canon has changed, and I think one of the big changes has to do with the impact of feminist criticism of Dickinson, because a lot of poems that we feminist critics direct attention to are not even in *Final Harvest.* I think it's time for a new, shorter version of Dickinson's poems with several hundred poems, but not quite the same several hundred.

Poem 754

My Life had stood — a Loaded Gun —
In Corners — till a Day
The Owner passed — identified —
And carried Me away —

And now We roam in Sovereign Woods —
And now We hunt the Doe —
And every time I speak for Him —
The Mountains straight reply —

And do I smile, such cordial light
Upon the Valley glow —
It is as a Vesuvian face
Had let its pleasure through —

And when at Night — Our good Day done —
I guard My Master's Head —
'Tis better than the Eider-Duck's
Deep Pillow — to have shared —

To foe of His — I'm deadly foe —
None stir the second time —
On whom I lay a Yellow Eye —
Or an emphatic Thumb —

Though I than He — may longer live
He longer must — than I —
For I have but the power to kill,
Without — the power to die — *c. 1863* *1929*

Women's Studies, 1989
Vol. 16, p. 115
Reprints available directly from the publisher

Poem 754: The Unreadable Poem

JOANNE DOBSON

Fordham University

"MY LIFE HAD stood — a Loaded Gun —," as well as being a superb work of art, is a frustratingly enigmatic utterance — a poem that defies understanding. Its singular images and intriguing obscurity, however, render it irresistible to commentators, as is attested to by the multitude of readings given it since its first published appearance in 1929. It is my contention, however, that reading this poem to determine its meaning becomes something in the nature of an exercise in futility. Dickinson's characteristic anxiety about expressing herself openly is at its height here, whatever her subject may be — whether it is anger, as it may well be, or ambition, as it could very well be, or sexuality, as it certainly might be, or some intertwined combination of the three. Here we see embodied both strong pressure to speak and an intense need to veil the subject. This expressive bind brings the poem to the brink of unintelligibility. As attested to by the conflicting conclusions of the many fine attempts to reconstruct it, the specific meaning of this poem is largely irrecoverable. My way of reading the poem, then, is not so much to try to understand what it "means," per se, but rather to attempt to determine the significance of its impediments to understanding.

My Life had stood — a Loaded Gun —
In Corners — till a Day
The Owner passed — identified —
And carried Me away —

And now We roam in Sovereign Woods —
And now We hunt the Doe —
And every time I speak for Him —
The Mountains straight reply —

Women's Studies, 1989
Vol. 16, pp. 117-120

And do I smile, such cordial light
Upon the Valley glow —
It is as a Vesuvian face
Had let its pleasure through —

And when at Night — Our good Day done —
I guard My Master's Head —
'Tis better than the Eider-Duck's
Deep Pillow — to have shared —

To foe of His — I'm deadly foe —
None stir the second time —
On whom I lay a Yellow Eye —
Or an emphatic Thumb —

Though I than He — may longer live
He longer must — than I —
For I have but the power to kill,
Without — the power to die —

(754)

The major problem here is not syntactical, but rather reflects disorder at the referential level. I refer to the omission of subject reference — that "omitted center" Jay Leyda finds so integral to the uniqueness of Dickinson's poetry. Here the vacuum at the center of the text is complete. Unlike other of Dickinson's elliptical poems, this seems impossible to reconstruct authoritatively. Even conjecture is problematic. A crucial feature of communication has been flouted; in her use of a powerful metaphor — the life that contains the explosive potential of a loaded gun — without the provision of markers to indicate its area of reference, Dickinson intrigues but does not enlighten the reader. She creates a radical disjuncture between text and meaning indicating that an experience of profound significance is being expressed, but refusing to name that experience.

Conjectures provided by Dickinson's commentators regarding the nature of this indicated experience are illuminating as we attempt to determine the significance of this poem. Sharon Cameron sees anger as its subject, "a fury grown larger than life ... [that] fantasizes its own immortality" (427). Adrienne Rich finds ambition central. She sees in the split between the active hunter and the passive gun an "ambivalence toward power which is extreme" (65). John Cody discusses a "fusion of sexuality and destructiveness" (402). Anger ... ambition ... sexuality ... This potent trio caused debilitating anxieties for the women writers of Dickinson's era, and "My Life had stood — a Loaded Gun" is rife with indications of all three — to the point where each of the above readers can develop his or her case convincingly and with authority. It is my proposal that the significance of this poem lies precisely here, in its embodiment of the expressive dilemma faced by any woman writer of Dickinson's time and place. The culture taught women that certain experiences were unnameable, specifically these three: the intensely personal and "selfish" desire for a sphere of achievement outside the circuit of domestic accomplishment; active, rather than passive sexual desire; and anger directed at personal rather than altruistic concerns. David Porter says that "the gun … is the emblem of her inordinate power of language" (215) and I think he is correct. This potent symbol — this gun-voice — embodies a superb ability and a pressing need to speak, filtered through a profound culturally conditioned anxiety about the acceptability of telling what she may well have considered deviant personal experience. For Dickinson, as for other women writers of her time, articulation of the self was a venture fraught with obscure dangers.

Although it is difficult to read this poem in a conventional way, one thing we can say for certain is that it is in some sense a poem about utterance, an expression of the explosive or incendiary potential of speech. We are given enough markers to indicate that: the gun that "speaks" as it fires, the mountains that echo that articulation, the "Vesuvian" or volcanic qualities we know from other poems are sometimes associated with speech. But how is it that this poem, with its lost field of reference, communicates? How does it speak to us? Because it certainly does speak to us. Important here are the tonal implications. The speaker's experience is one of dissociation. She is a speech object rather than a speech subject. Although she is the medium through which articulation occurs, she is not the instigator of the impulse to articulation. An extreme and compelling ambivalence characterizes the relationship between the passive "gun," the one who speaks, and the active owner, the one who initiates the speech. The gun/speaker is devoted, smiling with the "cordial light" of a massive pleasure. But that pleasure is "Vesuvian," in other words, volcanic and thus massively and horribly destructive. A fascinated yet horrific interplay is detailed. However, although both fascination and horror are indicated, neither predominates. The tension between them, the radical ambivalence, gives tonal articulation to a consciousness in conflict. And the concluding lines, without being specific, are imbued with a deep sense of tragic irony. To "have the power to kill / Without — the power to die," whatever it *means*, communicates to us more through tone than through statement or even through analogy. What an ironic fate: allowed power, but doomed to an unending eternity of destructiveness. Ambivalence and irony predominate over statement here. As in certain other women's writing of the era, they are extra-textual vehicles of expression that carry the communicative weight of this poem.

Is "My Life had stood — a Loaded Gun" a successful poem? Or is it a hyperbolic, convoluted, evasive failure? It all depends on how we read it. A good case for its success is going to depend heavily on awareness of the expressive impact of indirection of statement, in this case through tonal nuance, and I contend that Dickinson's resort to this mode of expression has much to do with the fact that she was writing as a woman in nineteenth-century America. Women's writing from that era is often faulted for being a failed literature. A knowledge of the anxiety-rife conditions under which women came to articulation, however, and of their need for indirection and selective expression, gives us both a new understanding of the debilitating omissions in the writing of most women, and a way of reading the best work of the era with increased skills of reconstruction. It also gives us new insight into how the characteristic indirection in the idiosyncratic poetry of America's greatest woman poet is related to her cultural milieu. She was indeed a loaded gun, and there were others, but with her "yellow eye" and her "emphatic thumb" she created a body of poetry singular not only in her time, but for all time "without the power to die."

Works Cited

Cameron, Sharon. "A Loaded Gun: Dickinson and and the Dialectic of Rage." *PMLA* 93 (1978): 423–37.

Cody, John. *After Great Pain: The Inner Life of Emily Dickinson.* Cambridge: Belknap P of Harvard U, 1971.

Dickinson, Emily. *The Poems of Emily Dickinson.* 3 vols. Ed. Thomas H. Johnson. Cambridge: Harvard UP, 1955.

Porter David T. *Dickinson: The Modern Idiom.* Cambridge: Harvard UP, 1981.

Rich, Adrienne. "Vesuvius at Home: The Power of Emily Dickinson." *Parnassus* 5.1 (1976): 49–74.

Poem 754 Ambivalent Heterosexuality in "My Life had stood — a Loaded Gun"

LILLIAN FADERMAN

California State University, Fresno

POEM 754, LIKE a number of other poems and letters by Emily Dickinson, is about her ambivalence toward heterosexuality, and particularly the role of a woman in a heterosexual relationship. Dickinson presents in this melodramatic poem three female victims: the hunted doe, the eider-duck (who makes her nest from the feathers that she plucks from her own breast), and, most *essentially*, the speaker herself. The females of the poem are victimized always in the service of the male: the doe is hunted at his behest, the eider-duck's feathers are a comfort only to him, and the Gun-wife speaker, who has virtually eradicated her life in order to execute her Master's wishes, is morally destroyed by her devotion to him. The major conceit of the poem, a Gun, which can do nothing unless activated by its owner, is a bold vehicle to suggest not only her passivity but also her perniciousness once she is placed in pernicious hands. She never resists the Master, who molds her as he wishes. One is tempted to read this complicity as being potentially autobiographical if one is familiar with the last Master letter. Apparently Dickinson, like the speaker in poem 754, could at some period in her life entertain the notion of abdicating all autonomy in the service of a "Master." Dickinson promises the recipient of that letter:

> I will never be noisy when you want to be still. I will be ... your best little girl — nobody else will see me but you — but that is enough — I shall not want any more. (II, 392)

Women's Studies, 1989
Vol. 16, pp. 121-125
Reprints available directly from the publisher

But such an obliteration of self in a heterosexual relationship was at other times in her life frightening. She suggests, for example, in an early letter to Sue Gilbert, who was a major love figure in Dickinson's life, that heterosexuality for women, though compelling, was paid for at too great a price:

> ... to the wife, Susie, sometimes the wife *forgotten*, our lives [as unmarried women] perhaps seem dearer than all others in the world; you have seen the flowers at morning, *satisfied* with the dew, and those same sweet flowers at noon with their heads bowed in anguish before the mighty sun; think you these thirsty blossoms will *now* need naught but — *dew*? No, they will cry for sunlight, and pine for the burning noon, tho' it scorches them, scathes them; they have got through with peace — they know that the man of noon is mightier than the morning and their life is henceforth to him. Oh, Susie, it is dangerous, and it is all too dear, these simple trusting spirits, and the spirits mightier, which we cannot resist. (I, 210).

Just as the wife's life is given up to the husband in this letter, so is the speaker's life given up to the Master in poem 754 — and in the context of the poem, too, "it is dangerous, and it is all too dear."

Dickinson maintained such ambivalence throughout her twenties and early thirties. A similar ambivalence is suggested in an 1860 poem (199), "I'm 'Wife' — I've finished that —." Although the speaker declares that being a wife is "safer" than "that other state," maidenhood, and she announces herself to be "Czar" through her wifehood, the second stanza of the poem makes clear that far from being a Czar, she is obliterated. The married state is described there as an "Eclipse." Just as in poem 754, the relationship with the master seems to give power, but it is a specious power, and, after all, it is all his.

The author's ambivalence is apparent from the first lines of 754, in which she has the Gun-wife speaker suggest that in her former single state she stood in corners, loaded with potential, though as yet undefined. "Corners," on first reading, would seem to imply that wherever the speaker was, she felt constricted, and yet we know that Dickinson herself chose to "constrict" much of her life to a single room in a single house, which undoubtedly permitted her to write more prolifically than she could have in most other situations. Apparent constriction takes on a different meaning when we remember the story Dickinson's niece Martha told of visiting Dickinson's room: Dickinson is said to have made as if to lock the door with an imaginary key, then to have turned to her niece and exclaimed, "Matty: here's freedom." Dickinson's room in her family home was, in fact, a corner room, which Adrienne Rich described in "Vesuvius at Home" as being "the best bedroom in the house ..., sunny, overlooking the main street of Amherst ..., white curtained, high ceilinged." And in Dickinson's poetry too "corners" seem to represent peace, comfort, freedom. Poem 1185, for example, describes "The Cat that in the Corner dwells/ Her martial Day forgot." Corners are thus far from constricting in Dickinson's language.

The Master, or the Owner as he is called in the first stanza of 754, appears in the speaker's life by chance — he *passes*, and in passing identifies her, who had before been undefined, as his, and carries her off. Henceforth, as a traditional Victorian wife, she gives up her will and does his bidding, whether for good or bad — and as the matter turns out, it is largely bad. She now belongs to a sinister gentleman who defines her. The tasks he puts her to are malevolent, but as the female member of the union her role is not to question but to please by obedience. She is amoral toward all else since "her life is henceforth to him" as Dickinson says in the "man of noon" letter, and she has allowed herself to have no existence apart from him, as Dickinson once wrote the Master: "Nobody else will see me, but you — but that is enough — I shall not want anymore."

The first specified service to her Master is hunting the doe, an image which stands for any despicable act. The pitying terms in which Dickinson describes the "consummate terror" of the hunted doe in poem 565 help to corroborate the notion of the author's separate consciousness which peers out from behind the poker-faced Gun-wife speaker of poem 754 and gives the poem its tenor of ambivalence. The doe, a most gentle and timorous creature, is destroyed, and while the speaker is too involved with the Master to see anything wrong in the deed, the reader is surely meant to understand that the speaker has now been corrupted by the union: in Tennyson's Victorian terms, "As the husband is, the wife is."

Dickinson emphasizes the misguided Gun-wife's loss of a moral sense in placing the Master so far above all else: The speaker proudly declares in the fifth stanza that none dare harm him a second time because of her deadly vengeance. Dickinson's repulsion towards those who feel justified in avenging themselves through verbal or physical violence is suggested in the wry satire of poem 118: "How martial is this place!/ Had I a mighty gun/ I think I'd shoot the human race/ And then to glory run!" The Gun-wife's chilling corruption is also emphasized by the ironic language in which she describes her foul deeds in his service. In terms of the conceit of the poem, the firing of the gun which kills is described as smiling, its flash is a "cordial light," its explosive power is "pleasure." And finally, a day devoted to destruction is described as "Our good day."

Of course, although her sinister spouse has made the speaker sinister, the marriage serves her well in terms of social standing. When she acts in his name ("And every time I speak for Him"), she is treated with respect, receiving immediate response from high and low (Mountains and Valley), as a young nineteenth-century single woman seldom would. However, while in stanza two she implies that she feels a sovereignty through their union (she projects that sovereignty on to the woods), it soon becomes clear that "sovereign" in this poem is as specious as "Czar" in poem 119. Although the speaker believes herself throughout much of 754 to have power (and may be treated by others as though she has power), she is in fact "eclipsed" since the power is all his. She is the *femme couvert* of nineteenth century marriage, in which husband and wife are one — and he is the one. Her real status in the relationship is dramatized in stanza four. There she devotes herself to his peaceful repose, but is apparently allowed no comfort herself, not even that of sharing his deep pillow (made of the feathers of another sacrificing female, the eider-duck).

The last, crucial stanza of the poem is a pathetic confession of her dependence and insignificance. Dickinson had ample opportunities to observe the economic and social difficulties of the nineteenth-century widow. The speaker fears to outlive her spouse. Although she knows it is possible that she will, she hopes that she won't: "Though I than He — may longer live/ he longer must — than I —." She realizes here that the only power she has is through him, as his servant and representative; but without him she is a non-entity. She cannot die herself, because she has not lived herself.

Finally, poem 754 is best understood in the light of a poem written two years earlier, 273. That poem too is about a wife who is taken over by her husband: "He put the Belt around my life —/ I heard the Buckle snap." Her "lifetime" is "fold[ed] up." Although she describes herself now as "imperial" that term is as specious as 'Czar" and "sovereign" in the other two marriage poems, and it is almost immediately contradicted. Henceforth she becomes only a "Dedicated sort." Her duty is "to come at call —/ And do the little Toils." She refers to "lives that stoop to notice mine," as illustrating her own insignificance. Like poem 754, "He put the Belt around my life" is about Dickinson's ambivalence toward heterosexual relationships. As so many of the poems and letters indicate, while Dickinson felt some attraction to such relationships, she feared to be taken over by a force that would define her instead of permitting her to define herself, eclipse her, overwhelm her. "My Life had stood — a Loaded Gun" is, above all, a cautionary tale.

Poem 754

ELLIN RINGLER-HENDERSON

Pitzer College

That "My Life had stood — a loaded Gun" is a highly significant poem in the Dickinson canon is attested to by the fact that nearly every serious critic of the poet feels obliged to have a go at this piece. Indeed, Adrienne Rich calls #754 "the central poem in understanding Dickinson;" in which case, the fact that most of the critics (including Rich) have *trouble* understanding "My Life" seems to augur ill for our comprehension of the poet herself.

Many of the more recent commentaries explore Emily Dickinson's ecstatic assumption of phallic power in the poem and connect this to her awareness of the dangers inherent in creativity, her gun's explosive potential. That Dickinson stood in awe of the power of the word is, indeed, indisputable. Such works as #1409, for example:

Could mortal lip divine
The undeveloped Freight
Of a delivered syllable
'Twould crumble with the weight.

demonstrate her strong sense of the risks inherent in "delivering syll-ables." Employing language which seems directly relevant to "My Life had stood," Dickinson echoes this idea in a letter to Louise Norcross in September, 1880.

What is it that instructs a hand lightly created, to impel shapes to eyes at a distance, which for them have the whole area of life or of death? Yet not a pencil in the street but has this awful power, though

Women's Studies, 1989
Vol. 16, pp. 127-131
Reprints available directly from the publisher
Photocopying permitted by license only

nobody arrests it. An earnest letter is or should be life-warrant or death-warrant, for what is each instant but a gun, harmless because 'unloaded,' but that touched 'goes off'? (L656)

The poet seems to imply here that each instant of our lives remains "harmless" so long as it is unexpressed, "unloaded"; the "loaded" instant — one infers — is that experience which has been recorded or written about, transformed into an "earnest letter," in which case it can become a life- or death-warrant. Still, the word will not actually "go off" — realize its potential explosiveness — until it has been "touched,' that is, received, "identified," "carried away." If one accepts this interpretation of Dickinson's passage, a possible approach to poem 754 is to view the speaker as, in fact, the potentially powerful written word and "He" as the receiver of the word, the "eyes at a distance" which read (identify) the letter and, in doing so, complete its meaning. Then "My Life had stood —" becomes a spelling-out of the dangerous, even lethal, consequences of the delivered letter, the power possible in language which has found its audience.

One of the more intriguing aspects of poem 754 is the kind of relationship Dickinson pictures here between the Owner and the word. It bears all the marks of the distinctly masculine, often aggressive, partnerships we have come to recognize as standard fare in much 19th and 20th century American literature, (from that between Ishmael and Queequeg through Huck and Jim, to Batman and Robin, Starsky and Hutch, *et al.*) Indeed, it is no surprise that "My Life" has been called "the most American poem Dickinson ever wrote" (Pollak, p. 154). With imaginative insight the poet characterizes different facets of male companionship: its hierarchical dimensions, as well as its shifts of power and the way in which speaker and Master become hunting partners, bed-fellows, guard and guarded, protector and defended.

The comradely team roams the "sovereign" woods, as we might imagine Robin Hood and Little John to have done, or, even more aptly, Natty Bumppo and Chingachook. Here a tone of jaunty cockiness is achieved in the repetitions of

And now we roam . . .
And now we hunt . . .
And every time . . .

Happy hunters together, Dickinson's pair chase the Doe, both as sexual quarry and as a source of food, one infers. In fact, one of the pleasures of this male friendship is its expression in a dominance over the natural world: the woods are freely "roamed;" the Doe is hunted; the mountains passively echo the gun's report; the Valley reflects its light.

Verses 2 and 3 describe, then, the "good day" enjoyed by these chums in terms suggestive of those boys' adventure stories which form a significant category of American literature. The irony in the phrase "our good day done," with its references to violent acts of hunting and shooting in the language of an evening prayer, is hard to miss. In verse 4 the "good day" has ended, but not the fraternity; for, with nightfall, speaker and Master form a firm community of guard and guarded, a bond deemed superior to the domesticated "pillow" (bosom) of the Eider-Duck. The contrast between the verbs "guard" and "shared" here, suggests all the difference between the fierce masculine tie and the softer, perhaps even debilitating, link with the female. The speaker's assumption of the protective role of watchguard over the Master's sleeping head leads logically to the vaunt about the ability to defend the Owner against any enemy. The militant and savage loyalty of the traditional male relationship is asserted directly with "To foe of His — I'm deadly foe —;" and all the violence and destructiveness underlying this fraternity come to a climax in the speaker's boast that

None stir a second time —
On whom I lay a Yellow Eye —
Or an emphatic Thumb —

The irony of the gun's "pleasurable glow" upon the valley in stanza 3 is deepened, as that "cordial" (or invigorating) "light" shifts here to the evil "Yellow Eye"; and all the earlier veiled politeness of the Vesuvian face is violently laid bare. The adjective "emphatic," suggestive of verbal intensity or stress, underscores the analogy between the gun and the word; and, with the lethal implications of lines 17-20, we are brought finally to a consideration of the life and death of the speaker and Owner themselves.

In fact, having begun with the line "My Life had stood —" expressed in the past perfect tense, poem 754 progresses from the "day," in the more recent past, of the speaker's identification — real beginnings — through a morning, noon and "Night" in the continuous present of roaming, glowing, guarding, and finally to the paradox of the "loaded gun's" ultimate future: its "power to kill" but not "to die." With a startling metaphorical leap, Dickinson has expressed her sense of the explosive potential of language through an adventure tale suggestive of the rough and ready male comradeship — a man's best friend is his gun — of the American frontier.

Stanza 6 of "My Life had stood" seems to have stretched the interpretive powers of Emily Dickinson's critics to their limit; and, given the general bewilderment, I feel quite tentative about offering any explanation of the riddle. Nevertheless, perhaps we might return to the idea of the speaker as the word and look to some other Dickinson poems for help. Number 1651, for example, seems to echo the final lines of 754:

A Word that breathes distinctly
Has not the power to die

Again, in poem 1212, she tells us:

A word is dead
When it is said,
Some say.

I say it just
Begins to live
That day.

Finally, the lethal and timeless potency of language has never been better expressed than in poem 1261:

A Word dropped careless on a Page
May stimulate an eye
When folded in perpetual seam
The Wrinkled Maker lie

Infection in the sentence breeds
We may inhale Despair
At distances of Centuries
From the Malaria —

These poems and Dickinson's letter to Louise Norcross offer a set of terms which should help to gloss the riddle of 754's final stanza. Both the word's power to "go off", to "stimulate an eye" at "distances of Centuries," and the fact that, once expressed, "breathed distinctly," it cannot die, are suggested in all of these pieces.

In one obvious sense, of course, the word "breathed distinctly" *is* immortal and may outlive any particular audience, as it does its "Wrinkled Maker." However, so long as it is left "careless on the Page," "standing in corners," the word's life remains incomplete; it has not yet been "inhaled," "touched," "carried away." The unapprehended word is mere unfinished action, a "loaded gun" which has not found its mark. To achieve meaning, then, the "impelled shapes" need to be "identified," to stimulate an eye," in other words, to be received and understood by a living consciousness. Another way of putting this is that the word is only instrumental, like the gun. It can transport meaning, have an impact, kill; but it cannot understand the *consequences* of its power: what it is to die. The "Owner" — "He" — (i.e. the identifier, the receiver of the letter) "must" live longer than the word so that there will be an audience: someone to transform (by understanding its full implications) the mere blind power of killing into what it *really* means: the power of death.

Knowing her own strength, Emily Dickinson might have gauged the distance that her poetry could travel; but, far less certain of her audience, she could hardly have imagined the numbers of eyes it would reach in a century.

Poem 754
Workshop Discussion

Speakers: JOANNE DOBSON, LILLIAN FADERMAN, ELLIN RINGLER-HENDERSON

YOU'VE BEEN TALKING about this poem defying interpretation, and I wonder if what it doesn't do is ask us to rethink what we mean by interpretation, because there is certainly a literary critical tradition of interpretation being coherent: you find an answer, it has a beginning, middle, and end . . .

Being right, exactly, and being righter than anybody else is — so that out of the three of you one was right.

To me it seemed like you gave interpretations. I find what's so exciting about Dickinson as well as — I work on Sylvia Plath — is that interpretation in a traditional sense becomes blurred. She's asking us to change our critical language and our critical categories.

Do you see that as something conscious?

I don't think that she is asking it. I don't know how quite to put it except that what you were saying made me realize that I felt tremendous relief that you weren't going to tell us what the poem was about. And then we would all argue with you about our interpretations.

I think what you mean when you say she's asking us to do this, is that she has provided for us a body of language that allows us to do nothing but play with it and give it interpretation. I was thinking this

Women's Studies, 1989
Vol. 16, pp. 133-148
Reprints available directly from the publisher
Photocopying permitted by license only

Printed in Great Britain

morning about what we're doing here as being something in the nature of a basball game. There are rules, there's a ball, there's this bat, and uniforms, and we all do it very skillfully with what we have. Perhaps that sounds anarchistic.

When you say baseball, are you saying that ironically — you really wish it weren't a baseball game that we're playing?

That image is trivializing and I don't mean it to be trivial. It is something in the nature of a very serious game that we're doing here: there are rules and we have a body of material to work on. And we do it one way one time and another way another time. But, of course, we have to take account of what's there. So I think there's coherence in what we've all said; we've all talked about ambivalence, we've all talked about pain and the polarization in the poem, but have come up with different answers.

I have a question, Ellin, about your reading, which I found very interesting. I liked very much your interpretation of the life as the text and the owner as the reader, but then your interpretation of the middle stanzas seemed more like Lillian's reading of the poem. The relationship between the owner and the gun seemed much less positive when you were interpreting the middle stanzas.

Yes, I had two ideas and I wanted to get them both in. Maybe what I ought to have done was to go back and work on each of those stanzas in terms of what in fact it does seem to say, that the owner, having interpreted the word or having received the word, roams freely in the woods and so on — except also to talk about the way in which the receiving of the word invigorates.

When you started out, I thought the point was going to be the female power that she confers on the reader who understands her, but then when you started interpreting the middle stanzas I began to think that maybe this was a male text for a male reader and it was about the relationship between those two.

I did see the "He" as male; I saw both the "He" and the word in male terms. When I was listening to Lilian — there is something about the loaded gun being a female that bothers me, I guess because it's such a phallic image that it was hard for me to see it as a female. So I read the relationship as pal-sy, with a certain tongue-in-cheek picture of that typical American Natty Bumpo-Chingachook kind of thing that seems to be pictured there. I don't see this as a positive relationship.

I would love to hear you or anyone talk about this whole issue of the loaded gun being phallic, because I find that certain images are assigned as phallic and everyone assumes they are; and I'm always very confused as to why they are. I would like to hear why you think that the loaded gun is phallic, or why you think that it isn't.

I think a post-Freudian necessarily makes that connection, but Dickinson was a pre-Freudian and she didn't have to. To me, it's not a phallic poem.

Not to me either. Do you think it's only because we have a Freudian language and therefore . . .?

Yes, I think it is. I think we're influenced by the popularization of Freud. We tend to interpret phallic symbols as the kinds of things that he described as phallic symbols. But it never occurred to me, until I read some critics, that a loaded gun necessarily had to be a phallic symbol.

I guess my sense of it is certainly associated with the male, the hunter — that's it, more than the phallic quality. In the letter that I quote, it's very clear that Dickinson wanted to use the shooting of the gun as a metaphor for writing her letters and for giving poems shapes, as she put it.

She's got so many images of explosion in her poems, like the bomb in the breast, the volcano. I'm fascinated by the contradiction. She's got all these images of fullness, something in her about to go off and, on the other hand, she has all these images of anorexia, where there's nothing inside her or she's going to make sure that things shrink to such an extent that there's nothing inside her. So, much more than phallic, I see the poem as this talk she's having with herself about fullness and emptiness.

In nineteenth-century American women's literature, there is a tradition of starvation, of images of starvation. I think perhaps the one that might be most familiar to people here is Rebecca Harding Davis's *Life in the Iron Mills*. Has anyone read that? [Remember] the statue that Hugh Wolf has made of korl, which is the refuse of the mine; it's a strong working class type woman lying on the ground with strong muscles. Somebody asks him what did he intend by it? "What is it that she wants?" And he says "She be hungry." "She's not hungry, man, look at those muscles." And he says, "No, no, she's hungry for something to make her live." I think Dickinson's picking up on that tradition of desiring something to make her live. She's got all those poems about hungering and starvation.

She and Davis treat images of starvation very much in the same way, but most of the other women writers are dealing with literal starvation; they're writing not about themselves but about other people, those masses out there for whom they feel responsible and who are literally starving. That was in the air. A woman's rhetoric of hunger — but always altruistic. She took it and made it personal. She tended to do that.

Did anyone else try that riddle — the last four lines to this? They had me up at four o'clock in the morning when I was trying to work it out.

She has the power to sleep.

I had a little extra passage which I left out. Reading a number of critics on the issue and discovering how many wonderful euphemisms there are for "this verse doesn't fit." You know, there was "outside the metaphorical context of the poem," etc. There were four or five wonderful phrases for "I don't know what the hell this means."

In other words, this poem is not a well-wrought poem.

Right, exactly. I don't know what to make of that final stanza. I found myself, as one would, I suppose, trying to complete a crossword puzzle or a jigsaw puzzle. Trying to make the thing fit.

My response to that goes along with the sense I have that a great deal of what was happening in her poetry was, for want of another term, extra-textual-things she wanted to say but embodied in another shape, in the implications of her language, in the ways that other women did. What some women did, and hid very well, was to disrupt sequences of their narratives. I'm talking particularly of women novelists now. The conventional novel was expected to have a certain beginning, middle and end. At that time, the novel began with a little girl who was in some sort of trouble and left alone and had to struggle on her own, and in the end was rewarded by an opportunity to renounce her success and get married. This was its expected shape. But some women, I'm thinking of two in particular, disrupted rather violently the sequence of that narrative structure to interject a space in which the woman could have her own story.

One novel by Mary Jane Holmes called *Marian Grey* begins with marriage. And you say, "OK, what could happen now?" because what happens after a woman gets married? But this woman is fifteen years old, she's undeveloped (it is made very clear that she has the body of a child), she's red-headed, she's freckled, she's ignorant, she's been living in the mountains, and what she doesn't know is that she's an heiress. So she gets married and between her marriage and her wedding night she overhears her husband say, or she reads a letter or something, in which he says that he is only marrying her for her fortune. She's a bride but she's not a wife yet — so she runs away and she goes to New York, and for five or six years she lives with a family in New York. She goes to an elite school, gets a fever and her red hair falls out, and she comes back with ravishing auburn hair and becomes beautiful. And during this whole period of time, he is looking for her, obsessively. She knows that and she has been monitoring him from afar. Finally one day he sits next to her on an omnibus and doesn't recognize her. So she realizes that she can go back home as governness to his — there's a point to all this, folks — his ward. He falls in love with her again as a woman — so he's in love with her doubly, as his lost young bride and as this ravishing woman. And finally at the end, after she's got it all her way, she reveals her identity, forces him to marry her again on her own terms and in her own home. She has had all this wonderful story, but it comes in that minute space between the wedding and the consummation of the marriage. This is disruption of sequence. And it seems to me that Dickinson is doing something like that in this last verse here, because it really is a disruption of sequence to say, "He — may longer live / He longer must — than I."

What you reminded me of was the "power to die." She died as the young bride. She went away and she died in that form, and she came back in another form. I've been free associating with that phrase, "the power to die." Thinking of it in Christian terms, there's a transformational power possible if you can die completely. We all understand what the power to kill is, but the power to die is something that's a little harder to think about.

My argument is that in fact we don't really understand what killing means unless we understand what the power to die is, what dying is. If we all understood what dying meant, then maybe we wouldn't kill. In other words, that thing which kills doesn't understand what it means to die.

But I go back to the transformation. When you dream about dying, it often has an association with new birth: death and birth, dying as one thing and being born as another.

That's of course the religious way, too; the notion of dying is to be translated into heaven.

I have a sense in this verse that the life sequence here, unlike the life sequence in those disrupted narratives, is not something positive. It seems to me to imply a life gone partly awry in some sense.

If she could die to it, maybe she could be reborn and transformed. But she can't. She has to be there forever not able to die, watching and being trapped by it.

I absolutely can't connect this feeling about the words to the rest of the poem. The word certainly has the power to kill and the word doesn't have the power to die, does it? Once the word's written it's out of your power and it is immortal.

When you're talking about living and dying, the "I" is "My life"; she doesn't say "I stood a loaded gun." Her life belongs entirely to someone else. She speaks for him, she smiles — but she smiles in a dangerous way. I suppose it's like if you shot a gun in the dark and would see a red glow, like a gun. She is a dangerous thing because she's full of power to kill, but she has no power of her own. The gun of itself can't walk anywhere or kill anybody. To do anything it has to be touched in some way. It can't go off unless you throw it or pull the trigger.

Another thing that's ambiguous to me is — several things! She sounds like his trusty squire or the dog or the Indian guide who will never leave his side, who will run along into battle with him holding the horse's bridle. Then she says she's a deadly foe, "none stirs" because she kills; and then she says "On whom I lay a Yellow Eye — Or an emphatic Thumb." The thumb is what pulls the trigger, right?

No, the thumb cocks the top of the gun, doesn't it . . .

Well then, what is the emphatic thumb?

It's a matter of language. You could not get "emphatic forefinger" in there with any sense, right? It's the word "thumb."

It has to do with the gun image still. Somebody else has to do it. In the entire poem, all this power belongs to somebody else that she is.

In those lines, though, it's "*I* lay a Yellow Eye — Or an emphatic Thumb."

Well, she could lay a yellow eye if once she'd shot it, a spurt of flame comes out.

It's not the eye that sights down the barrel?

This is interesting because I read the "yellow eye" as a kind of development of the irony in the third stanza, the glow that comes from the gun. But all of the cordiality of the third stanza has really been transformed by that evil "yellow eye." It is an interesting shift if you look at the yellow eye as being the eye that sights and remember that thumb becomes the thumb that cocks the top of the gun; you have shifted your image.

Have you shifted or are you conflating the two images? Perhaps the eye is the gun, the flash that comes from the barrel of the gun, and it's also the eye that sights down the gun.

It's a perfect identification, to use a word that she's used herself, a fusion of the gun and the "He." The gun and the master have been fused, "identified."

Could we go back to "Tis better than the Eider-Duck's Deep Pillow — to have shared," because those lines have been haunting me all day. It sounds as though the kind of relationship the gun has with the owner is not a sexual one but something that's preferable to a sexual one, either ironically or truly.

I see it as implying a certain kind of male homosexual relationship which is better than the debilitating relationship that one might have with a female.

There's a certain seductiveness about the eider duck . . .

I found Lillian's reading very good. I found both of your readings very good — almost as if anything that might have been feminine about her is now taken up and become masculine. The absences in Dickinson's poetry speak very loudly, and the absence of feminine images here, except ones that were destroyed, is compelling.

But if this were a heterosexual relationship wouldn't she have shared the eider duck's deep pillow?

I think it's interesting that it's not absolutely clear what the subject of "share" is. Whether it's that the master and she or it or the gun share the pillow, or the master shares the eider duck's pillow but the gun doesn't, or neither of them share the pillow because they're out there in the rough woods and neither of them is in bed. And that of course is rather fun.

Of course, in that the "power to die" can also be a Renaissance sexual "power to die," which could be female sexuality that she doesn't see herself as having. The power to kill, to be a loaded gun, is different, a much more dangerous power — but with something missing that would make it impossible for her to share the eider duck's deep pillow.

The power to kill without the power to love.

Right. Or to lose oneself in another. Or lose one's identity. He's sleeping and she's gone.

Isn't it also, too, that the feminine is always acted upon. She has no control without his control. She can't explode without his pulling the trigger. And finally she wants to get out from under that control.

Except that she acts against. She is acted upon but then she acts against in response to that. She shoots.

She hunts the doe.

He fires the gun. Guns are not dangerous to any deer if you leave them lying on the forest floor. Somebody carrying it and shooting it is what's dangerous. But the danger is inside of Emily Dickinson in the sense that we were talking about in the other group this morning: her demonstrations in her letters to men show great deference and were always talking about herself as if she were a tiny mouse or a daisy — images of tininess, frailty, apologizing for being alive; but she didn't write that way to women. She feels about herself that she's dangerous in some way to the opposite sex. I would guess, to be a post-Freudian, that her anger is what's dangerous. "A loaded gun," besides being a phallic symbol, is an expression: "Well, we wouldn't touch that, it's a loaded gun."

But I also think that there's a real assertion of the strength of the word. The power here is positive, as well. The danger's there, I think you're right, but there's also something very positive in a creative talent that says "I impel shapes at a [very far] distance." You may "inhale Despair . . . at distances of Centuries."

It shows a knowledge of power, but somehow I connect that knowledge of power with all this, to us. Somehow we're all stuck on this last stanza — why? Why does it seem if not ambivalent, confusing and mysterious. Somehow I connect that with her own feeling about her power and the danger. Whatever that power meant to her, clearly it must have meant writing. But a lot goes into whatever creative act you involve yourself in; there are other things leading into it, streaming into it, and those things make you feel afraid.

Mary Kelley has written a lovely history of nineteenth-century American women writers called *Private Woman, Public Stage*, and in it she talks about the tremendous, debilitating anxiety that women writers felt about putting themselves on a page and then being seen in public. She begins by talking about a writer named Caroline Gilman whose first published work was published without her knowledge, and Caroline Gilman said "I felt as if I'd been detected in a man's clothing." It's very much like what's happening in this poem. She was somehow becoming fused with the masculine by speaking.

I wanted to ask more about that, too. If you could refresh my memory — I know she had very few poems published and they found them all in a trunk — but who was her audience?

She was interested for a while in publication and had written to a contributor to the *Atlantic Monthly*, Thomas Higginson, apparently asking for his criticism, also very much wanting to interest him in her work. He was happy to offer criticism, particularly happy to tell her that the poems needed to be more orthodox in their style. Only seven of her poems were published during her lifetime. I think she had a secret wish, in fact she said to her sister-in-law and brother, that if she could make them proud someday with the publication of her poetry, it would give her "taller feet." She certainly had ambitions for a while, but I think she was sufficiently discouraged so that perhaps she wrote for posterity rather than for an immediate audience. Many of her poems were included in letters to friends, particularly to Sue. She sent a number of poems to Sue. But she also wrote variations of many of these poems to other friends.

I don't think Dickinson did want to be published. I think she had internalized the cultural standards of femininity to the point where to see herself in public would have been extremely problematic for her.

Why do you think she wrote to Higginson?

I think she "experienced admiration" for him, as she said when she wrote to him, and that she wanted to share her poems with him in a very innocent, uncalculating sort of way — that to our twentieth-century eyes seems impossible. I really do have the sense that she wanted to make a friend of him and this was her way of enticing his friendship, which she certainly did . . .

And her note to Sue and Austin about making them proud of her?

I have a kind of mixed theory about it. I think she began by wanting to publish but that when she saw the reaction — that the choice was either to publish and have her poetry edited, "straightened out," or to continue to write the way she wanted to — well, she obviously chose to write what she had to write the way she had to write it.

Karen Danderand discovered four or five more Dickinson publications that no one knew about — three of them published in 1864, I believe, in a Brooklyn newspaper that was put out by the United States Sanitary Commission, which was the agency that was running the hospitals for the soldiers in the Civil War. Evidently, she either had given the three poems to the editor or they had been communicated to him surreptitiously. And another one was published a couple of weeks later in another Brooklyn newspaper. They were then clipped by other newspapers, including the *Springfield Republican.* In 1864 there were ten Dickinson publications, four original and then several reprints — which indicates that her poetry was attractive to people at that time. And none of them were particularly mutilated by editing. Karen Danderand suggests that she might well have submitted those three poems to that charity magazine because it was for the purpose of doing good, and that that was an acceptable motivation to intrude yourself into the public sphere. She wrote to Higginson asking about publishing a poem, and said somebody had asked her for it to help homeless children or something — and she said "the name of child was a snare to me." In other words, she would have done it to help someone else, and it seems that she probably did submit these three poems to help soldiers. I really do think it was by her own choice that she didn't publish.

Do you think, then, that she didn't publish but that she was hoping someday to be published? She sewed all those packets up.

I thought that the most problematic thing that Dickinson did is leave that huge body of poetry in a dresser drawer with no instructions. And she told her sister to burn her correspondence. Her sister could very well have interpreted that to mean burn all her papers. And she didn't do it. But it seems that she could easily have done that, we could easily have lost this.

Were some of the poems destroyed, though, by the family?

Well, some of the letters were mutilated.

Wasn't there a huge amount of correspondence from Sue Gilbert to Dickinson . . .

Austin wanted Gilbert's letters destroyed.

By that time, of course, Austin had been involved with Mabel. From what I understand there was a real hate relationship caused by [that] with Sue.

Were those letters destroyed?

Yes. We don't have any idea of what Sue was saying.

That's like Sylvia Plath's journals . . .

Austin was a nineteenth-century Ted Hughes.

But Austin didn't burn Emily's letters. He censored them somewhat.

I'm still wondering about the lady-like gesture of having your verses published for charity. You said they weren't "particularly" edited. I had the feeling that Emily Dickinson was passionately attached to her dashes and capital letters and spellings and her lack of titles. Maybe she would suffer a little bit of pulling around in the interests of charity, but if she was going to publish it was going to be her way. I felt that had something to do with the fact that she didn't take Higginson's advice.

Isn't it true also that the few poems that were published were relatively conventional and accessible, such as the "little Tippler" and stuff?

Yes, but now I'm trying to remember ... I'm sorry, I don't have the list here and I can't remember precisely. But there were a couple of major poems that were published in Brooklyn. I think "Further in Summer than the Birds" was one of them.

Of course, in order to go along with my theory one has to think of Dickinson in some ways as being conventional, and I think in some ways she was, although she was clearly transcendent in many ways — but in conventional ideology of feminity there were two reasons to publish. One was to do good — Harriet Beecher Stowe spoke like "a Loaded Gun" in *Uncle Tom's Cabin*, in order to help the slaves. The other reason was because she needed the money. Many women writers were freed to have very exciting and stimulating careers by the fact that their husbands had the grace to die when they had three small children, or to desert them or something.

She doesn't have the power to die.

Dickinson was not in either of those camps. She did not have the desire to do good in the conventional way. I'm not saying her poetry is immoral or amoral, it certainly was moral, but she didn't want to go out there and change the society and address particular cultural issues. And she certainly didn't need the money. So she would not have had for herself any conventional reason to publish.

But one of her great heroines was Elizabeth Barrett.

She was certainly a model.

Did Barrett Browning need the money? Robert was earning a reasonably good income.

But the situation in Britain was very different from what it was in this country; the ideology of femininity had an iron grip in this country.

Todd published quite a bit, didn't she? And yet she, for all her carryings on, was still considered a lady, was she not?

Oh yes, but this was also later in the century. And yet, there were exceptions — Helen Hunt Jackson, who was born in Amherst two months before Emily Dickinson and went to school with her. But her husband died; she did not begin publishing until her husband died, and she published poems of grief. Then she became galvanized to do her most ambitious work once she took up the cause of the American Indian, and realized how they were being abused by the government. So she fits into the categories. It always astonished me that those two women were born in Amherst at the same time, and one of them went on to be called by Emerson the best woman poet of her time, and it wasn't Emily Dickinson.

I had a question for Lilian. The way you read this poem it was very much Dickinson's criticism of heterosexual marriage. What poems do you think she wrote to Sue Gilbert? Do you feel that there are any celebrations of homosexual love in them?

No, I don't think there are celebrations. They're often poems of complaint, like "Ourselves were wed one summer — dear —" in which Sue obviously deserts her for an easier, happier life. She often used bird imagery in those poems that she wrote to Sue, and frequently the bird that she cherishes flies away from her. Many of them are poems of desertion. I don't think she found that an ideal relationship either.

What about "Wild Nights"? Is that one she sent to Sue Gilbert?

I think she did, and certainly I think the imagery there is very female. It's soft and ...

— not phallic ...

No, but she says in that poem "Might I but moor — Tonight — / In Thee!" and I talk in an article that I did in a *Massachusetts Review* essay about the letters, about how that imagery is similar to the imagery in a letter she sends Sue, in which she talks about wild nights and a storm that they experienced together. So I think that poem was written for Sue. But I'm not suggesting at all that she saw the relationship with Sue as being easy. Although many of the letters are certainly impassioned, I don't think the relationship was a contented one.

Didn't someone suggest that the "Owner" was her muse or a poetic spirit that took possession of her life?

Adrienne Rich — to a certain extent . . .

What do you think of that theory?

I like it! I go along with that to a very great extent.

What does she make of the end?

I didn't think she said . . .

Here we go again, trying to explain the riddle. What [Rich] ends with in her discussion is something like "I do not pretend to have explained this poem, nor do I wish to." She ducks the ending, which is probably the smart thing to do, because if you don't you spend nights wondering . . .

"Wild Nights" . . .

I suppose, to get back to what Cheryl was saying this morning, it is terribly tempting — whether it's because our brain is fashioned that way or whether you do want to make some sort of logic of this — to try to make it work. I think probably it's a good caution to sort of "let it be."

Or perhaps experience it, experience the contradiction. Give the little shudder . . .

Instead of treating it like a question that better yield up the answer — one answer.

You have a similar problem in Shakespeare; I think the ending of the sonnets doesn't reveal how good the rest is. It seems a little pat, as if he's sort of teasing us and saying "ha, ha, perhaps you got that." And I think she feels a sensitivity at the end here that frustrates our desire for closure. The last two lines unravel it.

When she says "This World is not Conclusion," it should be something we listen to when we read her poems.

It seems to me that the last two lines are the meat of the whole poem; you were saying in your paper that the poem is about having something to say but having to veil it. The last two lines are a tremendous relief to me, because they're pure expression of that pain, of that inability to die. [She has] the mechanical ability to kill and to go on with life but without the spiritual ability to die and be reborn or ... to get rid of the pain.

One of the problems with "letting it be" comes in the way in which it is expressed. It does invite us to understand what the hell's going on; it's not like the kind of flowing thing in Whitman, where sometimes you're so completely overridden by Whitman's lines that you aren't forced into the intellectual game playing that it seems to me Emily Dickinson demands of you. This is aphorism. There is a sense that intellect is beautiful, [but it's] constantly teased. So that while I think you're right, that we ought not to try to keep concluding, there are ways in which Dickinson is frustrating because she invites you to come up with a conclusion: "For I have but the power to kill,/Without — the power to die." That's got to mean something!

Poem 1581

The farthest Thunder that I heard
Was nearer than the Sky
And rumbles still though torrid Noons
Have lain their missiles by —
The Lightning that preceded it
Struck no one but myself —
But I would not exchange the Bolt
For all the rest of Life —

Indebtedness to Oxygen
The Happy may repay,
But not the obligation
To Electricity —
It founds the Homes and decks the Days
And every clamor bright
Is but the gleam concomitant
Of that waylaying Light —
The Thought is quiet as a Flake —
A Crash without a Sound,
How Life's reverberation
Its Explanation found —

c. 1883 *1932*

Women's Studies, 1989
Vol. 16, p. 149
Reprints available directly from the publisher

Poem 1581
Kinds of Difficulty in "The farthest Thunder that I heard"

MARCIA FALK

Stanford University

THE FIRST THING I note as I read Emily Dickinson's poem 1581 is that it is difficult; and, perhaps because I have been asked to comment on this poem (rather than having chosen it myself because it was a favorite), I find myself focusing on its difficulty. After several readings, I discern that, indeed, this poem is difficult in at least three different ways, none of which will seem rare to the avid reader of Dickinson's lyrics. Perhaps it will not be useless, then, if I make the subject of my remarks the *kinds* of difficulty I encounter in this poem, even if I do not resolve the particular difficulties themselves.

A larger question that might flow from this subject would be: *Why* does Dickinson present her reader with so much difficulty, so much to be construed and figured before the poem can be understood? That the poem can be embraced without being thoroughly understood I take to be a given. But the poet, I believe, *invites* us to understand her, here as in other poems, luring us into her charged and compressed lyric world — and then, after gaining our attention, she thwarts our attempts to penetrate her with our intellect. Is she, perhaps, after another kind of appreciation, one that washes ashore only after the waves of the intellect retreat, having fully spent their energies? Does the poet sometimes seek a different kind of union with us, one that emerges out of our surrender rather than our conquest? These are the extra-textual questions that hover in the background as I notice with

Women's Studies, 1989
Vol. 16, pp. 151-154

what effort I try, as a first step toward interpretation, to translate this poem into a coherent paraphrase. And these are the questions that I will try ultimately to address in this brief discussion, even if I do not answer all the questions of meaning internal to the text.

The first kind of difficulty the poem presents is that of the indeterminate symbol. We sense that "Thunder" here is not real thunder, that "Lightning," "the Bolt," "Oxygen," "Electricity," and the like are private symbols for elements of the speaker's experience or world. But how do we determine what these images symbolize? It is hard to be definitive on the basis of this poem alone, which provides no internal definitions and little qualifying context; yet when we look for help to other of Dickinson's poems where similar images appear, we find a qualifying *range* of contexts rather than a unified picture (Dickinson, like Whitman, is not afraid to contradict herself; she might easily make Whitman's claim to contain multitudes). Thus in poem 1247, "Thunder" is associated with "Poetry" — or, the speaker hastens to add, "Love." In poem 505, the "Bolts" are "of Melody" — the poet's creation once again — but here the speaker claims she would rather be the listener than the poet. In poem 315, the "Thunderbolt" is dealt by an unnamed "He" who "fumbles at your soul/As players at the Keys" — another musical metaphor, but one which takes place in the context of an apocalyptic revelation. In 1581, the poem at hand, we may surmise that Thunder and Lightning refer to intense private experience, such as that of creative inspiration or spiritual enlightenment. But it is hard to be much more specific than this with any real measure of confidence; finally, it may be easier to say what these symbols are *not* about than what they are.

The second way in which this poem is difficult is in its logic. It is not just that the poem is full of paradox, seeming-paradox, and oxymoron; it is that, at several points, it is hard to follow its syllogistic connections. And yet we are teased into trying, for the poem takes the form of an argument, presenting information, making deductions, arriving at conclusions. Consider just the opening two lines — straightforward perhaps at first glance but, on reflection, nonsensical. For what kind of thunder is the "farthest" that the speaker has heard? If she means the real thunder of nature, why should she inform us of the scientific fact that it is "nearer than the Sky," an idea she does not go on to develop at all in the poem? Yet if she refers to another kind of thunder here — the internal thunder of poetic inspiration or spiritual revelation — why is this the *farthest* thunder she has heard? It would seem rather to be the *nearest*, or, at least, nearer, i.e., closer to the self, than that physical thunder of the sky with which it is compared. Or perhaps "farthest" doesn't mean "farthest" but something more like "farthest-reaching," most long-lasting, since the speaker will go on to say that it rumbles long after the rains have passed. But then why does the poet choose the word "farthest" — is it only to juxtapose the ideas of "near" and "far" and thus create an illusion of paradox where none in fact exists? Is it only to tell us, right at the outset, that this is not a poem that will make logical sense?

The poem is rife with this kind of perplexity. The "Lightning" that precedes "missiles" to strike only the speaker's self is a violent force that the speaker holds dearer than all the rest of life. Though paradoxical, this idea may still be easier to accept than the description of "Electricity" that follows. For the speaker goes on to portray a benevolent, domesticating energy that "founds the Homes and decks the Days," yet whose every manifestation — "clamor bright," a synaesthetic image which might well describe the brilliant noise of the poetic object — waylays, detains us in ambush. And what do we make of lines 9–12, wherein "the obligation/To Electricity" is contrasted with "Indebtedness to Oxygen"? Even if we can coherently interpret both the meaning of these symbols and the relationship between them — for example, "Oxygen" as the stuff of ordinary life, "Electricity" as the rare extraordinary moment — how do we understand what they have to do with being "Happy"? Do we repay Oxygen by being Happy, or are we Happy to have only it (and not Electricity) to repay? Is it an *un*-Happy endeavor to try to repay Electricity, or is it an impossible one? Or is it that the Happy are ordinary folk who, unlike the speaker, never know Electricity? Exactly what is the logic here? It is hard to say for sure, and the more one ponders it, the more one is teased out of thought.

Finally, we find in this poem — perhaps to a lesser extent than in some other poems, but present nonetheless — Dickinson's characteristically difficult, because exceedingly compressed, syntax. Thus the concluding two lines, "How Life's reverberation/Its Explanation found —," are attached to the rest of the poem by a wisp of a syllable, an exclamatory "How" that reveals little about how *we* might find an explanation to the poem's reverberating meanings. The conclusion of the poem seems to hang in the air, reverberating to itself in a self-satisfied way that leaves us all but crying for more explanation.

And yet, and yet. This poem, like a good many others in Dickinson's opus, is *not about* finding rational explanations; it is about experience that must be experienced to be known. It is about insight that strikes as rarely, as quickly, and as suddenly as a thunderbolt, and which therefore cannot be compared to the rest of ordinary life. It is about a moment that is intensely real and yet ineffable; to tell it is necessarily to distort it. Ultimately, such experience can *never be described in words*; it can only be alluded to, evoked by contrast with what it is not, teased up by means of paradox that baffles us out of our rational mode. Like a Zen koan — what is the sound of "A Crash without a Sound"? — this poem leads us into appreciation by thwarting our ability to fathom it with our intellect.

And this may be a clue to the method behind Dickinson's maddening persistence in serving us so much difficulty.

Poem 1581

BARBARA PACKER

University of California, Los Angeles

IT'S EASY ENOUGH to classify Dickinson's poem 1581 — it's one of those poems about poetic inspiration, or poetic election, that are her peculiar contribution to a familiar enough Romantic genre. Like them, it expresses both the glory and the cost of poetic "election" in a series of paradoxes; the lightning bolt seems a catastrophic sort of visitation, yet one she would not "exchange/For all the rest of life." Her own share of the celestial fire is small — "a gleam concomitant" of the larger light — yet in possessing it she is participating in the energy that gives life and light to the planet. The after-effects of its stroke continue to be felt even in the autumn of life, just as the revelation of meaning it offered made sense of all that followed.

But this paraphrase of the poem's "meaning" does not do justice to the alternation of bafflement and clarification that a reading of the poem necessarily involves, and whose intricacies are ambiguously represented in the poem's central trope: the relationship between lightning and thunder. The poem begins in a confusion both of space and of time. The poet, it will become clear, is remembering a single experience of lightning-and-thunder; but she remembers the thunder first, and what she remembers is both confusing and falsely precise:

The farthest Thunder that I heard
Was nearer than the Sky.

I say "falsely," because by the third line of the poem we have clearly been propelled from memory into allegory. Aristotle pointed out that one of the ways of making metaphor is by introducing an alien term and then denying one of its attributes, as when you call a shield first

Women's Studies, 1989
Vol. 16, pp. 155-158
Reprints available directly from the publisher
Photocopying permitted by license only

"the cup of Ares" and then "the wineless cup." Dickinson introduces a stopless thunder, a thunder that never ceases to reverberate, and in doing so switches the rest of the poem into a different mode, like one of those maddening computer programs that go on underlining when you have forgotten to tell them to stop. The simple past of the first line must be revised in light of the attribute denial of the third; this retroactive revision goes on all the time, in syntax, in the interpretation of poetry, in the understanding of life — but it is only one of the modes of knowledge, and not the one whose influence the poem exists to celebrate.

The next four lines, a perfectly conventional statement of the supreme value of this lightning bolt, offer nothing to disturb the reader's complacent sensations of comprehension — "I get it; it's a *metaphor.*" Like Frost's equally tricky "The Road Not Taken," it offers sentiments so unexceptionable and conventionally uplifting, cloaked in just the thinnest and most transparent of allegories, that it seems to plead for inclusion on wall plaques.

But the next four lines of Dickinson's poem plunge us into genuine difficulty. How may the Happy be said to repay their indebtedness to Oxygen? By respiring what they inspire? By restoring to the oxygen-producing plants the carbon dioxide they need for their own respiration? This happy image of symbiosis might seem an attractive one for a Romantic poet, who returns in song what she has received in joy. But Dickinson introduces the model only to reject it. The electricity she honors is *absolutely* prior, as lightning is always prior to thunder; it is only a source, never a receptacle. The cheerful slogan she invents for it — "It founds the homes and decks the days" — sounds almost like an advertising jingle, but the kennings she invents for individual electric power in the next line — "clamor bright" and "gleam concomitant" — return the diction to High Style with a vengeance. If "clamor bright" stands, as I think it does, for "human artifact," specifically for poems, then it represents a collapsing or synaesthetic blending of both lightning and thunder. "Gleam concomitant," with its noun-adjective reversal, not only qualifies as "poetic diction," it manages to sound rather like a technical term from heraldry: cf. lion rampant. The movement from the cheerful nineteenth-century designation of "electricity" as the stuff of all life, to the vague medievalism of "gleam concomitant" is one of those minor comedies of diction that Dickinson delights in. Like "clamor bright," it is a composite image, though it blends historical periods rather than sensory attributes.

The "waylaying Light" of the next line is Dickinson's spooky term for a sudden confrontation with supernal power, though it has the odd effect of making a conversion experience sound rather like getting mugged. As Saul was waylaid on the road to Damascus, Dickinson's divine electrocution has left rumblings behind that outlive the "torrid noons" of physical human life. Our obligation to this Electricity is immense and unpayable, like the "debt immense of endless gratitude" that so tormented Satan. Unlike Satan, Dickinson seems (in this poem, anyway) to feel only awe and gratitude, happy enough at being a "gleam concomitant" of that larger Power.

The final quatrain suggests why this might be so. The "Bolt" of the second quatrain is transformed into the "Thought" whose "Crash" is a purely internal affair. If the source of energy Dickinson worships is really within, then poetic election is in fact a moment of *self*-recognition whose terror and beauty derive from the awareness that it was involuntary. All the Transcendentalists payed homage to the power of the moment to counterbalance the whole of life — Emerson's beloved hydrostatic paradox — but Dickinson's more violent metaphors seem chosen from the language of religious mysticism, of seizure. The unshakeable conviction religious visionaries sometimes display — think of Fox, or of Blake — grows from the fact that experience has for them a status merely confirmatory; the pattern that makes sense of their experience has already been given.

So for Dickinson, too, the flash of revelation is *prior* to the experience whose meaning it reveals. Hence the curious confusion of the final lines. In general, the poet who is seeking a metaphor for the clarity that comes from comprehension would do well to avoid the lightning–thunder metaphor, since it is backwards, temporally speaking. Far better to begin, like Dante, in a dark wood, and only work up to the blinding revelation that ends Paradiso XXXIV through a series of neatly graduated steps.

But Dickinson classes herself among the elect whose dubious privilege it is to have received the explanation before the experience, the revelatory lightning before the reverberation most of us call "Life." And so the metaphor which makes no sense for us, because it is backwards, makes perfect sense for her:

How Life's reverberation
Its Explanation found —

Poem 1733, "No man saw awe," treats a similar theme in Biblical allegory. Moses' face-to-face confrontation with the physiognomy of awe leaves him with nothing left to do but breathe; his *acts* are over, dwarfed by the immensity of his vision.

But Dickinson knew that Moses told of his vision, and her enactment repeats again the experience of revelation that seems to me at the bottom of her intensity. At times she likes to repeat in the temporal structure of the poem the kind of lightning-flash with subsequent reverberations that she here indentifies as the central experience of her life. And so you have those terrifying poems that begin with a casual thunderclap — "I heard a fly buzz when I died," "Because I could not stop for Death" — and spend the rest of the poem listening to its reverberations. In other places Dickinson's very fondness for mystification — for ellipsis, catechresis, and so on — gives us as readers the pleasure she, as author, can never know — the pleasure of arriving at comprehension through confusion, of being troubled by the thunder before we finally see the blinding flash of light that silently explains it all.

Poem 1581
Workshop Discussion

Speakers: MARCIA FALK, BARBARA PACKER

THE POEM doesn't come to a power play. It talks about frustration, the frustration of recognizing cosmic possibilities and not being able to respond to that with equal dynamics. So at the end, she feels this lightning has struck her in maybe a random sort of way, and she doesn't know how to respond with gratitude to that. She relishes the experience and feels this enlivening sense of energy about herself. But she can't do anything with it. So, elliptically, you have no transition at the end, "The Thought is quiet as a Flake," which might be interpreted as something like a crash without a sound. But I think more than that, it is probably the microscopic response that she's having to the possibility of having a flash of epiphany; instead she has only this gleam or flake or the very tiniest kind of reductive response to it. So her little thoughts, she's saying, have the possibility of a crash but turn out to not have a sound. But yet they have the possibility of covering the entire landscape, as the flake in the snow, if you're going to take a seasonal kind of approach, "the torrid noons" of the cosmos being reduced to the flakes that might cover the landscape at the end of the day when the snow covers everything. There's a possibility of a grand kind of cover. But what it is, I see, is a response of frustration to the enormous possibilities of being energized with Emersonian transcendentalism that she finds reduced to the place of language.

It's interesting to me that the "I" disappears from the poem. At the beginning you have the "I," the speaker trying to locate herself in terms of this experience, but the "I" reaches its own personal climax at the moment early in the poem when it recognizes that it would not

Women's Studies, 1989
Vol. 16, pp. 159-174
Reprints available directly from the publisher
Photocopying permitted by license only

exchange the "Bolt/For all the rest of Life —." After that, "I" disappears.

Well, by the time of the end of the poem, it seems to me that the "I" has been totally absorbed into the flash of lightning and the reverberations; and that has become the comprehension of the experience and the light, from the lightning and thunder ... so she's no longer listening to what she is.

That sounds good. But I think her disappearing from the poem is more like her being further and further alienated from the experience rather than incorporated into it.

I think the problem, I think possibly the poem, as you say, is more coherent on the level of argument than it is of imagery, and that the feeling of frustration that you're noting is because it's not working on its own terms. For me the place where it breaks down is the business of the "Thought is quiet as a Flake." It introduces a realm of imagery which has nothing to do with the imagery of the poem as it has been set up so far. It's the problem of the first two lines, too; they seem to be introducing a subject which turns out to be irrelevant. I don't find them as hard to understand as you did. I mean it seems to me that she's talking in a way about the phenomenon of thunder, that it does seem somehow spatially closer to you than the sky. Although you couldn't locate either one of those things being precisely in space, you're actually hearing ...

Real thunder ...

Yes, real thunder. Like a New England thunder storm. It seems right over the house.

In contrast to what?

In contrast to the sky.

No, no, I mean in the first few lines she's making a point that she is then going to put into what?

That's the problem; she doesn't do anything with it. To me it sounds as if she's trying to introduce this fiction that she's going to work out later between sound and light, which the poem turns on, but she doesn't connect it enough with the rest of the poem.

That's very interesting. I think that's what threw me. I kept trying to look for this thunder as opposed to another thunder. You're saying, she's not saying that at all, she's describing thunder ...

This is real thunder, and the point is there's a difference between the sky over the thunder and the thunder, which is like the difference between the lightning and the thunder, which is like the difference between comprehension and experience. But although Dickinson in other poems that I can think of, takes a triple decker illusion like that and makes it work, in this one it doesn't ever quite seem to come together. And so you have an interesting idea I think the concept behind the poem is very interesting, the idea that whereas we normally think of clarification as coming at the end of an experience, which it then retroactively reveals, she's experiencing it the other way around. That seems to me very interesting.

Wait a minute, where do you get the fact that she's experiencing the revelation first?

The last two lines. It's a paradox, it's the reverberation that comes after, but the explanations come before.

I equate explanation with thought. The thought is of how life's reverberation later found its explanation.

I don't think it's later, though — I think it's before.

Isn't there a developmental sequence there and sort of a pyramidal structure, where you have the lightning bolt at the tip and the lightning bolt then becomes electricity, and the pyramid broadens and electricity becomes light, and then the final base of everything is light?

That's good, but she doesn't quite connect up with electricity and light, does she? I mean, light is oxygen, and that seems to be in a different realm from electricity.

Well, but it "founds the Homes and decks the Days."

I know, but that's just what...

We're using her own criterion: you know, if it's not taken off the top of your head then it's not working. Dickinson herself gives you the best argument for an experiential test of whether or not the poem works. I was just trying to come up with a coherent explanation of it on a logical level to see if I could do it. Because I had the same response to it when I first read it, which was "is it a good poem I ought to read? this isn't a poem I've ever paid much attention to." When I first read it, it didn't make any sense, and then I was trying to see if I *could* make sense out of it, but I still wouldn't want to defend it as one of my favorite Dickinson poems, although I can see in it techniques which she does use elsewhere.

Right. And one thing, the poem (because it isn't self-contained, we don't feel satisfied by it alone), forces us out into her other poems.

I was saying that this morning: that you always go from one Dickinson poem to another Dickinson poem for an explanation of the one you can't explain.

Which is very dangerous, though, because she may be saying exactly the opposite.

In 1775 poems you can't exactly expect consistency among them every time she uses an image.

We feel that we're imposing on the poem, and I think that in a reverse way the poem does impose those kinds of feelings on us. It makes us feel frustrated, and in that way, gives us the experience of the poem itself.

I am not sure I think the poem is about being frustrated and unable to pay back. One of the issues of the poem that I'd like to explore, if people are interested, is this relationship between being the receiver of the bolt and the creator, which is what she talks about in 315. Because the sense of experiencing being overtaken by power can make you feel powerless or empowered, and I think she's confused about it in this poem. This poem doesn't help me, but the poem did raise the issue which other poems, I think, deal with more successfully.

How about "My life had stood a Loaded Gun"? In some ways that situation is like powerlessness, but also it's the situation of being empowered.

I just wonder if she isn't trying to describe here that ineffable experience of the trance that one goes into for the split second before one begins writing. Once one begins writing, once the poetic process begins, one is a creator, however powerful or powerless one feels. Once in the process, you're active, you're doing it. But there is that moment, a split second, that you pick up the pen because "Ah!, it's coming," when you have the sense of being overtaken perhaps, and of receiving.... Now I think that's an inner experience, I think that the imagery that she uses to describe it is outer imagery, imagery of transcendence, but I think that psychologically if they were to do experiments on it, it is an inner thing, I mean something must happen in the brain. Nothing really comes from outside, and yet all of our language is all — you know, the language of the muse, the language of the thunderbolt and being struck by a bolt from the blue —

Remember what that Julia James person said, that primitive man was getting orders from one half of his brain and so it felt like it was coming from the outside.

Or is it we have to spit out, in other words we have to force out everything ... we have to feel that we're the receiver of something external before we can feel ...

That would be more Freudian ...

You raised an interesting question which I think comes up again and again in teaching Dickinson, which is that at the beginning of the class we have total bafflement, you know, just utterly defeated by all of

Dickinson's poetry. And then it gets to become something of a game; "can you interpret it"? And interestingly enough, I often find it is the non-humanities students, like the physicists and the mathematicians, who go absolutely ga-ga over Dickinson. One of them presented me with a series of worked out equations, which of course I was absolutely incapable of reading, dealing with Dickinson's concept of infinity, and he said it worked out mathematically and was absolutely perfect. But once they get into that, then it becomes easy for them to come up with readings of the poems, and sometimes quite brilliantly, and then toward the end they get very worried about precisely this question; how much of it is a pattern which they have imposed upon the poem?

Well, that's the incredible thing about Dickinson, isn't it, that she is very hard. I keep reiterating that, not in any way to discourage myself or others from reading her, but to allow myself to continue without feeling somehow inadequate, you know, and I say it to my students so that they don't have to feel, "Oh, my God, I just can't do this." I think she is difficult, but there's so much room in her. That is, there's so much latitude that it's almost impossible not to be creative with her work, not to engage in dialogue with her work, once you get past the initial hesitation. And it's very hard to be wrong about Dickinson. It may be impossible to be right about her ... but it's very hard to be wrong.

I agree, and I always like to use her analogy just as a subject matter, as a way of teaching interpretation of poetry. Because it's a whole gym, a whole Nautilus. And you can do a week on imagery, and on syntax, and on allegory, and the students find it very fascinating for that reason, because it's a kind of program of acquiring these skills. And yet, it seems to me almost at the end of the collected poems that the goal is the creation of the reader, rather than the assimilation of a certain body of poetic knowledge. The only way you can do it is just to go back and start all over again. It's not like you can walk away with a little bundle ...

What she really wanted was to have a dialogue.

Just as that poem that I was alluding to, the poem about Moses, ends by saying that "very physiognomy," she's talking about his contemplation and awe of God, and she says "very physiognomy I am convinced was this." And the pronoun can only be referring to the same thing. But you have the feeling that as she has been looking at Moses looking at God, now she's looking at God, and we're looking at her, who's looking at us, and it's a kind of communion that we're being invited into.

I'm curious about other people. When you originally read the poem, what did you think oxygen meant, what did you think electricity was, what was your first impulse on this?

I should say, too, since not all of you have the complete variorum text, that the earlier draft, the 1881 draft, has "indebtedness to oxygen/The chemist can repay." For what that's worth.

But what does "happy" have to do with it?

Except that you think that when you're happy you sort of have the sensation of the expansion of the chest.

I got the idea that the happy are the fortunate ones whose obligation is one that is reciprocal.

Who only need oxygen and who don't have these goals within them?

That's right, they can repay it, so they're happy.

Does that make it ironic?

It's like the happy pig.

The fortunate ones, the stupid ones ... yeah.

Woody Allen's famous shallow couple, right?

You keep reminding me of that speech of Satan's on Mount Mercedes in "Paradise Lost," because he gets involved in this whole discussion of gratitude and attainment and he's saying, "oh, I wish I could have been some inferior angel, then I wouldn't have wanted more than I had," and the logic keeps eating itself away. But it all has to do with the notion that the thing that was really bothering Satan was not the elevation of Jesus and all this, but just the notion that he was always having to be grateful for a debt which he could not possibly do anything to reciprocate.

Well, the alternatives are sort of provocative. Because the chemist, the happy, and then two others that are rejected, "the ransomed can repay" — she uses that in a very loaded way — and the last one, "a lover can repay."

What do people think that flake means?

I thought snowflake first, but I'm sitting here trying to think of one coherent thing I can say about this poem, I wondered whether it might not be a flake of light — at least that ties in with the other imagery.

Does light come in flakes?

I thought it came in winter fireplaces.

And is a crash without a sound an apositive to the flake?

I think that would be like lightning and thunder.

Lightning without the thunder. Lightning itself doesn't make any noise.

I thought it was the snowy flake that settles and melts, you know. Except that you're right, the seasons change, because toward noon certainly is not the time of snowflakes.

If it worked, it's going to dissipate, also. I'm not sure it works. I just want four lines of consistency here.

Explain to me, Barbara or anybody, the syntax, "How Life's reverberation/ It's Explanation found —." What does that attach to?

It isn't, it's a kind of colloquial syntax, ... it's when you say, "It's how a man gets rich," or "It's how a man finds his way to the top." It seems to me to explain the whole poem. It doesn't need to be connected syntactically to what comes immediately before.

But what about the thought?

The thought is the how of Life's reverberation.

This thought is quiet as a flake and this is the thought we are trying ...

Suddenly it hits her, suddenly: that that experience found its explanation.

But she still doesn't force the explanation.

No, I mean the poem fails to tell us ...

But thought could also mean, "Thought itself," and that the bolt we're talking about can be bolt of insight; it doesn't have to be necessarily that which precedes the writing of poetry, it can be that which precedes understanding. So that thought itself, as quiet as a crash without a sound.

But she says "the thought."

It seemed to me to go back to the bolt of lightning: it seems to be another metaphor for a bolt of lightning.

Right, but the bolt, the thought itself is what struck the bolt.

But it's not thought itself, because I think it's some isolatable experience in time and space, at this moment, this particular thought.

She seems to me to be writing again about a thing that a lot of the transcendentalists deal with, that your real life as it is visible in the world is not really where the significant moments are to be found. You know, that a quiet moment of walking around a lake, a thought that revises your whole life, Emerson says, is what to you gives the whole pattern. And when I read those lines they seemed to me confused lines, but she seemed to me to be writing about this kind of experience.

And that's why I think that the opening two lines are not talking about real thunder and are not . . .

No, they are, they are, they are!

. . . but are talking about that kind of charismal experience. I think the thunder and the lightning are just different ways of talking about that . . .

No, I think she's already saying, "we are using a metaphor, because I'm talking about a thunder that is not the same as the thunder that you know from the sky."

But my thunder does not come exclusively from the sky.

My thunder is closer than the sky. It's mine alone, it stays within me, it changes my whole life, and it can never be paid back . . . I think that the thunder and the lightning are the same thing. It waylays me at the same time that it is the foundation of my whole life, and it is my reverberation.

What about, as an apositive poem, what about "There's a certain Slant of light"? "Heavenly Hurt, it gives us —/We can find no scar,/ But internal difference,/Where the Meanings are." I mean, that's not precisely the kind of extreme she's describing, but it's similar in the sense that it's imperial affliction, it's something that changes the self internally in ways that can't be undone.

What do you mean by imperial?

Well, it's the lightning bolt that you wouldn't exchange for all the rest of Life. It's an oxymoron.

Right, it's a vertical experience . . . a slant of light coming down from above and then lightning coming down from above . . . but in that poem, she actually is moved by nature in a way that the romantics are, and put in touch with her own pain. I think she actually sees something out there in nature, is touched by it and changed. Here I don't think there is any real nature.

No, nature is just being used as an expression.

No, nature's being used here as simply a linguistic symbol; I mean, I don't think this poem is about nature in any way. Maybe that's where you and I are still disagreeing.

Well, if it weren't about nature in any way, we wouldn't be able to comprehend it. It seems to me that she's using nature as a 19th century local descriptive word for it. As illustration, with all of the weakness that poets like Wordsworth attacked. You know, in the "Preface" to the *Lyrical Ballads*, where people are simply using kind of stock phrases that describe natural objects, without really thinking about whether they go very well together. And that seems to me what's wrong with the poem.

I'm not sure if we're agreeing or disagreeing.

I don't think we're disagreeing.

What I'm trying to say is that I think that she is talking about an experience she has with nature in a slanted way ...

That's right ...

And here she's not ... here she's just been using nature as a metaphor.

That's right, we agree. All I'm saying is that no matter how clichéd your natural symbolism is, it does depend upon the experience of nature in the first place to comprehend it, and if you don't think that's true, try teaching Dickinson to a group of Southern California undergraduates. I remember teaching once that Frost poem and going through — it's a riddle poem, you know, about the blond assassin that goes through the garden, and wondering what was so wrong with them, why were they so stupid, not one in a class of thirty-five could figure it out — and finally, they kept saying "dew," "rain" — finally it dawned on me that of course none of them had ever seen frost or had any experience of what it could do to a garden in one night in New England. And so I give little weather lectures. But aside from that, I don't think this poem is about nature.

I think that's a fundamental difference.

So, that in those terms, what are the "torrid noons"?

Just a continuation of the extended metaphor. I think they are just a way of saying "the rain that is sometimes accompanied by thunder has long since passed."

I thought of the torrid noons ... I thought of them almost as being light.

Could they be illumination?

"The farthest thunder that I heard/Was nearer than the Sky" ... it was something internal, it was this thunder crash internally, and it continues although those noons, those moments of illumination, of understanding, have gone.

And then the missiles are ...

Shots of understanding?

Maybe, I don't know.

Maybe it's dry lightning, instead of lightning in a rain shower.

Well, it still seems to me that what she's doing in the first eight lines is what poetry frequently does, which is to first assert something, and then deny it, as as way of letting you know that the first was intended to be metaphorical in the first place. So she's sort of saying, "I'm still hearing the rumble of thunder, although the torrid noons that ordinarily produce thunder have long ago disappeared." I don't know what those missiles are either. I don't know whether they are light or rain or what, but the point is, this is not that kind of thunder.

No, of course not, but the effect of the torrid noons that produce thunder is still with her somehow in the rumble, in the reverberation. Because see then, this sudden inspiration, those torrid noons, could be the explanation at the end.

Say that again?

Well, if the torrid noons are somehow analogous to the way that she used noon in lots of other poems, where a perception of what the eternal and infinite, that moment of knowledge — they're gone now but they were a kind of explanation in the past . . .

They still reverberate . . .

At the end she's thinking now about something in the past, how that's reverberation.

Do you have the sense that she's describing a particular moment in a particular experience in this poem, or rather a continual . . . I debated that about the first two lines for a long time. Is this one moment that she's discussing . . . "The farthest thunder that I ever heard/was that day, July 5, 1879 . . .," or . . .

See, I do, I think that she is trying to say at this particular moment my whole life changed.

But it's still with me because it's still reverberating . . .

It does work for me, the notion of the distinction between, even in anyone's experience the arriving of thunder — there's the blinding flash of illumination which seems to take place in an instant, and then the rumble, rumble, rumble, going on afterward . . . and she seems to me to be trying to use that as a metaphor for the relation of this illumination rumbling after.

Maybe she's using the idea of the torrid noons as a repetitive experience? I mean, you can learn or get inspiration from or be struck by the impression of the violence of a terribly hot day, but it wouldn't be the same kind of heat that you would get from a lightning bolt, or that there would be two kinds of energy, two kinds of heat ... equally violent, and Dickinson used violence in dynamic ways in her poems. But so that the torrid noons are past, it could be a thing of the passage of time, too, that these were experiences that she had when she was writing. So it could be that she feels experience — repetitive experience has gone but she remembers this one moment in her past.

It's interesting that we've all been given this poem as an assignment and we all sort of admitted that we wouldn't have chosen it, and it's put me into the position of greater empathy with my students, who don't get to choose. And the only difference is that there's no one sitting in this room now who is the repository of wisdom, the answer! Who's going to give us the answer? So, in a way I find this whole discussion very, sort of liberating, because as I've had a chance to say, unembarrassedly, you know, I have more questions than I have answers here. I'm not sure how much I like this ... I remember discussing this with Cris earlier, when I said, I don't know what I'm going to say about this poem, and I think one of my issues is, I don't know what questions we're being asked to deal with. Are we being asked to say what does the poem mean, or maybe we're being asked to say "do I like it, or why do I like it?" And Cris originally said, oh, well, no, that's a far less interesting question, and I said "why?" And she said, wait, maybe that's right, maybe that is a valid question. Do I like this poem? Why do I like it? How does it read? — and I had to deal with all of that in this poem that I didn't basically like as much as the others, and I'm sure that's a lot of how my students feel. They sit there probably thinking "I don't like this very much."

I wanted to say, one of the things I always do is to give the last paper on evaluation, and I send them out to Winters just because he's such an opinionated old bastard. He sort of does things which most pious and reverential critics don't do. "I don't like these, they stink, but these are wonderful." But he usually gives reasons, and even if you think the reasons are crazy, you can see what they are. And the students find it very liberating because they feel in a sense that we encourage them in a kind of system of hypocrisy.

I really like your observation that interpreting Emily Dickinson becomes the creation of a reader. And what you're saying, and that's a commentary on what we're doing here, is that it does create a way of reading that enriches and validates what other people are doing. And so it's a very collaborative thing, an appreciation of each other.

I've had that experience really with a lot of writers, that at the beginning you're kind of feeling your way along, and working on somebody, and you're not quite sure how to interpret a given thing, but after you spend years with that person, you begin to have a sort of, a kind of rapport with the work. I didn't have it with Wordsworth and then I team taught with a Wordsworthian. He and I disagreed over something, and I said, I think it's this and he said, no, no, no, and a little further along, when I had spent a little more time, I said, "wow, I really think he's right there; he had that rapport which I didn't have which would allow him to say "it's probably this." And it really makes sense. So I think that it happens with a lot of writers, that you have that sense that you are being created as a reader. But there is something special about Dickinson's address to the reader, because it has that teasing, coy quality.

I also think what we're doing today is acknowledging that conversation teases thought out of us, and the model of this whole conference is so different from most academic conferences, in that way.

In the way that Dickinson is different from other poets!

Yes! In that it invites conversation and it allows for question, and I think there are really few pleasures greater for me than being able to talk about a poem with other people and let the meanings emerge. It's hell sitting alone in a room trying to figure out poems . . .

That's not what they're designed for . . .

Of course not, they're designed to be read out loud.

It seems to me that Dickinson is also making a point about the exercise of the reader being intimately connected with the structure of the metaphor itself, because the metaphor is essentially the riddle, based on a similar kind of thing, something that's suppressed, and you're not given all the information and you have to supply it in order to make the equation work. And that is why they're fun. They're like doing the New York Times crossword puzzle in miniature.

That's right. Dickinson takes that characteristic of poetry and intensifies it, so that her poems become part of a puzzle.

Only you don't ever get the solution.

Wait for next week! Wait for the next poem!

Poem 1651

A Word made Flesh is seldom
And tremblingly partook
Nor then perhaps reported
But have I not mistook
Each one of us has tasted
With ecstasies of stealth
The very food debated
To our specific strength —

A Word that breathes distinctly
Has not the power to die
Cohesive as the Spirit
It may expire if He —
"Made Flesh and dwelt among us"
Could condescension be
Like this consent of Language
This loved Philology.

1955

Women's Studies, 1989
Vol. 16, p. 175
Reprints available directly from the publisher

Poem 1651

Loving Language: The Poetics of Authority in "A Word made Flesh"

JOANNE FEIT DIEHL

Bowdoin College

"A WORD MADE FLESH" may be read as Dickinson's assertion of her alternative power in the face of a potentially crippling external authority, the sovereignty of a male-identified God. In poem 1651 Dickinson explicitly chooses the democratic mutuality of imaginative figuration over against the inherently hierarchic, hence con/descending "WORD OF GOD." In a stunning inversion of orthodoxy, Dickinson takes God's word and makes it her own, thereby establishing a criterion for measuring all power outside the self. Thus, transubstantiation becomes a trope for poetic inspiration. Such a rhetorical gesture constitutes a transference of authority to the self, for a "Word made Flesh" presents an alternative drama of mutuality that effaces the hieratic relations that characterize orthodox Christianity.

While adhering to the general outlines of this interpretation, I want now to attend to moments within the poem which articulate its self-doubts. My discussion centers on those textual moments of grammatical ellipsis or rhetorical indeterminacy to assess their possible significance as well as their implications for circumscribing or delimiting Dickinson's assertion of her alternative poetic authority. For, throughout the poem, rhetoric engenders as it interrogates the transference of Christological power by and to the self.

If one locates the original source of "A Word made Flesh" in the New Testament (John I, 1–14), there exists a more contemporaneous

Women's Studies, 1989
Vol. 16, pp. 177-180

source as well, for the phrase becomes Emerson's when in "Self-Reliance" he asserts that "a man is the word made flesh," "born to shed healing to the nations...." Here, as elsewhere, Emerson draws upon the resources of Christian sanctification to empower the man of imagination. Authority, as Emerson understands it, can be transferred from its Christian context to the new American religion of literature. If one conjoins the Emersonian and the New Testament echoes, "A Word made Flesh" creates a double sense of occasion, for Dickinson's poem may be responding not simply to the doctrine of transubstantiation, which she rejects in favor of a more demotic linguistic exchange, but also to the Emersonian transference of Christological power, the appropriation of a Christian miracle by and through the embodying imagination.

Does Dickinson subscribe to this Emersonian vision of self-divination, and, if not, how does her divergence appear in the poem? What does it signify? In its provisional, tentative, even vexed reassertion of Emersonian sanctification, Dickinson's poem more precisely locates her philosophical difference from her formidable precursor. Among the shadows of its rhetorical doubts, the poem locates the difference between a questioning, self-reflexive, delimited human subjectivity and the absolute authority that Emerson (if only in his early work) would assume. One might, indeed, read "A Word made Flesh" as Dickinson's choosing the Emerson of "Experience" and "Fate" over the more confident Emerson of the earlier essays.

To clarify this distinction, I turn to Dickinson's poem, observing not only the rarity and awe associated with this moment of transubstantiation, "A Word made Flesh is seldom/And tremblingly partook," but noting as well that the poem's attention is not directed toward the experience undergone by the word (the Emersonian interest) so much as it is toward the experience of the one who *receives* that word yet does not herself become it. Not only does the occasion of transubstantiation provoke trembling, it also raises conceptual issues of authenticity and the truth of the witness:

Nor then perhaps reported
But have I not mistook

If the occasions when word becomes flesh are marked by their infrequency and anxiety, they may not even be reported by those who provisionally experience such moments. Note, too, the play on "mis-took," with its suggestion that the speaker may have mistakenly interpreted events experienced by others and/or that she may somehow have erred in taking the communion wafer, that she "mis-took" by participating in the very process of transubstantiation. Surely, there is something both illicit and appetitive in the following description:

But have I not mistook
Each one of us has tasted
With ecstasies of stealth
The very food debated
To our specific strength —

The appetitive is rhetorically appropriate if one extends the metaphor of the wafer, but rather tellingly inappropriate for other reasons. If the speaker is not mistaken, then one may experience the word as flesh with an ecstasy that conveys the pleasures of the violatively erotic rather than an aura of chaste sanctification. The vocabulary of appetitive desire expresses as it re-inflects the Emersonian conviction that one is fulfilled according to one's capacities. To the doctrine of works and the doctrine of faith, add the Dickinsonian doctrine of desire. Thus, "tasting" acquires the thrill of stealth. Here Dickinson diverges from Emerson in her refusal to idealize the human through her introduction of the illicit and the appetitive into the rhetorical figurations of doctrinal Christianity. But a central question abides: where does Dickinson position herself in relation to this transubstantiation?

The poem's last eight lines may answer this question, for here Dickinson once again introduces the problematic into the sacred as the transubstantiated word, the word made flesh, discovers that it remains, despite or because of its metamorphosis, still dependent upon the other, upon "Spirit." Although the word has the power to breathe distinctly, (in its own voice), having won through to originality, it cannot itself voluntarily relinquish the life it has won. "Cohesive," it coheres to and with the Spirit, and can only fall back into a lifeless "word" if the Spirit itself expires. Is this, then, the anxiety of intermittent inspiration? Is this the risk run by the poet who acknowledges the inherent dependency of an inspirational model of poetic composition? If Dickinson remains skeptical of the Emersonian transference of the Divine into the human, she also rejects its orthodox alternative. To yoke transubstantiation to the individual's subjectivity is to acknowledge the anxious limitations of self-reliance. Thus Dickinson may be intensifying rather than freeing the self from such dependency. For, it is, finally, the redemptive power of the miraculous that it can transcend the limitations of both our appetites and our desires.

If Dickinson, therefore, undercuts both the orthodox and the Emersonian paradigms for poetic inspiration, what she instead privileges is significant in a number of ways. I shall suggest two: first, to write not from the word but from subjectivity of the one who receives the word is to present annunciation as an alternative primary trope for inspiration. Secondly, once having introduced this alternative, Dickinson makes a deliberate choice against any such essentially hierarchic, mystifying representations of experience, whether Emersonian or Christian:

A Word that breathes distinctly
Has not the power to die
Cohesive as the Spirit
It may expire if He —
'Made Flesh and Dwelt among us'
Could condescension be
Like this consent of Language
This loved Philology.

In these lines, Dickinson chooses the mutuality of the linguistic perceived as erotic exchange. Yet, what proves disturbing about this apparently humane affirmation is its inherent self-reflexivity; for the dialogue of linguistic consent occurs not between two human selves, but between the single imagination and language. Over against Christian salvation and Emersonian self-divination, therefore, Dickinson chooses a consensual solitude in which she selects the words that alone would not betray her.

Poem 1651

CRISTANNE MILLER

Pomona College

IN MY READING, this poem is above all about choice or choosing language, but it is also about a nearly Puritan sense of being chosen. I think this is a hard poem, primarily because the second stanza undercuts the reverence of the first — but even after seeing this, it seems to me difficult to read the first stanza any way but solemnly. The poem represents the power of language, or of some words in language, but it focuses on the experience first of receiving or hearing and only secondarily of using powerful words. The poem also, I think, distinguishes between the patriarchal language of God's word, represented in archetypal form by Christ, and the language of everyday use — which is less perfect and less powerful but ultimately, in Dickinson's mind, to be preferred because it is ours.

Although the language of stanza 1 can be read metaphorically as being about any kind of privileged language (for example, poetry) its connotations are so clearly and consistently Christian as to make me think Dickinson really is talking about the Christian word here — biblical or sacred or Adamic language. Even in this imagery, though, the poet provides occasional clues that we are not passive receivers of this word. The first two lines present a paradox: the line break after "seldom" isolates the first phrase and suggests that a word made flesh rarely occurs; the second line continues this possibility but suggests as well that we cause the scarcity by seldom partaking it (seldom becomes an adverb parallel to tremblingly instead of an adjective describing word). "Tremblingly" implies the taker's hesitation; "partook" recalls the language of the communion service, suggesting that the taking of any powerful word is as holy and as communal an act as

Women's Studies, 1989
Vol. 16, pp. 181-184

partaking of the Eucharist in the community of the church. As in "Your thoughts don't have words every day" (1452), this reverberating language comes "Like signal esoteric sips/Of the communion Wine."

The public nature or context of communion sets off the essential privacy of the partaking Dickinson describes but also underlines its universality. It makes no difference that no one we know has "reported" this experience, because each one of us have undoubtedly experienced language so powerful and illuminating that it seems synonymous with life — or with the promise of salvation.

Next comes another paradoxical claim, echoing the private/public paradox of partaking: we experience a word made flesh in "ecstasies of steath" — "ecstasies" suggesting an expansive lack of self-consciousness or even consciousness, as when one is ecstatic, but "stealth" returning us to deliberate, careful, highly selfconscious and secret action. This contrast between unconscious and conscious action echoes the opening ambiguity about the cause of the word's scarcity — are we simply receivers of this mysterious Word or do we in some way call for it? In how far are we responsible for what we receive? The final two lines of this stanza, more than any other moment in the poem, imply that we receive passively; we take what has been planned or "debated" for us. Like children still fed according to a watchful mother's dietary plan, we are given the kind and size of morsels she finds us ready for or needing. Some force above us determines "our specific strength" and feeds us accordingly. The end of the stanza underlines conventional notions of human spiritual reliance on God and gratitude toward God for sending his Word among us. Dickinson even presents the paternalism, or maternalism, of debating food to our strength without innuendo; the poet seems to be truly and deeply grateful to take or receive such a word.

The second stanza, however, differs right from the start. While it is hard not to think of Christ when reading of a "Word made Flesh," it is hard to think of Christ as a "word that breathes distinctly." This is a more secular description of powerful language. The first kind of word comes seldom and is enjoyed stealthily; the second word cannot die — implying that it is always among us, forever at our service. This contrast returns us to the implications of stanza 1 that point to an active human role in communication: this is the word we choose to experience and that we take communally, not a word that is occasionally bequeathed to us. Any impulse to make the "word that breathes distinctly" analogous to the "Word made Flesh," or understand it in terms of the Christian paradox in which Christ dies on earth but lives forever, is checked by the following lines: if Christ were the model for the word that breathes, it would make little sense to say that the word would be able to die if Christ acted differently. This word cannot be Christ. It is "cohesive as the Spirit" — that is, perhaps, as much a uniter of disparate entities, or perhaps simply as powerful — but it is not the same as any part of the Spirit's trinity.

The second stanza claims that this living word "may expire" if the Christ-Word "could" be condescension. The key word here, I think, is could. We already know that the word that breathes is limited; it cannot die (implying that this death is to be desired — in a paradox much like that at the end of "My Life had stood — a Loaded Gun," 754). The conditional "could," however, also calls into question whether Christ can do what we desire Him to. All know that the human word cannot do what God's word has done, but the poem questions whether divine language is capable of the service human language routinely performs.

Indirectly, the poem asks Christ to come among us again, but this time in different form, this time as "condescension" — a curious request, because it is less egalitarian than being made flesh. In "condescension," Dickinson plays on the words "descend," as the Spirit did in the form of a dove at Christ's baptism, and "condescend," with its glance at what may be either God's benign courtesy or His hierarchical system that keeps humanity low. In other words, it asks Christ to come down in visible form but suggests that such descent can never result in a relationship of equals — Christ's descent will always be a condescension.

The importance of the hierarchical distinction implied here reveals itself in the comparison of the last two lines of the poem, where Dickinson contrasts Christ's inability to be "condescension" with philology's ready "consent." God's Word dies on earth to take eternal life, to become one with patriarchal godhead and eternally assigned meanings in heaven; but it cannot live with us. The human word, in contrast, lives always, and lives in continual "consent." Because it cannot die (after all it can never become flesh, and only flesh dies), it can never share in the absolute knowledge and power of God's Word, the only word made flesh. The poem, then, seems indirectly to question what one would prefer: a word that will always fail to achieve ultimate or perfectly fulfilled meaning but that gives itself freely, or a word that is perfectly true and powerful but unattainable except in rare moments of ecstatic and stealthy communion. I think there is no question about which Dickinson would have us choose.

Rather than calling the repository of human or living words "language," Dickinson calls it "Philology" — a word representing human love and study of language, or human response to language's power, not authoritative creation or Adamic naming. Philology represents an exchange between speakers and the categorizable aspects of language, an exchange valued for its complexity and for its dependence on those to whom it 'consents.' Philology, that is, cannot exist in a vacuum the way a word made flesh might. As language, it depends absolutely on those who study or love it. Dickinson emphasizes the emotional tie inherent in such action by making human language in this poem twice "loved" — first, in the adjective and then etymologically, in *philo-logos*; language is loved because it communicates *with* us; it consents to our manipulation which in turn replenishes its meaning. As Dickinson says in another poem, a word "just begins to live" when it is spoken (1212). Together the two stanzas of "A Word made Flesh" suggest that Dickinson values the language of godhead; she recognizes its power. To the extent, however, that such language makes of its speakers mere recipients of its word, that is remains outside the realm of human power, Dickinson rejects it. Such language is ultimately inadequate because it allows no room for us to contribute to it; speaking in God's word is like speaking in tongues — not like writing a poem — because its meaning stems from ecstasy rather than from the poet's perception and experience. Dickinson chooses language that is hers, language that she can manipulate. One might say that she chooses poetry over salvation.

Dickinson is a poet of "consent," of the shifting transformation, not the authoritative establishment, of meaning. To put it in other words, Dickinson chooses to love and study imperfect words that breathe instead of turning her devotion to the word made flesh that occasionally chooses or "comes unsummoned" to her. "A Word made Flesh" celebrates the force of any language that lives, but by the end it seems to want us to discard, with Dickinson, the patriarchally assigned language of godhead and to be most grateful towards language in its human form, or towards our own activity in language, "this loved philology."

Poem 1651

MAURYA SIMON

University of California at Riverside

IT IS INTERESTING to note in this poem — as in others written near the end of Dickinson's life — that the notorious dashes have dwindled to an economical one or two per poem. The sparing use of dashes in the eighth and twelfth lines, and the emphatic period at the poem's end, lend the poem a forceful emotional conviction and an unequivocal stylistic assurance. A further formal consideration is the poem's steady use of iambic trimeter, which allows the rhythm to gather momentum gradually and evenly. Most important, however, is the poem's controlling metaphor: language is a sacrament; thus the poet's diction is linked with Christ's incarnation. The poem employs eucharistic imagery to dramatize the magical and transcendent forces of language. The lines "A Word made Flesh is seldom /And trembling partook" bring to mind St. John's identification of Christ as Logos, the incarnate Word, as well as the ritual of communion, whereby the host is transformed into the body of Christ. The lines also allude to God's covenant with man — or, rather, with woman — that is, the immaculate conception during which God impregnates Mary by entering her (as a word? A breath?) through her ear. (And I think, too, of Eve's fateful bite into the fruit plucked from the Tree of Knowledge.)

What a strange and persuasive poem this is! Dickinson, typically, has blanked out the real scene or situation that compels the poem and has reduced time and space to an indefinite eternity. The poem seems suspended in air like a crystalline bubble, an indestructable truism composed of equal portions of breath and sound. And yet, the poem's details, especially in its first eight lines, are quite specifically concrete. Here we have a supporting metaphor — that of eating — which

Women's Studies, 1989
Vol. 16, pp. 185-187
Reprints available directly from the publisher
Photocopying permitted by license only

complements and strengthens the religious metaphors.

"A Word made Flesh is seldom/And tremblingly partook," because to experience such divinity and power is a rare and awe-inspiring occurrence. So affecting is this taste of the Spirit, that most often the act goes publically unacknowledged, unreported. Still, Dickinson contends, "Each one of us has tasted/With ecstasies of stealth/ The very food debated/To our specific strength —" — each according to his or her own needs and abilities.

Now the poem breaks away from the food metaphor to elaborate on the idea of individuality, and to introduce and develop a new and related idea. "A Word that breathes distinctly/Has not the power to die/Cohesive as the Spirit" — in other words, the inspired individuality of expression in a poet's language secures for her verse a parallel kind of immortality to God's. And this literary immortality, i.e. the sacrament of poetry, is "Cohesive as the Spirit" — it has just as much staying power, just as much holy tenacity, as God's divinity.

By making such a contention, Dickinson has clearly parted with the Christianity of mid-nineteenth century Amherst. Committing a kind of sacrilege in her peer's eyes, Dickinson compares the poet's powers to God's. The poet, she argues, is a Maker who breathes life into clay, spirit into language, animus into ink.

How brilliantly and economically Dickinson presents her complex thesis. And yet, she is not done with it. For the poem proceeds and climbs steadily towards a crescendo of meaning. Yes, she states, poetry is a sacrament that defies mortality — but it "may expire," evaporate, "if He —/'Made Flesh and dwelt among us'" — if, in some distant moment, God again became incarnate, visible among us. Then, the need for the sacrament of poetry will disappear. Because God's incarnation on earth will grace us with divine knowledge, with the Word, we'll no longer need religiously inspired language (words).

Dickinson, who possessed a vast knowledge of Greek and Latin etymologies, plays with the dual denotations derived from the Greek word "pneuma," which means both "breath" and "spirit." Language "may expire," may cease to breathe in us, cease to enliven us spiritually, *only* when the Spirit becomes flesh (as Christ) on earth. Dickinson asserts that in Christ's absence, "language ... plays Christ's role, consenting to share its strength with those who love it, and condescending as a compound of humanity and divinity to fulfill [human] needs."[1]

The word "condescension" is used literally here; for the Spirit *steps down* from heaven, thus it consents to dwell among us "Like this consent of Language/This loved Philology." Dickinson delivers a double-whammy in this last line by using the word "loved" to modify "Philology" — which literally means "love of language." So, in effect, she's emphasizing the double-nature of an intense love of language, a love which is like Christ's intense love for humankind, to which he both consents and condescends.

The poem is an amazing tour de force. It speaks volumes in sixteen brief lines. Dickinson displays, once again, her phenomenal ability to compress emotions and ideas with the utmost precision. She deftly selects complex symbols and images that reverberate in the mind. She fuses Christian rhetoric with original language, thus creating a sense of reverence for words and for the vocation of being a poet. In short, she celebrates the vision and power in an art that reconciles the finite and the infinite.

Notes

1. Jane Donahue Eberwein, *Dickinson: Strategies of Limitation*, p. 19.

Poem 1651
Workshop Discussion

Speakers: JOANNE FEIT DIEHL, CRISTANNE MILLER, MAURYA SIMON

JOANNE, your statements were packed with thoughts ... part of what I wanted to do is to unpack some of them and look at them. I was just fascinated by the notion of a Dickinsonian doctrine of desire; could you complete that?

I'll try. Specifically in terms of this poem, I was struck this time around by the conflation, by the combining of language of sacrament, sacramental discourse, and language that one would associate with desire or eros, and I was wondering about how one reacts to the other. And one could take, one would ordinarily take it in terms of the sacrament, that kind of context "the word made flesh is seldom and tremblingly partook" — that sense of awesomeness ... of being a part of that sacramental kind of occasion, so that's where that trembling would come. But there is an erotic trembling as well, and a performative one, too. In terms of the erotic it seems that the discourse of the erotic continues and can be associated with appetite and with the desire ... with human desire, fleshly desire, corporeal desire ... the corporeal desire of sexual and oral needs. And I see that in the play with "mistook" and the notion of the wafer and eating the wafer. So that you can explain this appetitive kind of language coming from taking the wafer, "have I not mistook"; but "with ecstasies of stealth." Why should, I asked myself, communion be approached stealthily, with ecstasy? One thinks of other kinds of occasions, at least I did — "and have I not mistook?" — each one making so intensely personal the individualizing of these ... in other words each one of us is faced

Women's Studies, 1989
Vol. 16, pp. 189-206
Reprints available directly from the publisher
Photocopying permitted by license only

with ecstasies of stealth. It's done, it's prohibited, rather than being sanctified. I think that is for me erotically charged.
"The very word debated to our specific strength . . ." And then I think it breaks and is making another argument. I do think also that the erotic is a way of "de-idealizing" the Emersonian notion that we are able to fulfill ourselves according to our character . . . which seems to me in some senses inhumane, or at least it bans eros or desire from a sense of what a person is. Dickinson is responding against the idealization of the human and resexualizing the human. And so, when you talk about self-reliance and capacity, what about desire . . . what about affect, what about this whole aspect of the self, of the erotic self that is ignored? I think that's what the appetitive language is doing there.

I was going to say, why is it then you end with "consensual solitude"?

I don't think I end there; I think she ends there. What I would want her to choose is another human being; and I think instead she draws the circle around herself in language. I then take this leap, when I say (I quote myself again), "Over against Christian salvation, the Emersonian self-divination, Dickinson chooses therefore consensual solitude in which she selects the words that alone would not betray her." Here, indeed, I go beyond the poem and to my own understanding of Dickinson's desire for power over language to protect or defend against a human relationship. I think here that we come closer and farther apart at the same time.

That's what Cris's reading of the second stanza is closer to: it picks up on what you seemed to be reading in the first stanza.

Yes, and I think what I'm arguing is that what seems to be going on in the first stanza is taken apart in the second stanza, so that the human, the other, the erotic, is taken away from self and other; and it is through the beloved love of language, through the reiteration, the circularity of the syllables themselves, that it forms a circle between self and word. That's a kind of isolation of self and language.

But it's also erotic.

It's also erotic, yes. And it's desire between self and language. But I would argue, from a human point of view, that that's dangerous and perhaps not to be desired.

How would this be similar to Dickinson's identification in other places with Eve and eating the forbidden fruit? When you talk about the ecstasies of stealth and the erotic, it is language that has been denied her; and then thinking of the culmination, "the consent of language," that language is telling her 'yes," even though she's been told "no," no this isn't for you.

Is it a conscious or unconscious use of the language, to arouse erotic feeling as you see it, or to express erotic feeling? Do you think she's conscious? Because I can imagine that if she were conscious of what she was doing, it just wouldn't work in the time. This is after all the language of Christ. ... Thinking of food and all these things would not normally inspire in me, and I wonder if it would in her conscious mind ... or do you think it is an unconscious thing that she's doing here?

Well, it's more as I said, it's such a *tour de force*, it is such an occasion of conscious articulation, it is such a carefully presented poem. I wouldn't want to get into a discussion of intention.

No, but in a sense you have to ... somehow there has to be something that triggers to us, whatever it is, that this is not just the language of the Bible, or the communion service, the attitudes toward it. It's not about language, or it is about language, but that it has this, that it stirs in any of us, or particularly at that time, a sexual relation. I just can't quite understand how to get there.

This is just an observation, but it seems to me that it's not uncommon, or wasn't uncommon, for earlier mystics to blur the religious/erotic in religious imagery.

The ecstasy seems perfectly appropriate in the religious context as well as in the sexual context of desire.

I'd point to the use of "stealth," not just ecstasy, which I think would keep it orthodox.

I can see that in Herbert, for instance.

I think Herbert is extremely erotic.

I think Christian discourse is fairly erotic.

Well, what are you really saying here?

It was essentially a way of sublimating, and so using, incorporating erotic desire for its own ...

That's why I wonder how we know the difference between the way Herbert would use it and the way she uses it? Probably from different points? Is that your thought? Why do we interpret Herbert in one way and ...

What's different is that knotty question you sort of worked into this morning as you talked about the soul; when is the person being taken over by the Holy Spirit just being taken over, and when is the person reappropriating the power?

That's what I want to talk about. It brings up the Eve business. I never thought of it before, but in that myth what Eve does is to take this word ... she steals the word that's outside of herself ... it's taking somebody else's thing. And I think Dickinson ends this poem claiming her own thing. I see it as less isolating, I guess, because it seems to me when you talk about philology you're talking about an enormous endeavor and you're not talking about "my words." I think my reading of her poem is different from yours in that way, too; this poem seems to do a funny thing where Dickinson wants the language to be both the thing that she claims for herself and something that's outside of her, that's too large, that she can't control. There are other poems where I see her talk powerfully about "my poetry," but this one seems to me more about "the wonder of this thing that I am hoping to make."

I would agree, though I would emphasize that my thesis would flow differently. The consent of language invites a notion of exchange and mutuality. "This loved philology" describes or circumscribes an enormous enterprise, a vast enterprise. But its self-word, self-reflexive, loved philologies are turning in on herself and language.

Consent brings desire right back in, too, right?

Yes, but from whom do you get consent? Who is the other?

I wouldn't say the whole world, and I would say the "word."

You're right, in that what you say is the paradigm, the course, for her life's strategies. It's not that Dickinson was not a desiring person, or an erotic person, but that she chose to have it out at home, for all kinds of reasons that we all talk about.

That wouldn't say that she wasn't erotic or desiring.

No, that's what I'm saying. That in closing the door and reading the letter and making sure that her major intercourse with this person was through letters and not on the sofa, no matter what Sue said; she wasn't being any less desirous, but she controlled the situation and it becomes, it did become, what Joanne is saying. It's very hard for us to read that, when she "does it in her mind." That's where what you said goes, but what I liked so much was that it didn't make her somehow fleshless, sexless.

I like that, too.

That combination of the first and the second stanza still throws me.

How do you read the first two lines in the second stanza, in reference to 754?

"But not the power to die." That's what I was thinking about when I was saying that it seems to me that the power to die in Dickinson is really the power to be human. And language is not human. It belongs to us, it consents to us, but it's not people. And it's not even people in the abstract or religious way that you could say that Christ was people. So, even a word that breathes distinctly doesn't have the power to die.

So you think that in a way she's defining the limits of language here?

Yes, I think that what she does in the poem is to say God's word, Christ, is more powerful, is better, than human language, but human language is preferable because it consents to us, it is ours, and God's word isn't. I think that in the last stanza she points out two kinds of limitations: the limitation of the human word — it cannot die, therefore it cannot become one with God, therefore it will never have the power of God's word, which is the power of creation, "in the beginning was the Word." Human language will never have that power. But I think that what she says human language does have, that God's word doesn't — or what it gives us that God's word doesn't is consent. We love it; it's ours.

Then perhaps you would insert "even"; you would begin the second stanza, just in our minds, "Even a word that breathes distinctly."

Well, yes — even the most powerful of human language cannot die.

I think that we violently disagree.

I don't think so!

We violently disagree, because I would not put in "even." Take out "even!" Erase it! I would read "a word that reads distinctly" as standing in apositional relation to a "word made flesh," and I'll tell you why. I think "a word that breathes distinctly has not the power to die" because . . . a word is fine in a trinitarian sense: it is representational, it is the word made flesh, it is capitalized (which doesn't mean much); but "cohesive as the Spirit/It may expire if He —" . . .

If he what?

If he also expired. That it is dependent, that the transubstantiation of the word is dependent upon the survival of him.

You see it as completely linked? Now it makes sense why you think that "loved philology" turns in on itself. That didn't make sense to me before.

So what I think she's calling into question is the whole project of mystification or Christian orthodoxy; the divine word is dependent upon God; it still hasn't got it. The only thing that achieves real authority — she thinks — is the word that comes from the self and breaks with God's word.

But wait. You say the word may expire if He may expire and therefore the divine word is dependent upon God. Is that what you're saying?

The divine word in the sense that it discovers its origins in God, it remains dependent just as, in 754, she has the power to live but not the power to die. But the relationship is hierarchical, and she doesn't want it because it's limited.

I agree.

So we say that this spirit is cohesive in a sense, it coheres, it comes together, but its strengths are also necessarily its limitations — "Cohesive as the Spirit." But to cohere also means to depend upon, and I think she reacts against dependence. Her alternatives for hierarchical structures are an Emersonian dependence — and that's where the inspirational model comes in: "I need to have announced from out there, from something external to me"; the word comes, but to depend upon it ... I think she wants to overcome the victimization of an annunciatory paradigm.

There I entirely agree with you. What she wants instead is her own language. In the end we agree, but in the middle we have completely different ways of getting there.

But the human language didn't come out of nowhere. One of the things that the poem does, I think one of the reasons we have so much trouble trying to decide whether somebody is in apposition or in contradiction, is that the poem allows us to see that the human language and the divine language have a very important connection with one another. Language, patriarchy, the Christ as the Word — that whole number is a model for language, that human language both depends upon and maybe resists ... but they have a very close connection. You see what I'm trying to say?

Well, I think I disagree.

You can disagree with half of it? I was agreeing with you, but all of a sudden I was realizing that Cris was assuming that everybody knows that human language is one thing and divine language is something else. You have to push that a little harder.

I agree that divine language is "the very thing debated/To our specific strength" — "here you go, honey," you know? — this spoonful for you . . . Divine language may be extraordinarily powerful, but it's not to be counted on. Or, you don't like the dependence, if you do count on it, because it always leaves you hanging.

What's the difference between human and divine language if it's words, if it's sentences, if it's syntax? How do you know that you're doing human language?

I would suggest that human discourse can be seen as part of Christian discourse or sacred discourse, and that we partake of this same language; perhaps Dickinson is emphasizing the origin of that language, and in the beginning of the poem she talks about a model for origins for where our words come from. The paradigm that she invokes is a sacramental one, and it involves a descendantal movement, a coming down, a condescending. "Could condescension be" — if only condescension could be like this consent of language, "this loved Philology"; whether language comes from human or from divine sources is, in a sense, beyond the question that she is appropriating. She's posing another model for poetic origins. And I think that it's the way she imagines her relationship to linguistic origins over against what Emerson imagines or figures his relation to poetic origin is — the way an exclusively orthodox Christian poet would imagine her or his relation to inspiration.

In that reading, who's doing the debating about the "very food" that fits our "specific strength"? Who does Dickinson think is making that decision?

God.

My sense would be that she's saying "this is a subject under discussion," that it's a way of distancing the immediacy of the image of "the very food debated." To use the word "debating" is immediately to move the communal experience out of the realm of a sacred discourse. We're now debating this issue — it's an abstraction of it, it's a secularization.

That was very different from your reading of it.

Well, we violently disagree.

I think that the difference between divine and human language has to do with how language means, and that divine language is a kind of Puritanical notion of the word, where a word has a certain and clear and absolute meaning, and that meaning is so clear and so powerful it is as though the word were a thing. It's as though the word is made flesh, you know what it means. In human language, you don't know what it means. Which is the wonder and glory of poetry, right? That you cannot say "it means this and nothing else."

But there are limits within what you can say abut it, otherwise ...

You don't say that it has no meaning. It has a lot of meaning, but it doesn't have a one-to-one relationship with meaning. God's word means in that it is absolutely specific and singular. God says a word and there is the earth, he says another word and there is the sun — I forget what the order is — another word and it's Jesus. Human language is never like that.

I'm thinking now of reading the poem; in a sense what this discussion has done is helped me to follow this poem much more clearly. One of the problems with reading the poem is that it's often very difficult to tell which language she's talking about. The reading experience is fuzzy. When you explained this, often you picked different lines to show where the distinctions were being made. We're all aware of the distinctions, but I want to suggest that she's also aware of the difficulty of making these distinctions. That she is also aware of how hard it is to get the better kind of language, the human kind of language, her own kind of language.

I think basically she wants both.

So textually, the poem shows their differences, as well as their contiguities. What this made me think of was the whole debate we're all engaged in right now; "if it's all a patriarchal language, how do we use it, and can we use it, and did we use it and will we use it?" I'm one of those Americans — "I've got texts and I'm going to work on them, and you can't tell me that there are not women's writings." This poem is very interesting for us in terms of that contemporary debate about the nature of language, because she shows how hard it is to make the distinctions, too.

But I would be a little reluctant to make our difficulties hers. There are lacuni, there are moments in the text where we are presented with difficulties of interpretation. But I'm not convinced that our readerly difficulties can be immediately transferred to assert her writerly difficulties. I think the poem is tremendously powerful as statement, and I think one can discuss those moments of intermittent difficulty not as gesturing toward her own indecisivness or uncertainty, but rather — any number of reasons.

I wouldn't call it indecisive or uncertain. I would call it her own sense of multiplicity or her own sense of complexity.

But I think she's making a clear choice.

May I ask one naive question. "The Word made flesh" is Christ, you know, it's religion. Would there be in that day anything that would invoke that, and not a specific language of the Bible. I gather you're talking about the language of the Bible, the whole language of religion. And I agree that she is saying that is fine, but in this day and age, we have to dispense with it because it cannot consent and talk to human sense. I don't understand "the Word made flesh" as being a particular kind of biblical language, the whole patriarchal language, or the whole language of other people.

Suzanne, I think one of the things you're wanting to do is to say that these words are patriarchal.

Why? Why is "the word made flesh," because it refers to Christ, therefore patriarchal use of the language?

The reason that Cris and Joanne were explaining earlier: it orders a person around, it imposes a structure on the participant.

So any language that imposes a structure could be considered patriarchal? I don't want to simplify what you're saying, but all of you seem to me to be making the persona make a choice between what you see as patriarchal language and something that she writes as a poet, and I don't see where she chooses between them. I don't see where there's a value judgment being made between the first stanza and the second, that this is better than the other.

I agree very much with you. I think she's saying the power of language is equal to the power of God. When you commit a word to paper, you are making the spirit flesh, you are making the spirit incarnate with language. You put ink on the page.

But why does she set up this peculiar conundrum then in the second stanza, "It may expire if He —/Could condescension be/Like this consent of Language?"

That's a tough line to read.

There is no need for language if Christ returns to earth and brings the word of God. We have divine knowledge: there's no need for language.

What do you think?

Something that you said before, recurrent in Dickinson's poetry, is her evaluation of the power to die. In the sense that "consent of language" markedly does not have the power to die, at least the way that this is structured grammatically, it makes me stop and wonder whether or not she is in fact pointing towards that consent of language, or loved philology, as a marked preferential choice.

That depends upon how you identify the "word that breathes

distinctly." If you read "A Word that breathes distinctly" as being parallel to "a Word made flesh," if you say this is the word that comes from Christ, this is identified with the sacramental language, then "A Word that breathes distinctly/Has not the power to die/Cohesive as the spirit/It may expire if He —." What I'm saying is very radical — that God's word is limited, it is limited over against the power of her word, which is greater. And that's the way I would read "Cohesive as the Spirit/It may expire if He —/'Made Flesh and dwelt among us'" — that's a Christian allusion, and then she stands back from it; she positions it as if it were a quotation, and there are quotation marks. She looks at it and says *could* this — I would even put in "this" — *could* Christ or this condescension, this "made flesh and dwelt among us," could this scriptural word be only as good as "this consent of language, this loved philology."

You identify condescension and consent?

No, but what I'm suggesting is that "Could this condescension" of a Christological language only be as great as "this consent of language." In other words, I choose human linguistic exchange over against a hierarchical, victimization of any inspirational model, whether it be Emersonian or orthodox.

I still feel the need to question that, because I feel that she is leaning toward a "loved philology" in her preference, but that she feels on some level that "the consent of language/This loved philology" is still missing in some quality, even though she prefers it.

Where do you find that in the text?

Just referring back to the second line, "A Word that breathes distinctly/Has not the power to die."

But that's consistent ... "A Word that breathes distinctly" depends upon a transubstantiation having occurred. It's the making of the word flesh. So that I'm saying that that's a Christian model.

But Joanne, let me say what I think you're doing syntactically, and then you can tell me if I'm right or not. It seems to me that you say "A

Word that breathes distinctly (Christ's word) Has not the power to die; (It is) Cohesive as the Spirit — It (this word that breathes distinctly) may expire if He (may expire)." And then you start over again with He and you say, you seem to use, "If He" again. What is the subject of . . .

It's the quotation. The subject is "Made flesh and dwelt among us." Let's reify this. Let's look at this sanctification of an inspirational experience. "Made flesh and dwelt among us." Well, I challenge that. I don't like it's made flesh and dwelt among us. And then she says "Could condescension . . ." — I call this condescension, I don't call this sanctification — "Could condescension be" only. . . . I choose instead. . . .

I think that it's the "It", meaning the "Word that breathes distinctly," meaning the "Word made flesh" being Christ. And that he condescends from his dignity to come into the mortal world, and that she's saying that this condescension is like the consent of language. Her poetry is the spiritual creativity of her spirit.

I think that's a possible reading, but then you isolate "Could condescension be"; does it then have a line break?

"'Made flesh and dwelt among us'/Could condescension be", meaning Christ made flesh among us could be condescension.

It seems to me that syntactically "It may expire if He *could* condescension be" — which he can't; consequently "It may not expire."

Why would she have a dash after "He"?

"He" — "Made flesh and dwelt among us".

Why don't we accept the indeterminacy of these lines?

If we do, then the next question, it seems to me, is, for somebody who has such a command of language, why would she put us through this?

She does it all the time!

She does it all the time, not because she's an orthodox poet and is saying "I have derived my language from a Christological language ..."

You said there was a difference between Adamic language, which has one meaning for one word, and the fine, poetic language which she's attempting to use. That's what the difference is — what you're calling indeterminacy. It's not because she can't do it the other way, it's because she wants to do it this way. And this calls into question the sense of reading that has to do with whether two features, regardless whether they are single words or lines or stanzas, are in apposition or in contrast. What do we make of that?

Let me go back to something I said at the very beginning of my first little speech. It seems to me that she although she would choose the kind of language that I would call human language and you called her language, over God's language, she loves them both and she values both experiences. That's why I say that however I read the second stanza, the first stanza continues to sound to me as though she does value this communion experience in a sort of traditional way. And in spite of all the trouble she's got with it. I like what you do with "mis-took" and I like very much this notion of desire, but it seems to me still that somehow it reverberates sort of traditionally ... you know: "I hate that you can't control that experience and I resent that one can be dependent on it and I choose this instead, but it's still so powerful."

Certainly it's powerful in that it's invested with all that feeling and desire, and I think that's what makes it a felt poem; it is not a choice that is easy. It is hard and, "if only I didn't have to give up this, if only I could have it, but I can't because implicit in this experience, whether sacramentally or in terms of an Emersonian self, is a way in which I am victimized. I am the one that has to wait. There's a mystification that renders me less powerful than what I can be on the same ground, on the same level, when no one has to come down and make its descent to me."

See, I don't think she has to give it up. The fact that you can read the two languages as being parallel in the end suggests to me that she doesn't feel that she has to give up, that they can both reverberate.

You know how I always saw this poem before today? I saw that the "Word that breathed distinctly" was living poetic language celebrated here because it was immortal. And that she was using "power to die" in an ironic way. The reason that language to her is so wonderful is because it is immortal, and it doesn't die. That's why she loves it, because it's her trafficking in this immortality that's going to make it possible ultimately for some kind of communion she's going to have. And that if "He made flesh and dwelt among us," if He did ever condescend, that language, her use of this language, would no longer be necessary.

You revised that.

It's not that I revised that, but now I wonder ... the relationship between who's doing the consenting in the second to the last line and the debating in the second to the last line with the first stanza — you might see a real connection there.

Don't you think it's possible that the debating has to do with the fact that each of us has tasted, each of us are closet poets, each of us are writers to some extent, we've all had a chance to taste the ecstasy of writing, expressing ourselves, committing ourselves to language. And maybe that's why it follows, "To our specific strength."

But as a writer you're feeding yourself, nobody is meting out for you. Your sense of "what am I allowed" and "what's the right portion for me to eat" — that's the kind of pre-censorship that Dickinson is trying is transcend in her use of language, a kind of forbidden fruit. She's taking it upon herself, and that's a courageous, endearing thing.

But does she mete things out to us to "our specific strength"?

You mean as the writer, what she has taken unto herself, is she then making a communion with us the reader?

We're seeing her word here, "made flesh."

This is the word she's giving herself, as the poet.

But then why is it "our"?

Because each one of us, meaning writers, I think "Our specific strength" …

But first of all it seems to me that what is assumed in Emerson is — I think the quotation is not from John but it is exactly from Emerson, which is important to remember — is that as much as we are, or we discover out there, she introduces to that a qualified and tentative aspect. One of the many places where we could argue in this poem is about the sense of a mother meting out to a child; "ecstasy of stealth" doesn't sound to me like a maternal figure so much as a Christian one. What's being invoked is absolute orthodox Emersonianism. We as souls can discover in the natural world, in God, in spirit or the world as spirit, exactly what we ourselves have. And she calls that into question by her diction.

How do you think the diction there calls it into question?

Why not read contextually? "Nor then perhaps reported/But have I not mistook." You notice the kinds of qualifiers. "A Word made Flesh is seldom/and tremblingly partook" is incredibly absolute, but then, "Nor then perhaps reported" — who's doing the reporting? "If I haven't made a mistake, you ought to listen to me because I'm going to tell you the truth." Who would agree to that? Each one of us is faced with "Ecstasies of stealth/The very food debated/To our specific strength." I think "debated" reinforces the kind of questioning introduced by these weak lines, these lines that distance oneself or call into question the experience has been had and by whom.

But you have "Each one of us has tasted," which is an active verb, but "debated" is from the outside. If this is the same sentence, which it clearly is, then you can't have "has tasted" and "debated" be the act of the person. Each one of us has tasted … the food debated, the food that has been debated elsewhere.

I read that "Nor then perhaps reported" as "what's created may never be read, it may be hidden forever." And then, "But have I not mistook" meaning her realizing her own fallibility in understanding suggests that others may not completely understand what she's presenting, which furthers this "consent of language." That pulls down to the bottom, where there's a real creative spirit behind poetry that she is fully aware of and full of. She's full of the experience of creating it. But the consent of language is that, in the consent of her art and the consent of Christ being mortal, it's belittled to this mortal realm to be taken in, to be fulfilled as meaningful, to become a word made flesh, to become a word that breathes distinctly. If you can find one word in a poem that speaks clearly and immediately and communicates direct meaning without any question, that's attained. That I think is what her creative spirit is trying to find in this poem and what she feels is attained in her work. I think that she uses the Christian metaphor to develop; she shows how she has to suffer through the artistry of literature, the study of literature; and the art of making literature, of writing, suffers through it as well, but transcends all of that suffering because it attains something in its united form.

Terrific. That's what I say.

It's interesting to me that we can touch on so many points of agreement and yet be so far apart.

Joanne, I don't remember your first reading. You said you were commenting on your earlier one and you were making a distinction. I asked the question, because I was interested in the idea of having done a reading and coming back to it, having reassessed the problem.

Really quickly — in your volume that you edited, in which you accepted my essay, I suggested that Dickinson, as I remember, "in a stunning inversion of orthodoxy takes the word of God and makes it her own" (in other words I was essentially agreeing with everybody else in the room) — "makes it her own, which then serves as the criterion for measuring all power outside the self." It's as if one could see in her poem a reenactment of the sacrament, with the word from outside, where she indeed eats God's word and then creates a beautiful mutual consent. I thought that that was too idealizing, going back to it. I thought this is very neat, but I haven't accounted for my own problems in reading.

Great. I wanted just to hear that said, because I was thinking about the development of feminism and how it's very interesting that I think each one of us is doing that kind of work now. You know, we went in the beginning for this heroic figure and in doing that we had to simplify and idealize — what she just said so eloquently.

Plenary Panel

Reading the Poems: Three Accounts

Reading Evanescence

ROBIN RILEY FAST

University of Akron

DICKINSON GAVE her poems social, historical, and cultural contexts when she sent them in letters to her friends; she affirmed the poems themselves as context when she bound many of them into fascicles. Obviously, these two contexts overlap and are complementary. If one enables us to locate the poet and her concerns in time and space, the other both places the individual poems in a solid body of work, and paradoxically, but necessarily, reminds us of the transience or evanescence of the things that engage her, and her own resistance to being "placed."

I have come to see evanescence as central to Dickinson's poetry. Her concern with evanescence pervades and to some extent determines her treatment of the other major themes. My account of reading the poems, then, is an account of reading them in light of a central issue that crucially influences the poet's various perspectives, her approaches to the topics that attract her, even some of her poetic techniques. To move this account of reading evanescence towards concreteness, I'll read you some lines from poems that have become emblematic for me of Dickinson's work and of how I approach it:

(627) The Tint I cannot take — is best —

(405) It might be easier/To fail — with Land in Sight —/Than gain — My Blue Peninsula —/To perish — of Delight —

(666) Ah Teneriffe!/Retreating Mountain!/Purples of Ages — pause for *you* . . . Ah Teneriffe!/I'm kneeling — still —

(628) They called me to the Window, for/" 'Twas Sunset" — Some one said . . . This — too the Showman rubbed away —/And when I looked again —/Nor Farm — nor Opal Herd — was there —/Nor Mediterranean —

Women's Studies, 1989
Vol. 16, pp. 209-215
Reprints available directly from the publisher
Photocopying permitted by license only

(319) The nearest Dream recedes — unrealized —
(266) This — is the land — the Sunset washes . . . These — are the Western Mystery!
(1099) My Cocoon tightens — Colors Tease/I'm feeling for the air . . . So I must baffle at the Hint/And cipher at the Sign/And make much blunder, if at last/I take the clue divine —
(607) Of nearness of her sundered Things/The Soul has special times
(1221) Some we see no more, Tenements of Wonder/Occupy to us though perhaps to them/Simpler are the Days than the Supposition/Their removing Manners/Leave us to presume

Most of these poems have to do with evanescence as such, in relation to one of the settings or themes where it becomes an issue for Dickinson. They crystallize the awareness of evanescence that often lies under the surface of other poems, whose concerns may seem to be entirely different.

These poems also state (or imply) a central fact about Dickinson's poems *as such*: they elude us. Or to use her words again (#673), this poetry "invites — appalls — endows —/Flits — glimmers — proves — dissolves —." Yet hearing the echoes, seeing the connections, among the poems solidifies them in a sense, making them more accessible, so that provisionally at least (and perhaps at best) we can grasp the poetry as more than fragments of sensation and meaning. And recognizing the concern with evanescence in all its importance, we have, too, another ground for comprehending the poetic strategies that make the poems so elusive.

Dickinson aspires after objects that she knows she can grasp only momentarily, if at all. In fact, their elusiveness can be an attraction, so that it is often with a hint of relief that she watches them retreat from her. She approaches her goals indirectly; by pursuing opposites, probing her interior self, tracing natural cycles — that is, she seeks the ungraspable and the abstract through the evanescent qualities of immediate experience. Thus her pursuit of the ungraspable does not separate her from the concrete and particular, but rather suggests new relationships between the abstract and the concrete. Balancing audaciously on the edge of the unknown, between immediate experience and distant, impalpable goals, she simultaneously aspires to the evanescent and values the immediate. She repeatedly affirms the reality and value of "angled" experience — the "Chips of Blank — in Boyish Eyes," the "harrowing Iodine," the "ample Rhine" of exhilaration, and the "inns of Molten Blue." Yet the evanescent mysteries to which such concrete phenomena awaken her — the "finer Gravitations," "undepicted Realms," and "Moats of Mystery" — are equally real to her.

Dickinson's interest in the evanescent is grounded, in part, then, in her perception of the "real" world around her. Another source, undoubtedly, is her experience in a culture that simply did not allow her to live expansively. Her interest in evanescence derived too, that is, from needs unmet by her milieu. And we can imagine that she came to see her own daily losses, and the limits forced on her by her society, as analogous in some way to the inability to attain other kinds of goals.

Not surprisingly, her poetry records a variety of responses to the, for her, unavoidable fact of evanescence. Among them are despair and rebellion:

> Their Height in Heaven comforts not — . . .
> I'm finite — I can't see —
>
> (696)

There is comprehension of the value of evanescence itself:

> It is a lonesome Glee —
> Yet sanctifies the Mind
> . . . . .
> Delight without a Cause —
> Arrestless as invisible —
> A matter of the Skies.
>
> (774)

or

> In insecurity to lie
> Is Joy's insuring quality.
>
> (1434)

And there is celebration of "the sufficing Longing," the "sumptuous Destitution," the "departing light."

An ungraspable object, then, may pain us with knowledge of our incapacity, or delight us with its shimmering; cyclic mutability can reinforce our knowledge of the goal's inaccessibility, or assure us of its eventual reappearance. Confronting evanescence and its contradictory effects, one must struggle to maintain a precarious balance between the known and the unknown, assurance and doubt. Dickinson's poetry can be thought of as a balancing act. Two statements from her letters suggest the poles between which she balances, and the centrality of evanescence to this necessity:

> "Oh Matchless Earth — We underrate the chance to dwell in Thee" (Letter 347)

and

> "The unknown is the largest need of the intellect, though for it no one thinks to thank God" (Letter 471)

Dickinson's consuming interest in evanescence is evident in her treatment of her other major themes. Elsewhere, I've considered how this interest contributes to Dickinson's treatment of religious issues.[1] Now, I'm going to discuss how I see it at work in poems on love and art. By considering these themes, we can see that Dickinson's concern with the "ethereal" does not preclude serious social or theological criticism, *nor* does it keep her from affirming her individual creative power.

Many of Dickinson's poems can be seen as moments in ongoing dramas; they may represent the voices of different speakers, or different parts of one mind, or they may be shots of one scene, from different angles. This has been for me an especially helpful way of approaching Dickinson's poems on love. *If* we understand them all individually, we still — or I still — need a sense of the whole that can accommodate the contradictions and reversals they present. What has worked for me is to see the love poems (in which I include third-person poems *about* love, too) as a drama which enacts different versions of realized or "achieved" love, criticizes them, tries out alternatives, and "ends" with the conviction of love's evanescence ("ends" because I'm not convinced Dickinson really concludes, and I'm not in any case proposing a linear or chronological reading). This drama might be considered, then, as an enactment of love-as-evanescence, for while she may in a given poem be committed to one version of love, her poetry doesn't ever indicate that she's convinced she's grasped it entirely.

Dickinson's poems explore the meanings of love within the conventional romantic boundaries, and the possibilities for different kinds of love. In doing so, they make up an important part of her critique of women's situation in the nineteenth century, and of the sexual power struggle. The critique becomes even sharper, I would suggest, as the governing conditions make true love truly ungraspable.

In many poems she plays and replays a stereotypical heterosexual romantic scene, in which a shy, submissive, vulnerable female addresses or contemplates a powerful, usually unresponsive, male. In "Ah, Teneriffe!" (666) the masculine mountain, with "Thigh of Granite — and thew — of Steel" is "Heedless" of the woman (and the feminine sunset) paying him homage. The woman in these scenes has invested her whole being in the remote beloved: "If He *dissolve* — than — there is *nothing — more*" (236). In his absence she can barely accept her own vitality: "Thy flower — be gay —/Her Lord — away!/It ill becometh me —/ I'll dwell in Calyx — Gray —" (339). The fruits of this relationship, for her, are self-denial and self-doubt: "My Worthiness is all my Doubt —/His Merit — all my fear —" (751). Her absolute dependency makes her vulnerable to accusations of betrayal: "Doubt me! My Dim Companion!" (275). To such accusations, her response can only be a renewed offer of her all: "Oh Lover — Life could not convince — Might Death — enable Thee —" (537). Yearning for recognition and love, she is willing even to deny her existence if only he will notice her and acknowledge her love. In these poems, she herself seems almost to dissolve, to become evanescent. (Unfortunately the beloved does not pursue evanescence as she does.)

Dickinson doesn't necessarily accept or condone the situation that these poems seem uncritically to present. If she's attracted, if she's fully a participant in some poems, in others she explicitly criticizes this often-repeated scene, and the underlying assumption that love is a relation of sacrifice and exploitation. Her critique is apparent in the rose-and-bee poems, "Like Trains of Cars on Tracks of Plush" (1224) and "A Bee his burnished Carriage/Drove boldly to a Rose —." (1339). It is equally evident in "He put the Belt around my life —/I heard the Buckle snap —/And turned away, imperial,/My Lifetime folding up —" (273); in "He found my Being — set it up — . . . Then carved his name — upon it —" (603); and in "All that I do/Is in review/To his enamoured mind" (1496), where the woman finally becomes *other* to herself, her own identity fading out at the end.

Recognizing this conventional "love" as the damaging relationship it is, Dickinson not surprisingly often treats love as an evanescent, impossible dream. Her clearest statement of this is poem 453: "Love — thou art high —/I cannot climb thee —." In response, she proposes alternative ways of attaining the elusive goal. She imagines love between equals: "He was weak, and I was strong — then — . . ./I was weak and He was strong then —" (190). Or between a strong woman and a weak man: "I rose — because He sank —" (616). Or between women: "Her sweet Weight on my Heart a Night/Had scarcely deigned to lie —" (518). Yet frequently these alternative visions end in uncertainty and loss; at best they promise "Mutual — Risk" (580). When such visions can't be sustained, she adopts yet another strategy in her pursuit of evanescent love: imagining a heavenly reward and compensation for the woman's earthly suffering in love. Here the evanescence is doubled, as heaven itself is not something about which Dickinson is often certain. Throughout the poems, her love of love itself, and her desire for love's transforming power (evident in poems like — "Come slowly — Eden!," (211); "Wild Nights! Wild Nights!," 249; "He touched me, so I live to know," (506); and "To my small Hearth His fire came," (638) make her disappointments, and love's elusiveness more acutely painful.

Nonetheless, Dickinson and her poetry are empowered by her awareness of and responsiveness to the evanescent. The evanescence evident in nature becomes an acknowledged quality of the art that it inspires; and in poems like "I reckon — when I count at all —/First — Poets — . . ." (569), Dickinson defines her artistic power in terms of her ability to imagine the ungraspable:

Their Summer — lasts a Solid Year —
They can afford a Sun
The East would deem extravagant —
And if the Further Heaven —

Be Beautiful as they prepare
For Those who worship Them —
It is too difficult a Grace —
To justify the Dream —

In poem 291 she seems to question her ability to paint the "Western Mystery":

How the old Mountains drip with Sunset
How the Hemlocks burn —

How the Dun Brake is draped in Cinder
By the Wizard Sun —

How the old Steeples hand the Scarlet
Till the Ball is full —
Have I the lip of the Flamingo
That I dare to tell?

The answer is obviously "yes." Domenichino may have "dropped his pencil —/Paralyzed with Gold," but Dickinson continues with her "lip of ... Flamingo" to tell how "the Fire ebbs like Billows ... How a small Dusk crawls on the Village ... How it is Night."

In "There is a Zone whose even Years/No Solstice interrupt" (1056), she creates the poets' heavenly summer:

Whose Summer set in Summer, till
The Centuries of June
And Centuries of August cease
And Consciousness — is Noon.

Having done so, of course, does not guarantee permanent possession or insure against loss; in fact, she is not apparently "there" in this poem, surely as she has momentarily envisioned that "Summer."

Dickinson's consuming interest in evanescence can be detected in most of her poetry. Her conviction about the transient, provisional qualities of experience and meaning should also inform our efforts to understand *her*, as we acknowledge multiplicity at all levels of her creative endeavor. Dickinson doesn't demand that we discover a conclusive pattern in the multiple meanings of evanescence and the varied responses to it that she presents. She does demand that we, too, accept the risk of balancing on the edge between the familiar and the inscrutable, that we acknowledge the utter mystery that we face every day if we look at the world with open eyes, that we admit our inability fully to perceive either immediate experience or the evanescent, and that with her we commit ourselves to both, as we struggle to see "beyond the Vail" into Possibility — spreading wide our "narrow Hands —/To gather Paradise —"

Notes

1. "'The One Thing Needful': Dickinson's Dilemma of Home and Heaven," *ESQ: A Journal of the American Renaissance* 27 (1981): 157–169.

Reading Dickinson Doubly*

SUZANNE JUHASZ

University of Colorado, Boulder

MY WORK ON DICKINSON tends to focus on reading the poems. For whatever generalizations we wish to make about her as poet or person, our knowledge results primarily from, and is grounded in, her poems. And those poems are not self-evident. The minute one begins to read them carefully, they open up, flower, expand; so that suddenly all that may have seemed clear (oh, I know what this poem is about), becomes complicated, suggestive, dense, even downright contradictory.

In my recent thinking about Dickinson I have been concentrating upon how to admit and accommodate the essential presence in her texts of multiple meanings. I neither believe that all responses to a poem are "right," nor do I believe that there is really no such thing as "meaning." So I need to find ways to *use* the obscurity or actual doubleness that we find as a part of what we think of as the poem's meaning. Especially, I am concerned with what effect gender, and the woman poet's uneasy relationship with patriarchal forms, has to do with Dickinson's language. For example, we can understand the impulse towards simultaneous privateness and publicity, or the famous telling it slant, or even the making of alternative, contradictory, and, again, simultaneous messages in term of gender: its poetics and politics.

The close-reading process that I have developed for Dickinson over the years — in which each line is experienced as it comes, as it helps to accumulate towards an interpretation; in which metaphors are

*This paper, along with my other talk in this volume, "Reading of Poem 315," are earlier versions of my essay, "Reading Doubly: Dickinson, Gender, and Multiple Meaing," scheduled to appear in Robin Riley Fast and Christine Mack Gordon, Eds. *Approaches to Teaching the Poetry of Emily Dickinson*, New York: MLA.

Women's Studies, 1989
Vol. 16, pp. 217-221
Reprints available directly from the publisher

initially taken "literally," their dramatic reality coming before their symbolic implication; in which syntax is initially understood as normal, so that embedded or elided syntax may more readily be recovered — becomes a useful format for encountering and, as I have said, accommodating the significant presence of non-recoverable or multiple meaning. Such multiplicity is present at all levels of language in Dickinson's writing, from the definition of a single word through syntactic structures through theme or central idea. Consequently, reading Dickinson demands a technique, and a perspective, that can see doubly.

We should begin by asking why this multiplicity should exist at all. It is not enough to note its presence, as most readers of Dickinson are eventually forced to do, especially when they then proceed to phase it out of existence, to "solve" the problem it is seen to have created. Understanding its origin helps us to read it properly. One reason (there are no doubt others) derives from Dickinson's gender: her situation as a woman in a patriarchal culture. For the ontological condition of what anthropologists Shirley and Edwin Ardener call a "muted group" within a dominant culture is in essence one of doubleness, in that reality is experienced both from the dominant patriarchal perspective and, at the same time, from the muted female perspective.[1] In culture as it is presently constituted, gender designates difference; yet expression of that difference is controlled by hegemonic structures. Language itself can be understood as such a structure; certainly, writing as a profession as well as an art has been traditionally so regulated. When a woman writes at all, she speaks a difference customarily identified by its very silence. One way to grasp the contradictions, evasions, and ambiguities that characterize Dickinson's poetic language is that they derive from and textualize this profound doubleness, as her writing reveals both the abiding power of the patriarchal perspective and the manifold difference of the female perspective. Dickinson will accept a cultural "given," enact it, challenge it, transform it, even deny that transformation — often in the same poem. In this way her language expresses, not so much a system of overt and covert messages, as her multiple experience of different yet simultaneous realities. Consequently, doubleness *is* the meaning; and the way we read her poems should release rather than simplify or suppress it.

Slowing down the analytic process helps, because it allows us to recapture, or recreate, the original reading experience, when the poem happens without much predetermination about pattern, or point, or meaning. Of course, the poem rarely exists for us in a total vacuum: we know who wrote it, we have read other poems by her, we have studied American literature. Nevertheless, the first time through, what happens next, and then next, comes as a surprise (especially in Dickinson), and we are in a better position to permit the doubled perspective that the words so often initially engender, before we try to organize them better. Reading line by line, then, letting each line happen fully, discretely, like viewing a film frame by frame, is a way to be particularly receptive to the experiential nature of the poem's creation of meaning. This involves faking it, of course; first, because we really have read the poem before, so we do have some sense of where things are heading; and secondly, because we can never avoid this sense of direction, since the poem is always reaching past each individual moment to create an extended action in space and time. Nevertheless, the ploy, or technique, puts the now critical reader in a position to give each word and phrase its due.

Dickinson herself establishes an environment of suspended animation in her poetry by her peculiar use of punctuation: in particular, the dash. Her dashes, both within individual lines and at the end of them, imply both discreteness and connection. What connection, however, they do not, as do periods or semi-colons, signify. When dashes control syntactic relation, as they do in Dickinson poems, they reinforce and promote doubleness.

Encouraging what my students think of as a "literal" reading of the poem's figurative language also contributes to this experiential method. I think of it, rather, as letting the metaphors exist as action in their own right, with their own reality, before translating them into something abstract and symbolic. For example, when Dickinson, in poem 789, speaks of a "Columnar Self," we experience a sense of possible overlap between columns and selves having to do with mass, weight, texture, direction, before we come up with some interpretation like "self-reliance" or "self-integrity." In fact, either of these concepts are limited and limiting with reference to Dickinson's subject. They leave out information present in the metaphor, and, I would maintain, should not be encouraged this early on in the reading. Translating or decoding in this way bypasses the poem as it is written — and, frequently, *misses* the meaning. Or, think of another poem, number 352:

Perhaps I asked too large —
I take — no less than skies —
For Earths, grow thick as
Berries, in my native town —

My Basket holds — just — Firmaments —
Those — dangle easy — on my arm,
But smaller bundles — Cram.

It seems essential here that the reader entertain the presence of skies and firmaments, earths, berries, basket; the overlapping realities of berries in baskets/firmaments in baskets; the easy feel of the latter, the awkward fit of the former — before talking about the poem in terms of "ambition" or "aspiration" or even "rebellion."

Finally, a word about syntax, and Dickinson's private, idiosyncratic language. To some extent, this characterization is true; Dickinson's solitude, and isolation, as well as her genius, had something to do with the "shorthand" quality to her writing. And yet, at the same time, her messages were meant to be read, or heard, as reading the poems aloud instantly reveals. They don't sound like another language, but a peculiar dialect of our own. From this perspective, we can understand that ellisions are meant to be recovered, for the syntax is for the most part normal, regular. Consequently, when it's not, those differences make sense in terms of the changes they ring. For example, going back to #789, "On a Columnar Self," in the second line, "How ample to rely," the substitution of "ample" for "amply," or adjective for adverb, causes the amplitude to modify not only the act of relying but the columnar self, a doubling which is borne out later in the poem when the self becomes an "Us," a "Crowd."

Nevertheless, sometimes syntax is not recoverable, creating the confusion, or multiplicity, to which I have been referring. Double meanings can cancel one another out, or enrich one another, or provide a suggestive tension, or irony, or contradiction. For example, in the concluding stanza to #789, Dickinson defines the crowd constituted by the self as consisting of "Ourself — and Rectitude —/And that Assembly — not far off/From furthest Spirit — God —." The dash between furthest spirit and God makes it impossible to tell whether God is the furthest spirit or the assembly, which in turn offers two seemingly contradictory definitions of the self's relationship to God. In the first case, the self is everything but God; in the second case, God, too, is included in the self's society. These alternative meanings may be seen as cancelling one another out; or, taken *together*, as expanding our understanding of the central concern of the poem, the nature of the self. The point of the poem is that the self relies upon itself, not God, so that whether He is considered an aspect of self, or as the only thing in the universe that isn't comprised by the self, He becomes secondary to an understanding of where power resides. Reading both possibilities as valid, the two together suggesting the whole meaning, helps us understand the central attitude of the poem. This may be likened to the way plastic overlays in a medical textbook work. Individually, each means something in particular about the human body; taken together, they show a more complete meaning.

Taken all together, these elements of slow motion reading permit the reader to sustain a double perspective: to allow more than one thing to happen at the same time and to see what happens when they do. Especially, they encourage a sensitivity to the effects of gender upon language itself — which seems of major importance, if we are to study these issues in other than a superficial way.

[1] "Belief and the Problem of Women," in Shirley Ardener, ed. Perceiving Women (New York: Halsted P, 1978), p. 3.

Approaches to Reading Dickinson

CRISTANNE MILLER
Pomona College, Claremont, California

MARIANNE MOORE WRITES that "Omissions are not accidents." If this is true of any poet's work more than of Moore's own, I think it would be Dickinson's. More and more, I am becoming convinced that reading Dickinson's poetry primarily involves coming to terms with the omissions or spaces in her poetry that we cannot fill except through interpretation; that is, through inserting our own ideas and experience into the poem — as Emerson put it, "shooting the gaps" between one sentence or analogy and the next. To some extent, we must interpret all texts to understand them, but that general necessity has a greater urgency, I believe, when we read Dickinson's poems, because they are so cryptically metaphorical and so compressed. In "There's a certain Slant of light" (258), Dickinson writes of a phenomenon that creates "no scar,/But internal difference,/Where the Meanings, are —." To my mind, this "internal difference" in "Meaning" provides a kind of paradigm for what Dickinson intentionally creates: she describes the perimeters of her subject by creating a space of difference or uncertainty inside the closed circle of things we think we understand. She makes us question the adequacy of Meanings.

As the "Slant of light" poem suggests, Dickinson apparently believes that no literal description or adequate name exists for certain kinds of experience; the best she can do in depicting such experience or perception is to show how it upsets previous understanding and then allow individual readers to name that, or their own similar, perception of "difference" more literally if they can. In these cases, the

Women's Studies, 1989
Vol. 16, pp. 223-228
Reprints available directly from the publisher
Photocopying permitted by license only

gap in meaning marks what has not yet been, and perhaps cannot be, defined. More often, however, Dickinson deliberately creates "internal difference" among "Meanings" as a way of asserting her belief in the complexity of perception, feeling, and human relationship, and also as a way of blocking either directly biographical or sentimental readings of her work. Dickinson creates a blank space of "difference" from which to examine the various sources and common tools of our understanding.

What this paradigm suggests as a model for reading the poems is that readers, too, might proceed most effectively by perceiving difference, or by opposing alternate possibilities of meaning in a poem. Such reading requires, first, an understanding of those possibilities or meanings Dickinson marks as inadequate to her thought, and then a balancing of those partly rejected meanings against each other to measure the space they leave. Typically, reading a Dickinson poem involves tracing more than one line of interpretation through a stanza or the whole text and then trying to understand how the differences between the lines can be reconciled.

So far I've spoken mostly from the reader's position. Now I want to talk about what Dickinson does to create this necessity for the reader. On the largest scale, in the structure of an entire poem, there are a few well-known strategies Dickinson repeats to create a nonlexical definition or an analogical, explanatory circumference. For example, in "It was not Death, for I stood up" (510), Dickinson makes both the positive and negative aspects of her comparison explicit in describing but never naming "it." "It was not" Death, Night, Frost, Fire, "And yet, it tasted, like them all" — as well as like "Midnight," and "most, like Chaos" with its unjustified "Despair." Dickinson tells what the experience felt like and how it left her, but she either does not or cannot name it. In a different kind of example, Dickinson uses all positive analogies: "As the starved Maelstrom laps the Navies/As the Vulture teased/Forces the Broods in lonely Valleys/As the Tiger eased/By but a Crumb of Blood, fasts Scarlet/Till he meet a Man ..." so "I, of a finer Famine/Deem my Supper dry/For but a Berry of Domingo/And a Torrid Eye." (872). In comparing her hunger to that of a whirlpool, then a vulture, and finally a tiger, Dickinson becomes more specific about the kind of hunger she feels and the kind of food that would satisfy her, but she never describes either directly and none of these analogies are particularly helpful in explaining her chosen Berry and Eye. Dickinson's three analogies tell what the speaker's hunger is like but also unlike — leaving interpretation of the speaker's "finer Famine" in a middle ground that the reader must locate and describe.

These structural circles around a single event or meaning have been discussed at some length in different terms by other critics (particularly Robert Weisbuch and Suzanne Juhasz). What interests me in the practical context of reading a poem is how Dickinson creates "internal difference" through syntax and by overturning semantic selectional restrictions in putting words together (combining words that don't match). Curiously, the most difficult part of writing this talk was attempting to find a less metaphorical or impressionistic way to describe the phenomenon I've been calling "internal difference" — and I gave up. If you'll allow me the presumptuous analogy, like Dickinson, I will not give my subject a single name but will use several, first returning to the terms recoverable and nonrecoverable deletion, which I've used to describe her work before — this time, however, emphasizing how they limit descriptions of what a reader finds in the poems. (I borrow these terms from Samuel Levin's "The Analysis of Compression in Poetry," *Foundations of Language* 7 (1971):38–55).

To talk about holes in a text assumes there was, or could have been, a complete (whole) text from which the author deleted portions to create the holes. Sometimes this is the case in Dickinson's poems: the poet leaves out several auxiliary verbs, pronouns, articles, and repeated words that are syntactically recoverable under the rules of ordinary language use. Recoverable deletion rarely causes problems in meaning. For example, in the second line of "He fumbles at your Soul" ("As Players at the Keys") Dickinson has deleted the repeated verb (as players fumble) and the prepositional phrase modifying keys (as players fumble at the keys of a piano) — just as we often do in speech. The difficulty of these lines stems from the unusual quality of the metaphor, not from deletion.

The more interesting spaces or gaps in Dickinson's poetry, however, are nonrecoverable; they cannot be filled in with any certainty by simple reference to grammar and common sense. The text they stem from cannot be recreated from the evidence in the poem and, in fact, there is no evidence that a complete text could ever have existed, even in Dickinson's mind. Recovering the missing words or phrases in these cases does not involve an act of recovery *per se* but speculative interpretation of the poem. The word "deletion," then, has a questionable accuracy in describing the poet's act and, more to the point, questionable accuracy in pointing towards the reader's task in interpreting the poem. Nevertheless, I will continue using, and qualifying, the term.

A relatively simple and common nonrecoverable deletion occurs in Dickinson's use of assymetrical or incomplete comparisons. In "He fumbles at your Soul," Dickinson provides no initial point of comparison for the speaker's comparatives. The speaker hears Hammers "fainter," "further," "then nearer" — than anything she has ever experienced or imagined? or than they were previously (wherever they were then)? The scene has no external point of reference or context. Consequently, "nearer" could be any distance, and the threat could be of any magnitude. We know the speaker is expectant and anxious — there is no confusion in basically understanding the poem, but the deletion prevents us from locating the speaker in any way outside the poem's terms. It sets the poem off balance, outside the realm of ordinary experience.

Nonrecoverable deletion may also create larger questions of meaning in a poem — a larger space of internal difference. For example, in "To pile like Thunder to its close," Dickinson's use of an uninflected verb in the penultimate line makes the consequence of experiencing either poetry or love ambiguous: one consumes both poetry or love in experiencing either? or, one is consumed by the experience of either? Is the reader or lover overwhelmed by her experience or does she actively engulf its source within herself? The lack of direct object and the indefinite form of the verb force the reader to hypothesize various sentences that complete the line grammatically, and more than one recreation makes sense of the line in the context of the poem. A full reading must take each interpretation of the verb into account.

The most obvious nonrecoverable deletions occur between lines or stanzas of a poem where Dickinson omits all clues as to the relation of one claim or description to the next. For example, in "Safe in their Alabaster Chambers" (216), the scooping, rowing, dropping, surrendering Worlds above the "meek members of the Resurrection" seem "Soundless as dots — on a Disc of Snow" to them. In this poem, Dickinson clearly compares the world of the dead in stanza one with that of the living in stanza two, but she leaves the reader to determine the point of the contrast. A more puzzling example occurs with the closing couplet of "He fumbles at your Soul": "When Winds take Forests in their Paws —/The Universe — is still —". These lines may summarize what precedes them, or provide a kind of coda, or the event in nature they describe may stand in contrast to His scalping of "your naked Soul." Because there is no connecting phrase, we are not sure if the human realm of vulnerability and terror is like that of winds and forests or different from it.

The notion of deletion from a complete text, however, is too restrictive for the "internal difference" created by Dickinson's metaphors — even when we speak of nonrecoverable deletion and therefore imagine various potential complete texts for a poem. With metaphors, there is no conceivable complete or unambiguous underlying text; there is no other way to say what Dickinson has said. This is true, of course, of all metaphor, but I want to make a special case for certain kinds of Dickinson's metaphors as being particularly difficult to unravel into paraphrase. Meaning is nonrecoverable, or remains between its specified poles, when Dickinson mixes terms from contrasting realms: for example, when she combines an abstract and a concrete idea, or when she predicates the properties of one sense onto those of another (synesthesia), or when she uses terms from three realms instead of two, so that we have to keep the characteristics of three worlds in mind. Dickinson uses a sound adjective to modify a sight noun ("clamor bright"); she combines weight and music to describe a quality of light (the oppressive "Heft of Cathedral Tunes" to which Dickinson compares a "Slant of light"); song becomes visible and a quality of light becomes solid with "spectral Canticle" and "Furrow on the Glow" of "Further in Summer than the Birds" (1068); she personifies an abstract concept as an Indian and then assigns his shoe a property of nature in "The Doom's electric Moccasin" (1593) — giving a sense of stealth or silence but also of devastating, shocking presence, a lovely but hair-raising description of the soft approach and electrifyingly alien effect of a storm.

As with simpler metaphors, we begin unravelling these by looking for common properties between the terms, but finding common denominators is difficult. Heft, Cathedral tunes and light seem to overlap only in the possibility of their all being "oppressive" — a word Dickinson provides in the poem. Otherwise we must speculate fairly far afield to see connections: Cathedral suggests that the light has some religious connotation or context; the light has the same kind of physical weight that sound (hymns) might have, namely, no weight itself but a quality that makes the perceiver feel heavy. Or perhaps this slant of light strikes the senses of touch and hearing as well as sight; it dominates three of the primary senses of experience rather than affecting the single obvious one we associate with light. The slant of light affects us viscerally, in illogical and powerful ways — "like the Distance on the look of Death." Each single speculation is inadequate to explain what the metaphor means; the combination, however, gives a resonant idea of what this slant of light might feel like, and what it might suggest to a sensitive spectator.

It is difficult to measure the effect of structuring poetry that is about abstract or metaphorical topics ("the soul's identity," perception, words "made Flesh") around linguistic spaces of difference or moments when literal meaning fails. Again, of course, no poetry moves solely in the realm of literal meaning; but it seems to me that the compression of Dickinson's work brings individual moments of "difference" or of metaphorical density so close to each other that we are always having to leap back and forth between the gaps. Dickinson clearly intends to communicate the essence of what she knows about the world and about human psychology; even more clearly, however, she intends to disguise the circumstances and the events of her life that any moment of difference may describe. Furthermore, Dickinson believes in the extraordinary power of language, but she believes in its power both to open and to close the process of perceiving or of thinking, and she will not accept what she sees as inadequate closure. Perhaps for this reason, she creates poem after poem in which Meanings — those solid building blocks of our daily understanding — are never quite secure. They may dominate a poem, and they are always present as the road signs or life buoys for the reader's interpretive forays into a poem, but to depend only on them would be, I think, to miss the living heart of the poem — those recurring moments of "internal difference" that leave "no scar" but resonate with what she in other poems calls "Druidic" presence or "electric Rest."

Plenary Panel:

Two Views of the Poet

Emily Dickinson and the "Prickly Art" of Housekeeping

JOANNE DOBSON

Fordham University

IN SPITE OF many biographical similarities in the early, formative years between Emily Dickinson and the American women writers who were her contemporaries, Dickinson in the domestic seclusion and self-willed non-publication of her adulthood chose a very different way of life from that lived by the largely progressive and outgoing women writers who were her peers. Like Dickinson, many of these women had come from well-to-do homes and well-respected families. Like Dickinson they, for the most part, had received good educations. Some rejected — not without conflict — their religious unbringings. Others suffered debilitating emotional problems or had been disappointed, in one way or another, in love. These factors, gentility, religious conflict, emotional instability, and heartbreak, alone or in combination, have been mentioned as having been causes of Dickinson's withdrawal from society and from publication. Yet, in spite of the co-existence of these writers, in similar cultural conditions to Dickinson, not one reacted to her circumstances by choosing to withdraw her person and her writing from an active engagement with that culture. The surprising fact is that, while many other women writers did open battle with the restrictions that would have kept them silent and at home, Dickinson's life in many ways appears congruent with conservative norms for modest, domestic femininity.

As a group Dickinson's contemporaries present her with role models for a wide variety of experience; they traveled widely, led varied social lives among interesting people, spoke out on important

Women's Studies, 1989
Vol. 16, pp. 231-237
Reprints available directly from the publisher

social issues, were financially independent, published widely to much acclaim, and at least one, Frances Osgood, conducted what appears to have been a passionate and illicit public romance. In sum, these were women who took risks, and lived much freer lives than was usual for American women in that era. On the whole, although they for the most part did preach in their writing a gospel of domesticity, the momentum of their lives was *away* from the home, out toward an active involvement with society. The momentum of Dickinson's life, on the other hand, led her in the opposite direction — from a socially active childhood and youth to a virtual self-imprisonment within her home. For the last twenty-five years of her life, as far as we know, she left her home only for visits to Boston for medical treatments. Except for a few select visitors she refused to see anyone. And, except for ten poems that may well have been submitted without her knowledge, she did not publish. In Dickinson's life, the ethos of feminine domesticity and privacy pervading women's writing was lived in actuality, and to an extreme unimagined in the novels and poems of her contemporaries.

An understanding of the cultural ideal of feminine privacy and domesticity helps us to see that Dickinson's withdrawal into the home and her refusal to publish were not aberrations rooted in psychological alienation from her society. Rather — however deeply rooted in pressing personal needs they may have been — they were the logical extremes of compliance to contemporary codes of feminine behavior. In relation to contemporary women writers Dickinson seems to have followed the old adage: "Do as I say, not as I do." Although the ethos of ideal domesticity was at the heart of the message imparted by women's writing in that era, the lives of most women writers themselves were in conflict with, if not in direct contradiction to, this ethos. Lydia Sigourney, for example, was forced into the subterfuge of smuggling manuscripts out of the house in order to avoid her husband's displeasure. Finally, however, she openly defied her husband and published widely and with much public acclaim under her own name. Dickinson, however, because of the urgent demands of an idiosyncratic psychology, seems to have lived, with an almost reactionary integrity, a life congruent with the conservative message of feminine domesticity preached by the women writers whose progressive life styles she did not emulate.

In nineteenth-century America, domesticity was the arena in which a woman's active life was expected to be played out. It was a private arena as opposed to the great public forums of commerce and government, but it was not the less important for its privateness. It was through the moral influence of home and mother that the nation was to develop and maintain a viable set of moral values. As Alexis de Tocqueville said in 1835, "no free communities ever existed without morals . . . and morals are the work of women" (198). "Genius," as literary talent was almost inevitably called, transgressed the codes of "proper" feminine selflessness and caused personal conflict for the woman writer, placing contradictory claims on her time and energy and jeopardizing her sense of identity.

That Emily Dickinson was a domestic woman, we know. Her domestic obligations began early in her life. In a letter to Jane Humphrey in January of 1850, when she had just turned nineteen, she complained about the claims on her time that had kept her from writing to her friend: ". . . and my two hands but *two* — not four, or five as they ought to be — and so *many* wants — and me so *very* handy — and my time of so *little* account — and my writing so *very* needless . . ." (L 30). In May of the same year she wrote at length to Abiah Root about the arduous job of keeping the house while her mother was ill. During this ten-day to two-week period, she did the cooking, washed the dishes, dusted and cleaned, sat with the invalid, provided for her needs, and cared for her father and brother as well. "God keep me from what they call *households*" (L 36), she exclaimed to Abiah in summing up the experience. But this period of intense domestic labor was only the beginning of life-long responsibilities for Dickinson in the home.

The Dickinson family usually had a servant to do the heavier housework; Margaret O'Brien was with the family for ten years during the late 1850s and early 1860s, and Maggie Maher came in the late 1860s and stayed until Vinnie's death in 1899 (Sewall, 609–10). It still fell to the women of the family, however, to do much of the cooking and housecleaning. Dickinson made bread and desserts, and was known for her excellence in both. "People must have puddings," she told Thomas Wentworth Higginson on his first visit. "*Very* dreamily," he added, "as if they were comets" (L 342a). In her letters over the years she makes reference to, among other chores, cooking, washing dishes, dusting, cleaning lamps, knitting, and caring for her invalid mother. Doubtless she had many other daily tasks; social class did not always excuse a woman from domestic drudgery. Harriet Martineau, in 1837, noted the obligations at the highest social levels: "All American ladies should know how to clean-starch and iron: how to keep plate and glass: how to cook dainties: and, if they understand the making of bread and soup likewise, so much the better" (302). Since it was upon the quotidian chores of women that the comfort and order, and indeed, the health and harmony, of a household depended, the responsibility was a heavy one. That Dickinson took her domestic work seriously we can assume from a comment by Joseph Lyman, a friend of the Dickinson sisters in their youth, that, whereas Vinnie was sometimes "afraid of soiling her little fat hands," "Em is an excellent housekeeper" (Sewall, 87).

It is difficult for modern readers accustomed to labor-saving devices to have an adequate sense of just how all-consuming an obligation housework was in the nineteenth century. For Dickinson to have been "an excellent housekeeper" would have been far more arduous and time-consuming an occupation that it would today, and would seriously have fragmented the time she had available for writing poetry. Susan Strasser in *Never Done*, a fascinating study of American housework, investigates the many facets of daily domestic functions: baking, cooking, keeping the fires, heating the home, lighting the home, drawing water, disposing of water, washing and ironing clothes, making clothes, shopping, cleaning, nursing the sick, caring for and educating children — the list is endless. And each one of these functions breaks down into multiple tasks, most of them daily tasks. Strasser notes the complications that attended just one aspect of one of these jobs — the initial preparation of food. Merely to get food to the stage where one could *begin* to cook it was a job in itself!

> Few manufactured products relieved the housewives' tasks once they had brought the food home. All year round, food arrived in the kitchen unprepared. Shoppers returned from the market with live chickens that had to be killed, or dead ones that had to be plucked; their work at home matched that of the farmer or the poor urban chicken keeper. Even purchased fish had scales; even purchased hams had to be soaked or blanched. Roasting and grinding green coffee, grinding and sifting whole spices, cutting and pounding lump or loaf sugar, sifting heavy flour that might be full of impurities, soaking oatmeal overnight, shelling nuts, grinding cocoa shells, seeding raisins, making and nurturing yeast, drying herbs: tasks like these accompanied nearly every ingredient of every recipe, whether it came from the garden or the market. (29)

Along with her other housekeeping chores, Dickinson is known to have done much baking. Strasser's delineation of the multitudinous steps of food preparation helps us to understand just how much daily drudgery was involved in producing the family bread and baked goods, and enlightens us as to how much time Dickinson must have spent at this task. The conflict between literary talent and domestic claims may well have been a draining one for Dickinson; Apollo and Hestia are both demanding taskmasters. But we must remember that to some degree Dickinson chose that conflict. Like Catharine Maria Sedgwick, Dickinson as an unmarried woman from a well-to-do home was in a position where she might well have chosen to relinquish the domestic role.

Her spinsterhood, combined with her financial security, offered Sedgwick an autonomy of which she, unlike Dickinson, took full advantage. She travelled widely and had many friends. She maintained residences in New York City and in Stockbridge, where she was centrally involved in the literary comradery of what has come to be known as "The American Lake District." And she wrote and wrote well and published to much acclaim. For most women writers, however, such as autonomous life was not an option; the writing/housework conflict was the central struggle of their daily lives. Dickinson's contemporaries leave record that the struggle was often debilitating. "I did my best by my house, my school, my sick child, and my publisher," the novelist E.D.E.N. Southworth writes in an autobiographical note, "yet neither child, nor school, nor publisher received justice" (Hart, 214). Southworth, deserted by her husband, was attempting to support herself and her two children by working as a school teacher when she began her writing career, and she became seriously ill as a result of the struggle to balance responsibilities.

And Harriet Beecher Stowe, mother of six, in a letter to her sister-in-law at the time she was writing *Uncle Tom's Cabin*, delineates an arduous round of petty but essential domestic activities:

> During this time [the weeks after her last baby's birth] I have employed my leisure hours in making up my engagements with newspaper editors. I have written more than anybody, or I myself, would have thought. I have taught an hour a day in our school, and I have read two hours every evening to the children. The children study English history in school, and I am reading Scott's historic novels in their order. To-night I finish the "Abbot;" shall begin "Kenilworth" next week; yet I am consistently pursued and haunted by the idea that I don't do anything. Since I began this note I

have been called off at least a dozen times; once for the fish-man, to buy a codfish; once to see a man who had brought me some barrels of apples; once to see a book-man; then to Mrs. Upham, to see about a drawing I promised to make for her; then to nurse the baby; then into the kitchen to make a chowder for dinner; and now I am at it again, for nothing but deadly determination enables me ever to write; it is rowing against wind and tide. (*Life and Letters*, 128)

These are hardly the conditions under which we can conceive of great literature coming into being, but Stowe persevered, and *Uncle Tom's Cabin*, written amid this domestic chaos, is both a literary masterpiece and, in its day, was a political bombshell as well.

Dickinson's involvement with the "prickly art" (L 907) of house-keeping was probably not as all-consuming as it was for Southworth or Stowe. Dickinson had no children to make claims on her time and energies, but she did have a mother who for long periods was an invalid, requiring much careful attention. Dickinson, indeed, considered her mother's illness a "holy" claim. Further, her father's prominent position as a lawyer, community leader, and treasurer of Amherst College entailed a considerable amount of entertaining — every year, for instance, the Dickinsons hosted at their home an Amherst College Commencement tea that is said to have drawn up to 200 people. These entertainments would have required a great deal of work on the part of the women in the family. And the ordinary day to day maintenance of the Dickinson's large home would, in itself, have been a demanding responsibility. Dickinson did have serious domestic claims on her time. Unlike the women in the stories, but like the others writers in real life, she wrote and wrote prolifically, nonetheless. Whatever effect domestic conflict had upon the themes, images, and structure of her work, it did not keep her from writing. In fact, it is quite possible that the culturally sanctioned identity of domestic woman *empowered* her writing, serving to allay anxieties that the identify of *professional* writer might well have elicited. Dickinson's obvious commitment to home and family may have enabled her to write with the dedication and seriousness of purpose of a professional without experiencing the gender conflict that such a self-definition caused other women writers, and would most likely have caused her.

Domesticity seems to have played a different role in Dickinson's life than it played in the lives of most other women writers. Rather than taking advantage of her social and marital status to free herself from quotidian obligations as Sedgwick, to a large degree, did, Dickinson took her domesticity seriously. And she took it farther than other writers did: what women like Stowe and Southworth struggled to overcome, Dickinson seems to have acquiesced to, and perhaps exploited. She told Higginson she experienced "a Cowardice of Strangers" she could not control (L 735), and her life of severely limited social contact affirms that weakness. Her domesticity not only offered her a culturally acceptable identity definition, it also allowed her the extreme seclusion she evidently needed in order to protect herself from irrational anxieties induced by normal social contact.

The extent of Dickinson's break with society may well have been abnormal, but she would have found much in the ethos of feminine domestic privacy that women's writing generally extolled to sanction her self-restriction to the home; her sister-in-law, Susan Dickinson, in a *Springfield Republican* obituary (May 18, 1886) said that Dickinson's "instinct that a woman's hearthstone is her shrine" was "simple and strong." In the domestic obligations that went with the secluded domestic role, Dickinson found work at which she could well consider herself, not fearful and eccentric, but necessary and useful. In this way she would have been able to alleviate her extreme anxieties about social contact, to write with seriousness of purpose, and still allow herself a way of life that had the sanction of the cultural ideal.

Works Cited

Dickinson, Emily. *The Letters of Emily Dickinson.* 3 vols. Eds. Thomas H. Johnson and Theodora Ward. Cambridge: Harvard UP, 1958.

Hart, John Seely. *Female Prose Writers of America.* 1851. Philadelphia: E.H. Butler, 1855.

Martineau, Harriet. *Society in America.* 1837. Gloucester, Massachusetts: Peter Smith, 1968.

Sewall, Richard B. *The Life of Emily Dickinson.* 1974. New York: Farrar, Straus and Giroux, 1980.

Stowe, Harriet Beecher. *Life and Letters of Harriet Beecher Stowe.* Ed. Annie Fields. Boston: Houghton, Mifflin, 1898.

Strasser, Susan. *Never Done: A History of American Housework.* New York: Pantheon, 1982.

Tocqueville, Alexis de. *Democracy in America.* 1835. Ed. Phillips Bradley. New York: Alfred A. Knopf, 1945.

Double Exposures: Emily Dickinson's and Gertrude Stein's Anti-autobiographies

BARBARA MOSSBERG

U.S. Scholar in Residence, United States Information Agency
University of Oregon

"That is the way any autobiography has to be written" —
— Gertrude Stein, *Everybody's Autobiography*

"I have no life but this —
To lead it here ."
— Emily Dickinson, P. 1398

CAN WE IMAGINE two more unlikely coquettes than Emily Dickinson and Gertrude Stein? Yet their lyric self-representations, their liberties and flirtations with their readers, their "fan dances," as it were, a literary strip tease of words, suggest a case of literary coquettes. Dickinson and Stein do not at first suggest comparison; but if we examine their conscious use of the coquette's etiquette, aspects of Dickinson's use of autobiography come to light. Dickinson's poetry has an immediacy and intimacy and intensity about it that derives from its autobiographical format and tone. I do not know any other writer who takes us behind the scenes, backstage, as it were, to the same degree. Dickinson is always referring to "this" — the word, the page, the poem before our eyes, the hand holding the pen writing the words we see before us; she always makes us aware of the process of writing the poem, how it feels to write it, what it means that she writes it. She appears to be candid and trusting, perfectly forthright in her aspirations, her hopes about communicating to us, making herself felt, known, and understood, recognized and appreciated. We feel, as readers, that Emily Dickinson believes in us. At the same time, the

Women's Studies, 1989
Vol. 16, pp. 239-250

message she clearly communicates is that she dare not tell us "all," and that in fact she cannot, prefers not to, for reasons we never are told. We are left with the form of autobiography, a first-person persona, which in itself teases us with its verisimilitude. The lines seem felt, from "I Years had been from Home" (p. 609), "I had been hungry, all the Years" (p. 579), to

It would have starved a Gnat —
To live so small as I —
And yet I was a living Child —
With Food's necessity

Upon me — like a Claw — (from P. 612)

But Dickinson is metaphoric, and she lets us know that she cannot tell us "all the Truth" (P. 1129). Furthermore, she presents herself, bafflingly, as taking great moral risks in talking to us at all; and she suggests an identification with witches, necromancy, spiritual hanky-panky. We are hearing a story that no one else is going to tell us. Yet we are not going to get the full story. We are trusted, but not trustworthy; she is to be trusted, but neither is she trustworthy. But we believe her.

What can we do with this set of attitudes? Dickinson is doing something new, and different, with language. What in the literary and cultural tradition in which she worked could serve her purpose to use language in effective ways; and what in the tradition could be reworked, even subverted? In coming before us on the page, is she to be honest about how it feels; is she to pretend that she isn't even there? Is she to pretend that she is the ordinary generic (male or female) author before us? Is she going to try to cover herself up? And if not, how is she going to let us know who she is? What does she mean by "Disclosed — to be Denied"? How is she going to tell the truth? Let us remember that it is Dickinson who raises this issue. It might not occur to us to question a poet's veracity or perspective or even right to be speaking.

I think it is helpful to consider these questions in the context of literary tradition, on the one hand, and in the light of modernism, on the other. Focusing on how Dickinson makes deception an issue in her own writing provides a way to understand how she both illuminates the tradition and uses it to make her own voice, to express herself in her own terms. One of the most pervasive images of women in literature that the literate woman must encounter in coming to terms with herself as a creator, is that of a deceiver — someone who in the process of using creativity and intellect abuses reason and trust, and causes evil: it appears that simply the act of intellectual creativity, self-reliance, autonomy, is destructive: for, the implicit message has been, while women possess these faculties of reason and independence, women should not be exercising them.

To put Dickinson's approach to talking about herself in perspective, in the stories we tell ourselves to make a meaning of the world, women are deceptive, whether in Genesis, Greek legends, folk tales, or television: Pandora, whose little disobedience resulted in the unleashing of the world's evils; Eve, whose deceit lost Paradise for us all; the witch's treachery in Snow White; Portia's clever and heroic scheming in *The Merchant of Venice*; Blanche DuBois' "I want to deceive him enough to make him — want me" in Tennessee Williams' *Streetcar Named Desire*; Lucy Ricardo's conniving antics in "I Love Lucy." Women in our stories have few other roles to balance this portrayal — and they are not the ones telling the stories. Power is telling the story your way.

The presence of deceit in a literary plot may reflect social truths about a lack of equality in social relationships; women traditionally have been seen as dependent upon a male power structure for social status, economic security, and protection. That is, women have had to be tricky; it's a survival mechanism, an evolutionary trait. Whether we forgive Lucy, pity Blanche, or admire Portia, their deceit — their practice of creativity, by which I mean autonomy in the use of their brains — is understood by us as a defense, necessary in such a patriarchal structure; in each case deceit bespeaks an unauthorized, unapproved power, autonomy, and confidence.

But the image of feminine deceit in literature, folklore, popular culture, does not simply point to a collective lack of clout on the part of women or paranoia on the part of men when we devise stories to figure out where we have gone wrong as a species — why there is evil and death in the world, confusion in our minds and lives (a sort of Cultural Classified — "Wanted: Scapegoat — No Males Need Apply"). The image of feminine deceit springs directly from an etiquette specifically relegated to women which requires women to cover up those facts which belie their maturity (body hair, gray hair, sexual experience, facial lines, thick waists) which the culture considers undesirable. In other words, deceit for women has often been a function of the need to be desired by men as an inexperienced child.

This is a no-win situation, of course, for once the woman participates in the "cover up," she confirms the values that deny her maturity and perpetuates the sense of the legitimacy of the stereotype of the devious female, the rationale for punishing women as the original sinners.

Against this portrayal of a necessary use of feminine deceit in a patriarchal culture that undermines its user in its practice, Emily Dickinson and Gertrude Stein stand out. As a female author, each has the opportunity to present a different image of herself from any cultural stereotype. She can tell her story her way. But we see instead the appearance of deception, deception celebrated, deception defended as necessary. While neither Dickinson nor Stein can in any conventional sense be considered a coquette, both engage in similar deliberate and self-conscious practices of deception in their writings, covering up **coyly**. It seems at first as if Blanche's "I want to **deceive** him enough to make him — want me" speaks for both, if "him" refers to their Reader. But it is far more complex, I think, than using words to entice a reader.

For neither Dickinson nor Stein is the Reader "Gentle." The Reader is too important — the Prince who is going to rescue them from their ignorant milieu which does not recognize or support their genius; this Reader Prince will ride them off into the sunset of immortality. But the Reader is also a necessary antagonist they have to outwit in order to be not wed but read, and hence, immortal. Emily Dickinson's formula for artistic success curiously paraphrases the coquette's advice urging feminine deceit: "Tell all the Truth but tell it slant —/Success in Circuit lies" (p. 1129). Both she and Stein follow this advice, appearing in their writings to be compulsively autobiographical, telling All, confessing, alluding to secrets and intimate, private moments with their souls, bodies, minds. Emily Dickinson's readers are conscious of being let in on moods and thoughts that the poet does not share with others; we are privy to secrets. At the same time, both Dickinson and Stein make a show of obscuring their "All" with stylistic, syntactic, and grammatic ambiguity. References to the self are camouflaged by the use of **some, one, he, we, she,** even **this** (P. 358, for example, "If any sink, assure that this, now standing —").

Perhaps both Dickinson and Stein want to entice their Reader without incurring the social censure that they felt would inevitably arise if they were to reveal the truth about their identity as women artists, their own desires as women. In Dickinson's poetry, we see a sense of being a sexual freak, a contradiction in terms, a person who violates social, sexual, and literary taboos for women. Dickinson called identity a "hound" pursuing her; in P. 670, she not only haunts herself but chases herself in a gothic comedy: "Ourself behind ourself, concealed —/Should startle most —/Assassin hid in our Apartment/Be Horror's least." She narrates how 'The Body" borrows a gun in self-defense, but in vain; the mind, the brain is hunting **him** down. Identity is similarly sinister in P. 754, "My life had stood — a Loaded Gun;" the divided self turns upon itself with weapons, and speaking — the poet's activity, after all — can be fatal, both to those who receive the word and those who utter it. In "Me from Myself — to banish" (P. 642) the self is presented as assaulting itself, again, as always, in vain.

Less melodramatic, Stein wrote an understatement: "Identity is not a pleasure." The need to reveal and conceal painful truths about their identities is controlled by Dickinson's aesthetic strategy to tell the truth "Slant." We are made to feel that there are omissions, yet what is deleted? We are here, aren't we? It was enough; we got the message; we are satisfied; there are no missing links — we simply are made to think there are. We know that meaning is there for us, if we keep at it. I would not be writing this, you would not be reading this, if Dickinson truly had deleted her messages and obscured her meanings.

But the point is that both Dickinson and Stein have made an issue of setting out to defeat and to demoralize the reader even as we are made to feel privileged by the intimate promise of disclosures. What we see with Stein and Dickinson is how a writer works within a culture, works within and against a tradition. What seems to link Dickinson and Stein is their straightforward, candid, unabashed use — even celebration of — deceit. They exploit their readers' expectations of feminine deception, telling us that that they are playing Hide and Seek: the author has hidden the truth and the Reader is It. Dickinson writes,

Good to hide, and hear 'em hunt!
Better, to be found,
If one care to, that is,
The fox fits the Hound —

Good to know, and not tell,
Best, to know and tell,
Can one find the rare Ear
Not too dull — (P. 842)

Should the Reader be unaware that the confessions are not true or full confessions, or that a secret lurks somewhere in the fractured syntax, Dickinson and Stein indulge in what I term an exhibitionistic reticence — we could simply say "coyness" — in which she constantly alludes to forbidden, untellable, topics. In P. 155, for example,

The Murmur of a Bee
A Witchcraft — yieldeth me —
If any ask me why —
'Twere easier to die —
Than tell —

In P. 157, she raises questions, only to say she cannot answer them: "Please God — shall Ascertain!" In the most dramatic of poems about her identity conflict (P. 1737) Dickinson imagines her readers at her literary autopsy, trying to determine who she was, given the fact that she is a poet; we will discover that she was not a typical woman; we may in fact try to figure out whom she loved, and what her sexual identity was like. We may deduce that she was really a man; is she challenging us when she says, "Amputate my freckled Bosom!/Make me bearded like a man!"). Or is she sarcastic? Or despairing of our understanding? She concludes,

Big my Secret, but it's *bandaged* —
It will never get away
Till the Day its Weary Keeper
Leads it through the Grave to thee.

We can be trusted with the secret, it seems, since we are the "thee" addressed here, but we still do not know what the "Big ... Secret" is. We only know that there is one.

Fifty years later, in another country where she can live a freer and more open existence as a woman who wants power, as a woman who loves another woman, Gertrude Stein writes,

I have been so careful. I will not say what I feel.
I do not wish to write down what I hear.
I am sadly tormented by flies, I do not mean flies.
We eat our breakfast and smoke a cigar. That is not so because we call it by another name.

This is not deception: this is being honest about being unwilling or unable to tell the truth. The effect of such lines is to focus the Reader's attention on what is not being said, and the fact that the author feels she cannot say it. It is a focus on absence; the presence of absence is the text.

There is the sense that Dickinson and Stein are in some ways forced into duplicity by a tradition enjoining them to be "still" and to "shut up." Dickinson tells us how she fights against this tradition:

They shut me up in Prose —
As when a little Girl
They put me in the Closet —
Because they liked me "still" —

Still! Could themself have peeped —
And seen my Brain — go round —
They might as wise have lodged a Bird
For Treason — in the Pound —

Himself has but to will
And easy as a Star
Abolish his Captivity —
And laugh — No more have I — (P. 613)

Even as she does not speak up, speak out, speak at all, her brain is intact; her silence is only a cover for the loud and vigorous mental activity that goes on within, and on the page before us. She is subversive within the tradition, rebellious — not a model of duty, of "Prose," of conventional ways of expressing herself in life and in literature. She does not compromise herself in the process; every poem before us is a testament to that integrity, to that necessary subversion.

Looking at how Gertrude Stein dealt with similar efforts to make her "still" and "Prose" and "shut up" suggests another way to read and re-read Dickinson's dutiful life strategies and poems about these strategies — staying home, living the life of a dutiful daughter, preserving the fiction that she was unknown in her true capacities by her world. Stein acknowledges the need for duplicity, for slanting truths. The titles of Stein's autobiographies are oxymoronic, self-cancelling and for that reason compelling: *Everybody's Autobiography, The Autobiography of Alice B. Toklas.* Autobiography itself, as a form, is the subject of the works; and yet Stein reveals her ambivalence towards the subject of the self by purporting to be speaking for other people. She takes liberties with the form; when she says Alice B.

Toklas objects to liberties taken with her name in the "autobiography," she replies "That is the way any autobiography has to be written" — as if for her, autobiography is a process of transforming objective truths. She makes her subject the problem of autobiography, her problems with telling about herself, her fascination with the form. The autobiography is about autobiography, the plot is the process of telling, how she feels about telling.

Even in *The Geographical History of America* Stein subversively uses linguistic means to include herself in history, make herself historical: "In the month of February were born Washington, Lincoln, and I." She does not not lie; she was born in February. But by including herself syntactically in autobiographical form ("and I") she makes of history autobiography, and she changes "history" — his story — in the process. She is creating a new form, challenging our definition of autobiography, clarifying the form, letting us see how fictive it is in its traditional format, bringing up questions about who writes it and why, who chooses history or biography (someone else's story) or the novel instead. How are we to read autobiography? Or history? Who is doing the deceiving? "This is my deception," Stein writes: what is yours? what is theirs? All her writings are autobiographical, but the question of authority, authorship, remains extant. From her point of view, does she have authority to write at all? Yet she affirms her actual "authority" as she describes her problems as an author, being revealing rather than deceiving. She celebrates how "true" one can be in words, even one's need to cover up.

Stein lures the Reader into a deceptively familiar landscape, which quickly becomes not "prose" but a maze in which the Reader is perhaps a trespasser, perhaps unwelcome, perhaps laughed at. The Reader is not deliberately misled, but is rather "misled about" by the hostess author, made to feel misled, lost, mistaken, disoriented, perhaps demoralized. Titles in Stein's work can be signposts for destinations that don't exist. She says they are "made for defense" — and hence the reader is the Enemy whose understanding of the subject will ostensibly hurt the author.

Tender Buttons, for example, at first seems to have a semantically incongruous title, preventing us from intimating the subject of the book. The book's three categories, Food, Objects, and Rooms, as organizational principles are misleading, for food discussions are found under Objects and Rooms, and such non-food entries are listed under Food as "A Center in a Table" and "End of Summer." Even when the Food section includes such logical items as Oranges and Salad Dressing and an Artichoke, these titles themselves do not necessarily illuminate what follows: "Build is all right;" "Why is a feel oyster an egg stir. A type oh new new not no not knealer knealer;" Titles, definitions, categories, headings — all are deceptive, all serve obscurity. If titles are made for defense, the book is a fort, and the Reader wonders for whom the fort has been erected, what kind of enemy is anticipated in these grounds. Stein's meaning seems to be safe, if the Reader gives up in demoralized confusion, as even Richard Bridgeman did, in *Gertrude Stein in Pieces*, convinced either that there is no there there, or that she simply and perversely means to confound.

But the vulnerable subject Stein is trying to protect is apparent if we examine the nature of what is being so defined. We see that the promise of order, signified by the book's organization, disintegrates into a chaos of furniture, accessories, kitchen appliances, and food; the book's structure is a metaphor of interiors, a feminine conception of space and time in which conventional boundaries have broken down, aspects of domesticity, the feminine domain, traditional "woman's work." Indeed, the book is a portrait of a household, houselife, taken apart and re-arranged, much as Stein's friend Picasso would rearrange the parts of the body, putting both eyes on one side of the face. Stein in writing this piece is not engaging in traditional woman's work. The title could refer to the way in which language is being used by a woman who is ambivalent about expressing herself and her own sexual role and identity. She has taken the words of the household and thrown them up into the air to see them land where they may; she has made us take new looks at household objects, out of context of their use; she has liberated the objects of the house from traditional and confining meanings. The title could refer to her own discreet, feminine ("tender") use of language to "button up" or enclose naked, provocative, vulnerable meaning which cannot flap open. Stein may in fact be revealing her identity conflict as a woman artist in the guise of Cubist non-sense: telling all Slant. Linguistically, she is messing up the room, a liberating act, and subversive as well: this is no conventional house wife.

The subject of *Tender Buttons* is Stein's identity as a woman artist. But if her identity is the vulnerable subject for Stein, she does not avoid the subject, and I think that this is the point. Like Dickinson, she structures her narratives around her sense of self. As Dickinson did in her first poem (P. 1), Stein began her writing career writing straightforwardly enough — writing "prose" — being so explicit in her themes about sexual conflict that her instructor wrote across one paper, "unpleasant in the extreme ... [but] not without psychological interest." Her first novel, which deals with a triangular love affair Stein experienced with two women while she was at Johns Hopkins Medical School, is written in relatively conventional prose. The subject was taboo in 1900 when she wrote the book (*Q.E.D.*), and perhaps because she did express herself so clearly, Stein censored the book herself, putting it away with no hope or desire of publishing it. Thirty-two years later, she mentions it for the first time in *The Autobiography of Alice B. Toklas.* Here she says on three different occasions that she had "completely forgotten" the book and that she had not mentioned it before. While she tells the reader that she was "Very bashful and hesitant about it, did not really want to read it," she does not tell why not nor further disclose what it is about. She says only that she handed it to a friend and told him, "you read it." In 1941, nearly fifty years after she had written the story, Robert Haas, in preparing the *Yale Catalogue*, wrote Stein to ask if the story could be included. Stein replied, "No."

This is typical of how Stein, like Dickinson, engineers telling the truth about the self. She brings the story to her readers' attention only to say that she can't tell us about it, and then she tries to close the subject. As Stein's reply to Haas makes clear, she really had no intention or desire of having that revealing story be read: she just wanted her readers to know that there were things she wasn't telling them. She never does close the subject, or even "tenderly button" it, for it is this story which is the basis of later works, including "Melanctha," *The Making of Americans*, and *Everybody's Autobiography*. And like Dickinson, Stein never leaves off telling about her identity problems as a woman, never lets her reader forget what is absent and must be absent in her text.

But Stein, like Dickinson, had a sense of purpose in the untraditional use of deception. In *What Are Masterpieces*, Stein implies that the practice, the look of deception is necessary for her to create: "I am I because my little dog knows me but creatively speaking the little dog knowing that you are you and your recognition that he knows, that is what destroys creation. This is what makes school." School — where one practices what one is taught — is the antithesis of creativity. Creation, then, for Stein, is the use of language in ways that one has not been taught. By definition, it is independent, even defiant.

Emily Dickinson defined this aspect of creativity for herself in P. 326, where she says she cannot "dance upon my Toes" because "No Man instructed me," but nevertheless, and in fact because of this, she does a kind of dance that is "full as Opera". She notes that she does not follow the fashion for performing, for treating audiences to their expectations in her art ("Nor hopped to Audiences — like Birds,/One Claw upon the Air,") and that, significantly, no one knows "I know the Art/I mention — easy — Here —." This reference to the fact that the poem before our eyes is a secret, its practice is a secret, her sense of its success is a secret, makes the true subject of the poem the process of deception itself. We are taken behind the scenes; backstage is the stage.

Stein had written, "I do not wish to write down what I hear." "If you do write as you have heard it said then you have to change it." That is, if you do tell the truth, you have to transform that truth — in Dickinson's words, make it "slant," "bandage" it. But the slant is the truth — the truth is the slant. It seems to be a case of eating your cake and having it too; of saying that one is being deceptive, but of being open about the need to say and to present oneself as deceptive. Emily Dickinson was accused posthumously by Higginson of having misled him for thirty years, of having misrepresented herself in her letters and poems, "with a naive skill such as the most experienced and wordly coquette might envy." The irony, of course, is that Dickinson consciously practiced such coquetry. In P. 443, she discusses the process:

We cannot put Ourself away
As a completed Man
Or Woman —
. . .
To simulate — is stinging work —
To cover what we are
From Science — and from Surgery —
Too Telescopic Eyes
To bear on us unshaded —
For their — sake — not for Ours —
'Twould start them —

The stylistic, structural innovations of Dickinson's work, and Stein's, what makes them unusual, what makes them great, and speak powerfully to us today, come from a sense of traditional behavior of women, who are so untrustworthy as a type that they must be constantly enjoined to stifle their creativity, their voices, their capacity for independent thinking. Neither Dickinson nor Stein could write given this tradition without being aware of herself as offensive — in Anne Bradstreet's words, "obnoxious to each carping tongue/Who says my hand a needle better fits."[5] What is remarkable about both Dickinson and Stein is that they used this tradition as a foil for their own creativity.

While they are superficially different in image and form — Dickinson the Yankee in white, self-enclosed in her bedroom, Stein, a monk-like, formidable, open, disclosing presence — to see Dickinson and Stein together illuminates a crucial aspect of their work. In fact, Dickinson and Stein are not such an ill-fitting pair. Both share a common reception of their work; both were deemed initially incomprehensible and aesthetically incompetent by people — men — who were supposedly competent to judge such matters. Both were supported by women in their lives. Both led privileged existences; both were served by other women; both identified themselves with royalty and power: Dickinson, with queens, Stein, with generals. Both lived essentially in exile, in chosen countries away from patriarchies: Stein in Paris, Dickinson in her room, in her mind. Both had powerful fathers, absent and weak mothers, well-educated and favored brothers. Both identified themselves with younger, weaker family members — a child, "baby." Both were originals in language, with vocabulary and grammar; both looked askance at a history and politics that excluded them; both were self-confident against the odds.

Dickinson wrote "I had the glory, that will do." Stein said she liked a view, but she liked to sit with her back to it. I think this notion — accepting the premise of a view, knowing how it is valued and approached in traditional ways, and "turning one's back" on those ways — defines both Dickinson's and Stein's approach to traditional ways of representing women and of writing about the self. Neither ignores the view, and in fact, the presence of the view gives them a stance, something to turn against, a background to define their achievement. Thus like Stein, Dickinson becomes, in self-portrait, part of the view. In fact, she is the view, the center of the image, facing us, giving us the truth about her abilities to talk to us and face us in this straightforward way.